CARTAGENA & COLOMBIA'S CARIBBEAN COAST

ANDREW DIER

Punta Gallinas

Bahía Hondo

Nazareth

Bahía Portete

Cabo de la Vela

PNN Macuira

Uribia

Riohacha

Maicao

Golfo de Venezuela

SFF Los
Flamencos

**Parque Nacional
Natural Tayrona**

anga

Palomino

nta
arta

Distracción

Minca

**PNN Sierra Nevada
de Santa Marta**

Ciénaga

Maracaibo

Atanquez

VENEZUELA

Nabusímake

Aracataca

Valledupar

Pueblo
Bello

*Lago de
Maracaibo*

Mariangola

Bosconia

Brazo la Loba

Aguachica

To Bucaramanga
and Bogotá

Cordillera Oriental

0   75 mi

0   75 km

© AVALON TRAVEL

Contents

DISCOVER

Cartagena and Colombia's Caribbean Coast

According to Gabriel García Márquez, Cartagena is a city of "amethyst afternoons and nights of antic breezes." After a sunset walk along the Old City's fortifications, you'll understand what he meant. Feel the caress of the Caribbean breeze, see the vivid pink bougainvillea cascading from balconies of Old World mansions, and taste tangy sweet tropical fruits. After dark, once the sounds of salsa and *champeta* rhythms begin to spill out from the city's nightspots, you'll surrender to the infatuation.

But there's more to discover—much more—if you have a sense of adventure, a trusty backpack, a little patience, and a sense of humor.

Beachside *cabañas* and hammocks await at ecofriendly hotels—but you'll have to find them first. Mountains and jungles rise abruptly from pristine beaches, creating a natural playground. Virtually untouched villages keep you busy with bird-watching, mountain hikes, and organic coffee and cocoa farms. Then there's the Ciudad Perdida trek: a multiday hike to the ruins of an ancient city.

Clockwise from top left: dancer preparing for Carnaval in Barranquilla; beach near Palomino; *mochilas* (handwoven bags) made by indigenous Caribbean women; trekking to Ciudad Perdida; hummingbird in the Sierra Nevada near Minca; plaza in Cartagena.

Over time indigenous people, African slaves, Spanish colonists, and Arab, European, and Jewish immigrants have made the Caribbean coast one of the most diverse regions in Colombia. All in all you'll find the people of this vast region to be generous, friendly, and shall we say…relaxed?

And really, that's the key to success here in the Caribbean: relaxing. Isn't that why you're here?

Clockwise from top left: toucan, Minca; Lover's Lane, Providencia; Catedral Basílica Menor, Cartagena; Palenquera woman selling tropical fruit in Cartagena.

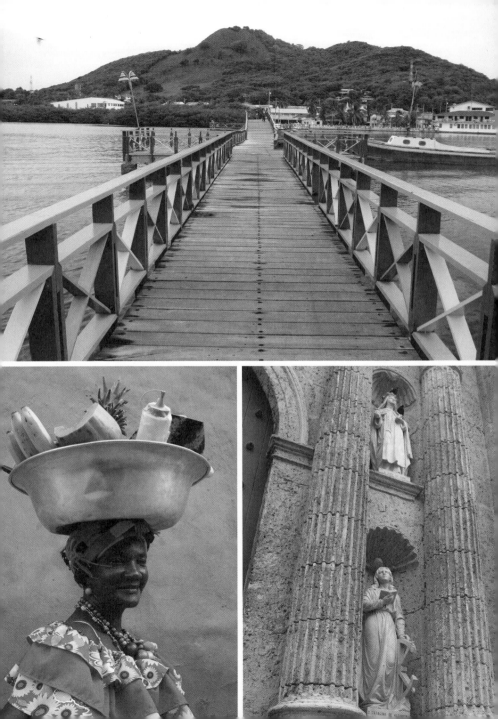

Planning Your Trip

Where to Go

Cartagena

With its narrow, bougainvillea-draped streets, **bustling plazas,** and Spanish architecture, Cartagena is the **colonial jewel** of the Caribbean. This walled city offers **luxurious hotels,** raucous **nightlife,** and delicious seafood.

Take to the water across the Bahía de Cartagena and past old Spanish forts to chill out on a **secluded Caribbean island** at the **Islas del Rosario.** Or slow down the pace in a sultry **colonial river town** by heading inland to **Mompox.**

Santa Marta and La Guajira

The Sierra Nevada de Santa Marta stands apart—literally. Separate from the Andes Mountains, this isolated range rises from the pleasant **colonial city** of **Santa Marta** upward to the **Ciudad Perdida,** the ruins of an ancient civilization set amid **jungle and mountains.** Surrounding towns offer myriad activities, from a bacchanalian celebration of **Carnaval** in **Barranquilla** to **secluded beaches** in **Taganga.**

In the **deserts** of **La Guajira** in the far northeast of Colombia, the Wayúu indigenous people have lived for centuries. The remote beaches of **Cabo de la Vela** and **Punta Gallinas** boast stunning landscapes where **windswept dunes** fall dramatically into the Caribbean waters.

Western Caribbean Coast

The Caribbean coast west of Cartagena beckons adventurous spirits. Off the coast of quiet **beach town Tolú** are the **Islas de San Bernardo,** the perfect setting for an **island getaway.**

One of the least-visited areas of Colombia can be found amid the **untamed jungles** and **rocky coasts** of the Darién Gap, home to remote **Capurganá** and **Sapzurro,** where transportation is by foot or boat.

San Andrés and Providencia

The paradise islands of San Andrés and Providencia offer everything you'd expect from a Caribbean vacation. **Fantastic diving** will keep you occupied for days off sunny San Andrés. The daily routine of lounging on **remote beaches,** eating fresh seafood, lazing in hammocks, and **stargazing** on the beach in sleepy Providencia will have you hooked.

When to Go

Because Colombia straddles the equator, the warm temperatures and short days are constant throughout the year. There are, however, distinct dry and rainy seasons. Throughout most of the country, **December through February** and **July through August** are considered *verano* **(dry season).** *Invierno* **(rainy season)** is usually between **April and May** and again between **September and November.** In San Andrés and Providencia, June through November is rainy and from February through April it's drier. From late December to early February the waters can be rough along the Caribbean coast, especially around Capurganá.

High tourist seasons run from **mid-December through mid-January,** during **Semana Santa (Holy Week)** and, to a lesser extent, school vacations from **June to August.**

During high season, hotel rates and airline ticket prices soar. Colombians from the interior flock to Cartagena, the Caribbean coast, and the San Andrés Archipelago during the New Year's holidays through the second week of January. Hotels and flights can also get booked up on the 10 or so *puentes* (long weekends) of the year.

Many of the major festivals and celebrations take place between December and February, with the **Carnaval de Barranquilla** occurring over the four days before Ash Wednesday each year. **Semana Santa** celebrations and the Jazz Festival in early October are big in colonial Mompox, while Valledupar relishes its moment in the spotlight during its **Festival del Vallenato** in April.

Before You Go

Passports and Visas

Travelers to Colombia who intend to visit as tourists for a period of less than 90 days will need only to present a **valid passport** upon entry in the country. You may be asked to show **proof of a return ticket.** Tell the immigration officer if you intend to stay up to 90 days, otherwise they will probably give you a stamp permitting a stay of 60 days. Language schools and universities will be able to assist those who may require a yearlong **student visa.**

Vaccinations

There are **no obligatory vaccination requirements** for visiting Colombia.

However, as a precautionary measure the Centers for Disease Control and Prevention (CDC) recommends travelers to have all of the **basic vaccinations** up to date (such as MMR), and additionally **hepatitis A, typhoid, hepatitis B, rabies,** and **yellow fever.** Proof of a yellow fever vaccination is no longer required at national parks, but may be needed for entry to other countries following a trip to Colombia; travel is made easier with this vaccination.

If you plan on spending a lot of time outdoors in lowland tropical areas, consider taking antimalarial drugs.

Transportation

Most travelers arrive by plane to Colombia, with the vast majority arriving at the **Aeropuerto Internacional El Dorado** in Bogotá, a modern airport with numerous nonstop flights from the Eastern Seaboard of the United States, Canada, and Europe. **Cartagena** and **Barranquilla** host nonstop flights from Fort Lauderdale, Miami, Atlanta, and New York.

Intra-country flights are easy, safe, and increasingly economical. Smaller airports in Santa Marta, Riohacha, Valledupar, and Montería have numerous daily flights from Bogotá.

Taking the **bus** to just about anywhere in the country is an inexpensive and popular (but slower) option. There are numerous options for public transportation between Cartagena, Barranquilla, and Santa Marta.

What to Pack

For jungle exploration, **waterproof hiking boots** and **lightweight gear** to shield against the rain, sun, and mosquitoes are a must. To protect your electronics, a **waterproof camera bag** and **silica gel** may prevent the heartache of a ruined camera. For finding your way at night, a **small flashlight** is useful. To spot wildlife, **binoculars** will be great to have. If you plan on spending much time on the coast, bring your own **snorkeling gear.** To dissuade pesky mosquitoes, wear lightweight and light-colored long-sleeved shirts and bring some strong repellent, especially if you plan on visiting lowland rural areas.

Luggage locks will provide peace of mind on long bus rides and at hostels. English is widely spoken at most hotels and some restaurants in Cartagena and Santa Marta and at most hostels. Taxi drivers, bus drivers, and boat captains usually only speak Spanish. A **Latin American Spanish dictionary** will help you get your point across.

Casual attire is fine at most restaurants and religious venues. Some restaurants in Cartagena may expect more of an effort, and you'll want to **dress to impress** in bars and clubs. **Modest clothing** is a good idea in indigenous communities and rural areas.

The Best of Colombia's Caribbean Coast

This weeklong Caribbean adventure includes plenty of time to soak up the seductive atmosphere of Cartagena's Old City, lounge on the idyllic beaches of the Islas del Rosario, and explore Parque Nacional Natural Tayrona, the country's most popular national park. If the pace feels too rushed, skip the Islas del Rosario (there are beaches in PNN Tayrona) or Santa Marta.

Consider flying into Cartagena and departing via Santa Marta or Barranquilla, which both offer easy international connections via Bogotá. Otherwise, give yourself another day to catch a flight home out of Cartagena.

Day 1 Sunday

Cartagena is an easy flight from the Eastern Seaboard of the United States. After landing, change into sandals before enjoying a sunset stroll along *las murallas,* the massive ramparts built by the Spaniards to protect the city during the colonial era.

Have dinner and mojitos accompanied by live music at **La Vitrola,** an elegant seafood restaurant. Spend the night in luxury at the understated but posh **Hotel LM** or at **Casa Blue,** a comfortable budget option in the heart of the **Centro.**

Day 2 Monday Portland

After a late breakfast of tropical fruit, *arepa de huevo,* and Colombian coffee at **Mila Pastelería,** get lost and found again as you amble around town, from the leafy **Parque de Bolívar** to the **Plaza de Santo Domingo.** Next, peruse the stalls of **Las Bóvedas,** nestled within the city's walls. Reenergize with a cool *agua de coco* (coconut water), sold by street vendors.

Stop for a Caribbean lunch at **La Mulata** and a siesta back at your room, then cab it to **Castillo**

the Old City of Cartagena

de San Felipe, outside the Old City, in the late afternoon. Once you've finished exploring the fort, head back toward the Centro to **Marea by Rausch** for an inventive seafood dinner overlooking the bay.

After dinner, join the hipsters, backpackers, and even a few locals several blocks away at the Plaza de la Trinidad in the heart of hip and happening **Getsemaní** before hitting **Café Havana** up the street for live music, drinks, and fun.

Day 3 *Sat*

After checking out of your hotel, you'll be ready for some beach time. Board a boat at the Marina Santa Cruz in Manga at 9am. From here you're headed on a day trip to the luxurious **Hotel San Pedro de Majagua** on the **Islas del Rosario.** After the included seafood lunch, perhaps some diving or snorkeling will be in order, although be sure to make time for relaxing in your hammock.

Take the afternoon boat back to Cartagena. Dinner tonight is at **Carmen,** where a five-course tasting menu awaits. Say goodbye to the city with a drink at **Café del Mar** on the wall.

Days 4-5 *Tus / Wed*

Today you're off to **Parque Nacional Natural Tayrona.** Take the direct early bus at 6am out of the Old City. The journey takes five hours, getting you to the park at 11am. (The bus will pass by Santa Marta, but don't worry—you'll hit it on your way out of the park.)

Upon arrival at the park, take the gorgeous path from Cañaveral to Arrecifes to get a taste of the park before you settle in at your campsite or in a high-end Ecohab.

The next morning, get an early start for the hike to **El Pueblito,** the remnants of an old Tayrona settlement within the park. Relax at **La Piscina,** a cove of calm water, on the way back. Buy a simple seafood lunch from one of the food stalls nearby, then while away the rest of the day on the beach. Dinner is at one of the park's two restaurants, where you'll enjoy more fresh seafood. After dinner, grab a flashlight and stroll along the beach.

Day 6 *Thr*

In the morning, make your way back to the park entrance, then hop a bus to **Santa Marta.** The

Parque Nacional Natural Tayrona

There are many ways to enjoy the landscape of the Caribbean coast.

- **Diving and snorkeling:** The island of **San Andrés** (page 123) is surrounded by a well-preserved coral reef that's teeming with marine life and perfect for both snorkelers and divers. Neighboring **Providencia** (page 134) is great place to learn how to dive, thanks to its fantastic visibility.

- **Kitesurfing:** In La Guajira, **Cabo de la Vela** (page 99) is a world-class destination for kitesurfing, thanks to the ample winds and smooth water.

- **Wildlife-watching:** Colombia's national parks are home to animals like sloths, bats, toucans, macaws, and monkeys. Visit **Parque Nacional Natural Tayrona** (page 79) or **Parque Nacional Natural Macuira** (page 101) and try to spot 'em all!

- **Hiking:** In Parque Nacional Natural Sierra Nevada de Santa Marta, you can trek to the ruins of an ancient civilization called **Ciudad Perdida** (page 87). Or, hike to the top of **The Peak** (page 137), the highest point on the island of Providencia.

- **Beaches:** Off the coast of Cartagena, **Playa Blanca and the Islas del Rosario** (page

Spectacular diving awaits off of San Andrés.

54) offer some of the region's most beautiful beaches. Or visit the spectacular beaches of **Parque Nacional Natural Tayrona** (page 79) if you're headed off the beaten path.

ride takes about an hour. Check into the boutique **Casa de Isabella** or budget **Aluna.**

Have lunch or a snack at **Ratatouille.** Stroll through the city's **Centro Histórico,** visit the **Museo del Oro Tairona,** and then check out the views from the pier.

For an upscale evening, opt for dinner at **Ouzo.** If you're in the mood for exquisite Italian, head to **La Casona/Donde L'Italiano.**

Day 7

Before taking a flight out of Santa Marta or hopping a *buseta* for the five-hour trip back to

Cartagena, have breakfast and a cappuccino at **Ikaro** in the Centro Histórico.

Excursion to La Guajira

If you have 4-5 extra days, consider taking a trip to **La Guajira,** a desert peninsula that is home to the Wayúu people. This trip is best planned out of Santa Marta with a tour group. Book your tour a few days in advance.

From Santa Marta, take the three-hour bus ride to **Riohacha,** then meet up with your tour group to head for the **Alta Guajira** region. After a dusty ride past countless cacti and lonely goats,

Social-Impact Tourism

The annual number of international visitors to Colombia increased almost threefold from 2000 to 2012. This boom has fostered a growth of community and ecotourism options. Here are several ways to support the local people, plants, or animals, all while having the vacation of your dreams.

- **Stay in a *posada nativa.*** The interior of **San Andrés** (page 131) is home to *posadas nativas* (native guesthouses) that are owned and operated by locals, many of whom have deep roots on the island. Stay at a *posada nativa* and you'll get to know the local culture.

- **Visit a national park.** Colombia's system of natural parks and protected areas cover around 13.4 percent of the country. The Parks Service actively engages local communities, with much of the ecotourism infrastructure being operated by community-based organizations. Some of the region's best parks are **Parque Nacional Natural Tayrona** (page 79) near Santa Marta and **Parque Nacional Natural Old Providence McBean Lagoon** (page 134) on Providencia.

- **Save the animals.** At the **Bahía de Cispatá refuge** (page 108) in San Antero, local fishers are helping to protect crocodiles and turtles, once hunted for their meat and

flamingos at Santuario de Fauna y Flora Los Flamencos

eggs. Visit the **Santuario de Fauna y Flora Los Flamencos** (page 97), most famously known for its population of migratory flamingos. Here, conservationists also work to keep threatened sea turtles safe.

---

you'll arrive at **Cabo de la Vela,** where you can take a dip in the Caribbean Sea or try your luck wind- or kitesurfing.

The next stop is **Punta Gallinas,** the northernmost point of South America. Spend a day or two on a photo safari of the unusual landscape of desert dunes that drop dramatically into the sea.

Upon returning to Riohacha, visit the **Santuario de Fauna y Flora Los Flamencos** for an early-morning or late-afternoon canoe ride in search of flamingos.

Excursion to San Andrés and Providencia

If you're looking to get away from it all, go to the islands of San Andrés and Providencia, off the coast of Nicaragua. Allot at least four days for some solid beach relaxation time.

Fly into San Andrés from Cartagena. To continue to Providencia, it's just a short flight. Once in Providencia, stay at the **Hotel Sirius,** where dive experts can take you to the reef for a few underwater adventures.

Take a hike up **The Peak,** kayak among the mangroves of **Parque Nacional Natural Old Providence McBean Lagoon,** and laze away an afternoon on the beach. For your last night in Providencia, dine under the stars at **Deep Blue Hotel Restaurant.**

Add another day or two in San Andrés to spend more time snorkeling, diving, and drinking *coco locos.*

The Untamed Coast

From Cartagena, it's possible to visit some of Colombia's wildest stretches of coastline. This weeklong itinerary takes you to lesser-known points along the coast. Try this itinerary in September or October when the waters are calm and the tourists have gone back to work and school.

Be prepared to take several modes of transportation in order to get around. If you don't have a full week, prioritize a visit to Capurganá or Río Cedro.

Day 1

From Cartagena, board a bus for the three-hour ride to sleepy **Tolú.** Upon arrival, hop on a tour of the **Islas de San Bernardo.** Soak up the sun, splash about in the Caribbean, and settle in for the night at the resort **Punta Faro** or **Casa en el Agua,** a fun floating hotel.

Day 2

Today is all about the beach. When you're done worshipping the sun, take a tour of the neighboring islands, including **Santa Cruz del Islote,** considered the most densely populated island in the world.

Take a boat back to Tolú and spend the night at **Villa Babilla,** where you can prepare your own dinner and soak up the silence.

Day 3

In the morning, take a minibus to **Bahía de Cispatá,** a turtle and crocodile refuge run by local fishers near the town of San Antero. Once you've worked up an appetite, have a fresh seafood lunch at **Pesecar,** which is perched on Bahía de Cispatá.

From here, it's a three-hour trip to **Río Cedro.** Take a minibus from San Antero to Lorica, then transfer to a bus headed for Moñitos. From there, you can arrange for a motorbike to take you to Reserva Natural Viento Solar. You'll arrive at this private reserve on undeveloped coastline in time to take a walk on the secluded beaches and go for a dip in the calm waters. Settle into one of the

rugged coast near Tolú

thatched-roof cabins, lulled to sleep by the sounds of the jungle and sea.

Days 4-5

Wake up early and take a walk through the tropical dry forest of the reserve. If you're lucky, you may spot an *oso perezoso* (sloth) clinging to a tree. Enjoy a quiet breakfast before hitting the road to the **Darién Gap,** a region that straddles the Colombia-Panama border. It's a five-hour trip to the beach town of Necoclí. Take a motorbike to Montería, then hop on a bus headed for Necoclí. Check into the **Hotel Panorama Suite** for the night.

The next morning, take a fast boat across the gulf to **Capurganá,** which takes about 1.5 hours. Once you arrive in Capurganá, stay at the friendly **Cabañas El Tucán, Cabañas Darius,** or at the secluded, honeymoon-worthy **Bahía Lodge.**

Day 6

Get up nice and early for a day of hiking and exploration. Hike through the jungle surrounding Capurganá to El Cielo waterfall and splash around in the water before heading back into town. Next, take the two-hour hike to the neighboring town of **Sapzurro,** letting the howler monkeys guide you. Have lunch at the **Gata Negra.**

Head back to Capurganá and have a gourmet dinner on the beach at **Donde Josefina.**

For those more interested in exploring the water, spend the day on a **snorkel or dive trip.** This region has over 30 diving sites to choose from, so expect a full day on the water.

Day 7

Today you return to Cartagena. Take a boat to Necoclí, and then a long bus ride back to Cartagena. Alternatively you could fly to Medellín, if you're traveling onward in Colombia.

a canoe trip in the Darién Gap

Cartagena

Look for ★ to find recommended sights, activities, dining, and lodging.

Highlights

★ *Las Murallas:* Stroll the centuries-old stone ramparts of the Old City and savor the moment with a sundowner cocktail at one of the wall's breezy bars (page 25).

★ **Colonial Churches:** Catholicism was a driving force for the Spanish colonists. The photogenic churches on practically every plaza of the Centro stand not only as testaments to their will but remain as vital houses of worship for devout locals (page 28).

★ **Palacio de la Inquisición:** This spectacular 17th-century building was where Catholic authorities once meted out punishment to accused heretics during the Spanish colonial era. Today it's a fine history museum (page 30).

★ **Museo del Oro Zenú:** This museum provides visitors a taste of highly detailed and spectacularly preserved golden ceremonial jewelry and earthenware from ancient Caribbean cultures (page 31).

★ **Castillo de San Felipe:** Wander through the tunnels of this 17th-century Spanish fortress built to protect the city and its gold from English pirates (page 33).

★ **Playa Blanca and Islas del Rosario:** Make it a true Caribbean holiday at this group

© AVALON TRAVEL

of 25 coral islands, known for their white-sand beaches, turquoise waters, and gentle breezes (page 54).

Magical Cartagena wastes no time in seducing its visitors. It's a majestic walled city full of magnificent churches and palaces, picturesque balcony-lined streets, and romantic plazas.

The main attraction is the Old City (Cartagena's *centro histórico*). The magnificent walls of the Ciudad Amurallada (the Walled City) enclose narrow streets lined with magnificent *casas altas* (two-story houses once home to wealthy merchants) with bougainvillea spilling out over their balconies. Getsemaní is an old working-class colonial neighborhood (also once enclosed by a wall) that today lures visitors with its many lodging, dining, and night-life options. Near the Old City is the magnificent Castillo de San Felipe, one of the most impressive Spanish fortifications in the New World.

Outside the Old City, Cartagena is a large, poor, and sprawling city of almost one million people. If you want to get a sense of its size, visit La Popa (The Hill) for expansive views of the city and the bay. To get to know the real Cartagena firsthand, visit the frenetic Mercado de Bazurto to the southeast of the Old City and then, for contrast, take a stroll through flashy Bocagrande.

If you're looking to play at the beach, escape to the white sands of Islas del Rosario or to Barú, as the gray beaches of Cartagena are unappealing.

Colombia's colonial past lives on in Mompox, a once-thriving inland port on the Río Magdalena where it feels as if time has stopped.

HISTORY

Cartagena de Indias was founded in 1533 by Spanish conquistador Pedro de Heredia on a small Carib indigenous settlement. During the 16th century, the city was sacked by pirates numerous times, most notably by Sir Francis Drake in 1568. Pairs of forts were constructed at various passage points in the harbor to stop intruders. The construction of the fortifications took almost two centuries and was completed by the mid-1700s.

Previous: colonial buildings in the Old City; rooftop view of Cartagena. **Above:** Iglesia de Santa Bárbara, Mompox.

Cartagena

© AVALON TRAVEL

Caribbean Sea

EL LAGUITO

HILTON HOTEL

HOSPITAL/ BOATS TO TIERRABOMBA ISLAND

BOCAGRANDE

Bocagrande Beaches

BOCAGRANDE MALL

AV SAN MARTIN

Castillo Grande Jogging Path

CLUB NAVAL/ CASTILLOGRANDE FORT

PRESIDENTIAL GUESTHOUSE/ MANZANILLO FORT

Cartagena Bay

NAVAL BASE

MUELLE DE MANGA

MANGA

CLUB DE PESCA/ PASTELILLO FORT

CRUISE SHIP TERMINAL

CARIBE PLAZA MALL

MERCADO DE BAZURTO

SEE "CENTRO AND SAN DIEGO" MAP

SEE "GETSEMANÍ" MAP

CENTRO

SAN DIEGO

GETSEMANÍ

CASTILLO DE SAN FELIPE

MARBELLA

EL CABRERO

AVENIDA SANTANDER

LA POPA

To PLAYA BLANCA AND ISLAS DEL ROSARIO

To La Boquilla, Las Américas, Playa Manzanillo, and Barranquilla

AIRPORT

DIAGONAL 22

AVENIDA PEDRO DE HEREDIA

TRANSVERSAL 54

BULLFIGHTING RING, SOCCER, BASEBALL STADIUM

To Turbaco

To Barranquilla

TERMINAL DE TRANSPORTES (BUS STATION)

0
1 km
0
1 mi

Caribbean Sea

PLAYA BLANCA AND ISLAS DEL ROSARIO

Isla de Tierra Bomba

Bocachica

Cartagena

Barú

Ciénaga de la Virgen

MAP AREA

The city prospered as one of the main slave ports in Spanish America. It is estimated that more than one million slaves passed through the city. Slaves often escaped and created free communities known as *palenques,* such as the town of San Basilio, south of Cartagena.

Cartagena formally declared independence from Spain in 1812. In 1815, it was recaptured by the Spanish. Cartagena was retaken by revolutionaries in 1821. During the 19th century, Cartagena lost its status as one of Spain's main ports. The economic decline had one good side effect: preserving the colonial past. The Old City remained largely intact through the 20th century, prompting UNESCO to declare it a World Heritage Site.

Cartagena remained relatively peaceful even during the worst periods of violence in the 1980s and 1990s. In the past decade, Cartagena has become a major international tourist destination, with a proliferation of chic, five-star hotels in the Old City, glitzy condominiums and hotels in Bocagrande, and new resorts along the coast north of the city.

PLANNING YOUR TIME

Cartagena is an easy destination to visit even during a **weekend.** That's enough time to stroll the streets of the Old City, experience some fine restaurants, and be pampered in a boutique hotel. Two days will suffice, but three days is ideal. For a quick beach getaway, head to Barú or the Islas del Rosario archipelago—preferably overnight, but they're also doable as a day trip.

To venture farther afield, a **week** is optimal, but you may not be able to hit every top destination. Getting to the town of Mompox involves five hours of travel by road and river, so staying two nights there is necessary. To the northeast of Cartagena, Barranquilla and Santa Marta are an easy day or overnight trip. Farther east is the Parque Nacional Natural Tayrona, where travelers often spend 2-3 days. For those looking for the quintessential Colombian jungle experience, continue to the Parque Nacional Natural Sierra Nevada de Santa Marta, where the famed Ciudad Perdida trek requires 4-5 days.

Peak tourist seasons are the last week of November (when the city celebrates its independence from Spain and hosts the Miss Colombia beauty pageant), from mid-December to mid-January, Semana Santa (Holy Week) in March or April, June to July (school vacations), and during any of the long weekends when Monday is a holiday (check a

Las Bóvedas in the Old City is the most atmospheric place to browse handicrafts and souvenirs.

Colombian calendar). Holidays aren't kind to wallets: Room rates spike dramatically.

SAFETY

The crown jewel of Colombian tourism, Cartagena is quite safe to visit. Be mindful while walking on the walls after dark. It's easy to be distracted while strolling the streets, so keep your valuables close to your body.

While reports are rare, police have been known to stop and frisk young non-Colombian men in the evening, purportedly out of suspicion of drug possession—in actuality they are looking for money. This has occurred most commonly late at night in Getsemaní. Some people have found that calling attention to the officer and getting others to record the episode on their phone defuses the situation.

Some of the poor fishing villages on islands near Cartagena, such as Tierrabomba (close to the entrance to Bocachica), are best visited in a group. Keep an eye on drinks at late-night watering holes.

By far the greatest annoyances in Cartagena are persistent street vendors, who have even been known to latch on to walking tours. In the evening, some vendors will pitch less legal items on male passersby. Saying *"No, gracias,"* may or may not help ward off these nuisances. Don't allow them to get under your skin.

Most taxi drivers, bartenders, and vendors are honest, but there are always a few who will try to take advantage of visitors by overcharging or not returning the proper amount of change to a non-Colombian visitor who may not hold a strong grasp of the language. Always try to pay with small notes or coins when possible—keep those COP$20,000 and COP$50,000 notes only for emergencies, or change them. Request to see the drinks menu (*carta de tragos*) at bars before ordering. Before getting into a cab, have an idea of what you'll be paying, and confirm the amount with the driver upfront.

ORIENTATION

Cartagena de Indias is a sprawling city located on the Caribbean coast of Colombia

at the north end of a large bay with the same name. The city's tourist focus is a relatively small area: the Old City (Centro Histórico), the original Spanish settlement that was once completely enclosed by massive stone walls. The Old City comprises two main districts: the Centro, with its magnificent walls, narrow streets, colorful bougainvillea dangling from balconies, activity-packed plazas, and myriad churches and palaces; and Getsemaní, an old colonial neighborhood that was also enclosed by its own wall and fortifications. Today it is the hot new address for lodging, restaurant, and nightlife options.

Centro and San Diego

The Centro (from *centro histórico;* also called the Old City or the Walled City) is the historic core of Cartagena; it's surrounded by the most impressive sections of the city walls. This is where most of Cartagena's sights are located, including its most famous churches and museums. The southern part of the Walled City boasts magnificent two-story *casas altas* (tall houses) built by merchants and government officials. Today, the Centro is where many upscale hotels, restaurants, shops, and nightclubs are found. The Plaza de Santo Domingo, filled with cafés, is one of the liveliest parts of town.

The northeastern half of the Centro is known as San Diego. In colonial times, this neighborhood was where artisans and laborers lived. Here the architecture is more modest. There are a few attractions in San Diego, notably the Iglesia de Santo Toribio de Mogrovejo and Las Bóvedas, a shopping arcade located in a section of the walls. The charm of San Diego lies in its quiet streets and pleasant bars and restaurants, particularly around the Plaza de San Diego.

The Centro is organized in a general grid with numerous plazas. Even many residents don't know or use official street names, as they change from block to block. Orient yourself by identifying the main squares—Torre de los Coches, Plaza de la Aduana, Plaza de Santo Domingo, Parque de Bolívar, and Plaza

Fernández de Madrid—and making your way from one to the other. Walking these charming streets (and even getting lost on occasion) is a pleasure.

El Cabrero

Just north of the Old City is the 19th-century district of El Cabrero. The neighborhood's sole attraction is the Casa Museo Rafael Núñez, once the home of conservative president Rafael Núñez, who governed from Cartagena.

Getsemaní

The neighborhood of Getsemaní lies to the southeast of the Centro. During colonial times, Getsemaní was where poor residents lived, and the architecture here is much more modest than in the Centro. The epicenter of the neighborhood today is the Plaza de la Trinidad, in front of Iglesia de la Santísima Trinidad, where backpackers, street performers, and longtime residents congregate in the evenings. Along the waterfront is the modern Centro de Convenciones.

La Matuna

In the late 19th and early 20th centuries, the mangroves and marshes separating the Centro and Getsemaní were filled, resulting in the neighborhood called La Matuna. During the mid-20th century, many high-rises were built in La Matuna, but it's still home to colorful open-air markets. La Matuna may be the next slice of the city to become gentrified.

Today the Muelle de los Pegasos (also known as the Muelle de la Bodeguita) is the departure point for tourist boats headed to the Islas del Rosario.

Manga

To the southeast of Getsemaní, across the Puente Roman (Roman Bridge) is the island of Manga, a residential district. The only destination in Manga is the Club de Pesca restaurant, housed in the well-preserved Fuerte de San Sebastián del Pastelillo, one of many forts that once protected the bay.

The boardwalk along Calle 24, with its magnificent views across the bay, is a pleasant place to walk at sunset. Many yachts and boats depart from Manga to go to the Islas del Rosario and Barú.

Bocagrande

South of the Old City is upscale Bocagrande, a skinny peninsula with many high-rise hotels, malls, and residential buildings. The main attractions here are the beaches, which get packed on weekends with Colombian families, vendors, and masseuses. These gray-sand beaches in no way compare to the beautiful beaches of the Islas del Rosario and Barú.

Sights

CENTRO
★ Las Murallas

Referring to Cartagena's *murallas* (walls), Colombians endearingly call the city "El Corralito de Piedra" (little stone corral). These walls are one of the most salient features of the city. After Drake sacked the city in 1568, the Spanish started fortifying access to the bay and the perimeter wall around the city. The effort took almost two centuries to complete. The walls that can be seen today are mostly from the 17th and 18th centuries.

The most impressive part of the wall is the stretch that runs parallel to the sea. This includes three *baluartes* (bulwarks, or ramparts) where Spaniards stood ready to defend the city from attack. The massive **Baluartes de San Lucas y de Santa Catalina,** built in the very north of the city to repel attacks from land, are known as Las Tenazas because they are shaped like pincers. When the sea

Centro and San Diego

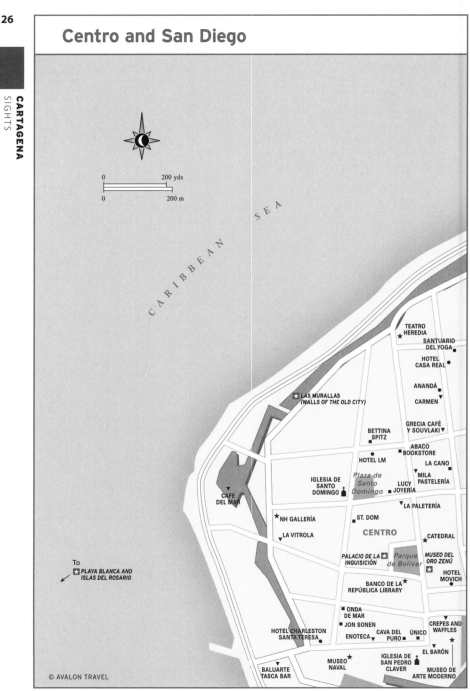

CARIBBEAN SEA

0 — 200 yds
0 — 200 m

TEATRO HEREDIA
★ SANTUARIO DEL YOGA
HOTEL CASA REAL ●
ANANDÁ ▼
★ LAS MURALLAS (WALLS OF THE OLD CITY)
CARMEN
GRECIA CAFÉ Y SOUVLAKI ▼
BETTINA SPITZ ■
ABACO BOOKSTORE ■
HOTEL LM ●
LA CANO ■
MILA PASTELERÍA ▼
IGLESIA DE SANTO DOMINGO
Plaza de Santo Domingo
LUCY JOYERÍA ■
CAFÉ DEL MAR ▼
▼ LA PALETERÍA
★ NH GALLERÍA
■ ST. DOM
CENTRO
LA VITROLA ▼
CATEDRAL ★
MUSEO DEL ORO ZENÚ
PALACIO DE LA INQUISICIÓN
Parque de Bolívar
To ★ PLAYA BLANCA AND ISLAS DEL ROSARIO
HOTEL MOVICH ●
BANCO DE LA REPÚBLICA LIBRARY ★
■ ONDA DE MAR
■ JON SONEN
CREPES AND WAFFLES
HOTEL CHARLESTON SANTA TERESA ●
ENOTECA ▼
CAVA DEL PURO ■
ÚNICO ■
★
EL BARÓN ▼
MUSEO NAVAL ★
IGLESIA DE SAN PEDRO CLAVER
MUSEO DE ARTE MODERNO
BALUARTE TASCA BAR ▼

© AVALON TRAVEL

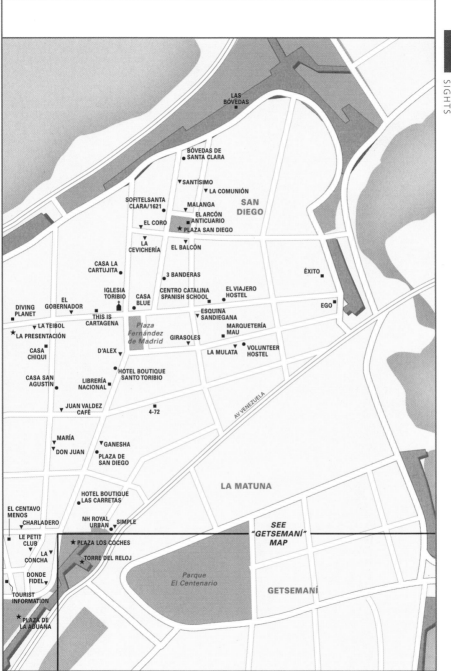

LAS BÓVEDAS

BÓVEDAS DE SANTA CLARA

SANTÍSIMO

LA COMUNIÓN

SOFITELSANTA CLARA/1621

MALANGA

EL ARCÓN ANTICUARIO

SAN DIEGO

EL CORO

PLAZA SAN DIEGO

LA CEVICHERÍA

EL BALCÓN

CASA LA CARTUJITA

3 BANDERAS

ÉXITO

IGLESIA TORIBIO

CASA BLUE

CENTRO CATALINA SPANISH SCHOOL

EL VIAJERO HOSTEL

DIVING PLANET

EL GOBERNADOR

EGO

THIS IS CARTAGENA

ESQUINA SANDIEGANA

LA TEIBOL

LA PRESENTACIÓN

Plaza Fernández de Madrid

MARQUETERÍA MAU

CASA CHIQUI

D'ALEX

GIRASOLES

LA MULATA

VOLUNTEER HOSTEL

HOTEL BOUTIQUE SANTO TORIBIO

CASA SAN AGUSTÍN

LIBRERÍA NACIONAL

JUAN VALDEZ CAFÉ

4-72

AV. VENEZUELA

MARÍA

GANESHA

DON JUAN

PLAZA DE SAN DIEGO

LA MATUNA

HOTEL BOUTIQUE LAS CARRETAS

EL CENTAVO MENOS

CHARLADERO

NH ROYAL URBAN

SIMPLE

SEE "GETSEMANÍ" MAP

LE PETIT CLUB

LA CONCHA

PLAZA LOS COCHES

TORRE DEL RELOJ

DONDE FIDEL

TOURIST INFORMATION

Parque El Centenario

GETSEMANÍ

PLAZA DE LA ADUANA

Getsemaní

© AVALON TRAVEL

started depositing sediments and expanding the seashore, thus enabling the enemy to maneuver south along the wall, the Spanish built a spike to halt them. This defensive structure, known as El Espigón de la Tenaza, is now home to the **Museo de las Fortificaciones** (Baluarte de Santa Catalina, tel. 5/656-0591, www.fortificacionesdecartagena.com, 8am-6pm daily, COP$7,000). At the westernmost tip of the walls, facing the sea, is the equally impressive **Baluarte Santo Domingo,** now home to swank drinking hole Café del Mar. At the southern tip of the segment of walls facing the sea, next to the Plaza de Santa Teresa, are the **Baluartes de San Ignacio y de San**

Francisco Javier, also home to a pleasant outdoor bar.

A *paseo* (walk) on the walls is the quintessential Cartagena experience, enjoyed by international visitors, Colombian honeymooners, and Cartagenan high school students. The best time for this is in the early evening hours. Avoid walking the walls alone late at night.

★ Colonial Churches
CLAUSTRO AND IGLESIA DE SAN PEDRO CLAVER
The **Claustro de San Pedro Claver** (Plaza de San Pedro Claver No. 30-01, tel. 5/664-4991,

8am-5:30pm Mon.-Fri., 8am-4:30pm Sat.-Sun., COP$9,000) is a former Jesuit monastery turned museum, where Pedro Claver served as a priest. He is remembered for his compassion toward newly arrived African slaves, and is said to have baptized thousands of them. The priest was the first person to be canonized in the New World. The museum has relics and art from the colonial era. The cloister, where San Pedro Claver lived, has a courtyard brimming with flowers and trees.

Adjacent to the monastery is the **Iglesia de San Pedro Claver** (Plaza de San Pedro Claver No. 30-01, tel. 5/664-4991, masses 6:45am and 6pm Mon.-Sat., 7am, 10am, noon, and 6pm Sun.), which is adorned by a beautiful marble altar and is the final resting place for San Pedro Claver.

CATEDRAL BASÍLICA MENOR

Diagonal to the Parque de Bolívar is the built-to-last **Catedral Basílica Menor** or **Catedral de Santa Catalina de Alejandría** (tel. 5/665-0211, mass 10am, noon, and 5pm Mon.-Sat., 8am and 7pm Sun., COP$13,000, free during mass). It was built in the 16th century and doubled as a fortress. It was attacked by Sir Francis Drake in 1586. The facade, along with most of the interior, has been stripped of the Italianate stucco exterior that was added in the 20th century and restored to its former austere stone look. The cathedral's pink and orange bell tower dates to the early 20th century, and can be seen from throughout the Old City. Stroll the ornate cathedral before or during a mass to skip the entry fee. Audio guides (included with admission) are available.

IGLESIA DE SANTO TORIBIO DE MOGROVEJO

The gorgeous **Iglesia de Santo Toribio de Mogrovejo** (Plaza Fernández de Madrid at Cl. Sargento Mayor and Cl. del Curato, tel. 5/664-5347, mass 6:30am, noon, and 6pm Mon.-Sat., 8am, 10am, 6pm, and 7pm Sun.) is elegant in its simplicity. This small, early-18th-century church has a stone entrance, a Mudejar-style ceiling, and baroque high altar. On display is a cannonball launched by English pirate Edward Vernon. The church hosts mass several times each day.

Museo de Arte Moderno de Cartagena de Indias

Cartagena's main art museum, the **Museo de Arte Moderno de Cartagena de Indias** (Cl. 30 No. 4-08, Plaza de San Pedro Claver,

Iglesia de San Pedro Claver

tel. 5/664-5815, 9am-noon and 3pm-6pm Mon.-Fri., 10am-1pm Sat., COP$5,000, Tues. free) is on the square in front of Plaza de San Pedro Claver, which contains several metallic sculptures by Cartagenero Edgardo Carmona that depict quotidian scenes of Cartagena life. The museum has a small permanent collection of works from 20th-century Colombian artists, including native sons Alejandro Obregón and Enrique Grau. The museum is in the old Customs House. For more detailed information on the museum and its collections, download Soundwalkrs, a free smartphone app.

Museo Naval del Caribe

Adjoining the rear of the Iglesia de San Pedro Claver is the **Museo Naval del Caribe** (Cl. San Juan de Dios No. 3-62, tel. 5/664-2440, www.museonavaldelcaribe.com, 10am-5:30pm daily, COP$8,000). This museum provides a history lesson of the earliest indigenous dwellers who lived in the area, continuing through the Spanish conquest and including a bit about the many (mostly English) pirates who tried to steal the Spaniards' gold loot, which they had absconded with from all across South America. The second floor has a lot of replicas of grand ships from the period

and a history of the Colombian navy (you may be surprised to learn of its participation in the Korean War). There are few explanations in English. Part of the building dates to the 17th century and was a Jesuit convent; after the Jesuits were expelled by the king, the building was converted into a hospital. Pushing buttons in the submarine upstairs makes the price of admission worth it.

Parque de Bolívar

One of the city's most pleasant and lively squares is the **Parque de Bolívar,** which once served as a bullfighting ring. A statue of Simón Bolívar on horseback presides over the center of the lush park. Take a break on a bench under the shade of the rubber trees.

★ Palacio de la Inquisición

On the south side of the plaza is the **Palacio de la Inquisición** (Parque de Bolívar, tel. 5/664-4570, 9am-6pm Mon.-Sat., 10am-4pm Sun., COP$16,000). This remarkable 18th-century construction, one of the finest extant examples of colonial architecture in the city, was the headquarters of the Spanish Inquisition in Cartagena. In this building was housed the Tribunal del Santo Oficio, whose purpose was to exert control over the

Parque de Bolívar

Palacio de la Inquisición

colonial Cartagena could anonymously report others for various and sundry heresies.

★ Museo del Oro Zenú

The **Museo del Oro Zenú** (Cra. 4 No. 33-26, Parque de Bolívar, tel. 5/660-0778, 9am-5pm Tues.-Sat., 10am-3pm Sun., free), on the east side of the Parque de Bolívar, exhibits gold jewelry and funerary objects from the Zenú indigenous people, who were the original dwellers of the Río Magdalena area and Río Sinú valley, to the southwest of Cartagena. It has excellent explanations in both English and Spanish. A smaller version of the Museo del Oro in Bogotá, this museum has a regional focus and is one of the few tributes to indigenous culture in Cartagena.

GETSEMANÍ

The *murallas* extend along the edge of Getsemaní, but strolling along them is not nearly as pleasant as in the Centro. You can, however, check out the **Baluarte del Reducto,** where there is a bar and sweeping bay views. This bulwark, part of the city's system of walls, once protected the city from potential enemies.

Paseo de los Mártires and Parque del Centenario

Paseo de los Mártires was once the main corridor that led from the Walled City to Getsemaní and today features nine marble statues of important historical figures. Adjacent to the corridor is the **Parque del Centenario,** which was opened in 1911 in commemoration of Colombia's first century of independence. It's a pleasant place for a stroll, and you just might spot enormous iguanas scurrying from tree to tree. On the northern edge of the park are a series of stalls where vendors sell used books.

Churches

There are two colonial-era churches in Getsemaní worth a peek. The first is the **Iglesia de la Santísima Trinidad** (Plaza de la Trinidad, tel. 5/664-2050, mass 6pm

Indians, mestizos, and African slaves not only in Nueva Granada but also in New World colonies in Central America, the Caribbean, and Venezuela. The tribunal was active from 1610 until the late 17th century. There were two other tribunals in the New World: one in Lima and another in Mexico City.

The first floor of the building is a museum displaying the weapons of torture employed by authorities as part of the Inquisition. In Cartagena as elsewhere, the most common punishable crime was "witchcraft," and hundreds of supposed heretics (indigenous people were excluded from punishment) were condemned here. On the second floor are exhibition spaces dedicated to the restoration of the building and to the history of Cartagena. Most explanations are written in Spanish; you may decide to hire one of the English-speaking guides (COP$35,000 for a group up to five persons). On your way out, take a right and then another right onto Calle de la Inquisición and look for a small window on the palace wall. This was a secret spot where citizens of

Plaza-to-Plaza Walking Tour

Total Distance: 1.6 kilometers (1 mile)
Walking Time: 25-30 minutes
The best way to get to know Cartagena is to go for a morning stroll, finding your way from plaza to plaza, and even getting lost a couple of times. This tour starts in the Centro and ends in San Diego.

1. Start at the **Plaza de los Coches** (west of Av. Venezuela, opposite Getsemaní), once the main entry point to the city. It is easily identifiable by the iconic 19th-century **Torre del Reloj** (clock tower) that tops the entrance through the wall. Inside stands a statue of Cartagena's founder, Pedro de Heredia. During the colonial period, this plaza was the site of the city's slave market. Today, the plaza is filled with watering holes catering to visitors. Along the main corridor is the **Portal de las Dulces,** a row of stands where Afro-Colombian women sell homemade sweets, often made from coconut and tamarind.

Torre del Reloj in the Plaza de los Coches

2. Immediately to the southwest is the large triangular **Plaza de la Aduana,** once the seat of power in colonial Cartagena. It is surrounded by stately colonial mansions. A statue of Christopher Columbus presides in the center. It has its fair share of ATMs and is where the main tourist office is located.

3. Adjacent to Plaza de la Aduana to the southwest is the **Plaza de San Pedro,** a small but charming square, located in front of the imposing **Iglesia de San Pedro Claver** and attached cloister.

4. Walk two blocks north on Calle de San Pedro and you'll arrive at the city's heart, the leafy **Parque de Bolívar,** a shady park with benches, fountains, and a statue of Simón Bolívar in the middle. Surrounding this lovely park are some of the most important buildings of the city, including the **Catedral Basílica Menor** and the **Palacio de la Inquisición.**

5. Continue north on Calle de los Santos de Piedra for one block. Take the first left onto Calle de Ayos. One block west is the **Plaza de Santo Domingo,** in the heart of the former upper-class quarter. You will notice many superb two-story *casas altas* built by rich merchants. The plaza is dominated by the austere **Iglesia de Santo Domingo.** A rotund nude bronze sculpture by famous Colombian sculptor Fernando Botero, live musical performances, and many outdoor cafés liven up the popular plaza.

6. Walk north along Calle de Santo Domingo for a block, then turn right and head east for four blocks on Calle de la Mantilla until you reach Calle Segunda de Badillo. Turn left and half a block north is the large, green **Plaza Fernández de Madrid** in the San Diego district. On the northwest side is the charming **Iglesia de Santo Toribio de Mogrovejo,** with its magnificent wooden ceiling.

7. Head east on Calle del Santísimo for two blocks, then turn left on Calle Cochera del Hobo and go north just over a block to the **Plaza de San Diego,** which is surrounded by inviting restaurants. It's also where artisans sell handicrafts under the shade of a tree.

8. Walk north for one block on Calle de las Bóvedas, which will deposit you at the **Plaza de las Bóvedas** at the extreme northeast of the city. Once the location of a military storehouse, this is where you can browse handicrafts under the golden arched walls of the Galería de las Bóvedas.

Mon.-Sat., 9am and 6pm Sun.), completed in the mid-17th century. This bright yellow church of three naves has as its model the city's cathedral. The church is often open during the day, and visitors are welcome to sit on a pew in front of a massive fan and cool off. In the evenings the colorful Plaza de la Trinidad is a hub of activity.

In response to the deadly cholera outbreak that was ravaging Cartagena at the time, church leaders committed to building a church dedicated to Saint Roch, protector of those afflicted with the plague. Construction on the simple **Iglesia de San Roque** (Cl. de la Media Luna and Cl. Espíritu Santo, tel. 5/664-2512, mass 7pm Mon.-Sat., 8:30am and 7pm Sun.) began in 1651.

EL CABRERO
Casa Museo Rafael Núñez

Just beyond the wall in the Cabrero neighborhood is the **Casa Museo Rafael Núñez** (Cl. Real del Cabrero No. 41-89, tel. 5/660-9058, 9am-5pm Tues.-Fri., 10am-4pm Sat.-Sun., free). This is the house of Rafael Núñez, the four-time former president of Colombia, author of the 1886 Colombian constitution, and author of the 11 verses of Colombia's national anthem. Núñez governed Colombia from this,

his coastal home. The museum has memorabilia from his political life and is a beautiful example of 19th-century Cartagena architecture. Núñez's grave is in the Ermita de Nuestra Señora de las Mercedes across the street.

★ CASTILLO DE SAN FELIPE

The largest Spanish fort in the New World, the magnificent **Castillo de San Felipe** (Cerro de San Lázaro, east of Old City, tel. 5/656-6803, www.patrimoniodecartagena.com, 8am-6pm daily, COP$17,000) must have given pirates pause as they contemplated an attack on the city. While the walls around the city fended off maritime attacks, this fort was built atop the Cerro de San Lázaro to repel attacks by land at the Media Luna gate. Construction was begun in 1639 and completed more than a century later. Tunnels enabled soldiers to quickly move about without being noticed, and cells housed the occasional unlucky prisoner.

Today, visitors ramble through 890 meters (0.5 mile) of tunnels and secret passages (a flashlight will come in quite handy). Views from the highest points of the fort are magnificent. The best time to visit the fort is in the late afternoon, when the intense sun abates.

Castillo de San Felipe, one of the most impressive forts in the New World

Audio tours (COP$10,000) are available. For many, the view of the fort from a distance suffices, especially at nighttime when it is lit up.

If you want to do things up for a special celebration, you can rent out the entire *castillo* or space on the *murallas*. Contact the **Sociedad de Mejoras Públicas de Cartagena** (Castillo de San Felipe de Barajas, tel. 5/656-0590, www.fortificacionesdecartagena.com) for more information.

To get to the fort, take a cab (COP$6,000), a bus (COP$1,500) from Avenida Santander, or the TransCaribe (COP$2,000) from Avenida Venezuela.

LA POPA

La Popa is a 150-meter-high (500-foot-high) hill east of Castillo de San Felipe, so named because of its resemblance to a ship's stern (*popa* in Spanish). La Popa is home to the **Convento Nuestra Señora de la Candelaria** (Cra. 20A 29D-16, tel. 5/666-0976, 9am-5:30pm daily, COP$5,000), which was built by Augustinian monks, reportedly on a pagan site of worship. The monastery has a courtyard abloom with flowers, a small chapel where faithful pray to the Virgen de la Candelaria, and memorabilia from Pope John Paul II's visit to the monastery in 1986. For many, the view of Cartagena is the biggest attraction. Cruise ship passengers arrive by the busload at La Popa, so be prepared for crowds. You can take a taxi there from the Old City for COP$50,000-60,000 round-trip. Arrange the price in advance and make sure the driver will wait for you there. Many visitors combine a visit to La Popa with the Castillo de San Felipe, which is nearby (although not within walking distance).

MERCADO DE BAZURTO

Not for the faint of heart, a visit to the sprawling, grimy **Mercado de Bazurto** (Av. Pedro Heredia, 5am-4pm daily) is the best way to connect with the real Cartagena. On the periphery of this covered market, be sure to peruse the seafood area, where women sell the catch of the day to restaurant owners. Be amazed at all the different kinds of fruit on offer. Don't be afraid to barter a little and don't be shy: The hundreds of vendors generally enjoy interacting with foreign visitors. The market is at its liveliest in the morning; expect to spend a few hours here. Dress down and keep an eye on your valuables.

The market is in the Pie de la Popa neighborhood southeast of the Old City. The best way to get there is via taxi (COP$8,000). It's possible to take a bus (COP$1,500) from Avenida Santander and there is also a TransCaribe rapid bus station here.

Another way of visiting the market is the **Mercado de Bazurto Tour** (tel. 5/660-1492, cell tel. 315/655-4120, cevicheria@hotmail.com, COP$250,000 pp), organized by La Cevichería and Bazurto Social Club. On the tour, you'll learn about the ingredients that make Caribbean cuisine special, particularly seafood and exotic fruits. You'll also meet the vendors who have worked their entire lives behind a stall at the market. Afterward you'll head to a beach house and have a gourmet lunch featuring lobster and other delicacies.

SIGHTSEEING TOURS

Bursting with insider tips on the city and its environs, **This Is Cartagena** (Cl. Sargento Mayor, No. 6-107, Of. 104, cell tel. 318/516-7767, www.ticartagena.com, 9am-6pm Mon.-Fri.) offers unconventional tours of the city. In addition to a top-notch walking tour of the Old City (US$52), the company also offers a tour devoted to the art scene (US$55), a bizarre-foods tour (US$85), a day of luxurious island-hopping on a yacht (US$750), and a drinking tour (US$75).

A fund-raising project for the nonprofit FEM (www.femcolombia.org), **Cartagena Insider** (Cl. del Quero No. 9-64, tel. 5/643-4185, cartagenainsider@gmail.com) takes visitors beyond the boutique hotels and fancy restaurants of the Old City to experience the "real" Cartagena and its people. Tour options include a night of salsa, a day trip to La Boquilla fishing community, a walking tour of the Mercado de Bazurto, and a tour focusing on the Champeta music culture unique to Cartagena. Proceeds go directly to the nonprofit's social programs in and around the city. Tours can also be arranged to communities such as Tuchín, Córdoba, Leticia (a town on Barú), Palmerito, and San Bacile de Palenque.

With an extensive array of interesting tours, **Alternative Travel Cartagena** (tel. 5/646-0701, www.alternativetravelcartagena. com) aims to take visitors to lesser-known areas in and around Cartagena for a unique experience. They are based in the fishing village of La Boquilla and offer horseback rides on the beach, cooking classes, and canoe rides through mangroves.

Photographer Joaquin Saramiento offers various tours of the city with **Fototour** (cell tel. 317/365-4021, http://fototour.co, US$80), during which amateur photographers can hone their skills, learn about Cartagena's history and culture, and explore the city.

Entertainment and Events

NIGHTLIFE

Cartagena's nightspots tend to close at 3am weekdays, with some staying open until 5am on weekends. Expect to pay a cover fee, but groups can ask for a discount.

The city's favorite music styles are old-school salsa and *son cubano,* along with the Afro beats of *champeta.*

Centro and San Diego

With the Caribbean breeze kissing your face, enjoying a drink on the *murallas* is an experience that shouldn't be missed. There are three official options for this activity, one of them a cheapie. First, the **Baluarte Tasca-Bar** (Cl. San Juan de Dios, tel. 5/660-0468, 5:30pm-2am daily, no cover) is an open-air restaurant-bar on the wall across from the Plaza de Santa Teresa. It's chilled-out here, not trendy—but the drink prices are on the steep side: COP$24,000 for a margarita. The most happening spot is the **Café del Mar** (Baluarte Santo Domingo, tel. 5/664-6515, 5pm-3am daily, no cover), on the wall near the entrance to the Plaza de Santo Domingo. The music is loungey and electronic, and it stays busy until late. It's a cool place, but it's not great for mingling, as patrons are all seated in bulky furniture, and the drinks are pricey. The third option is also good for your budget: Buy an Águila beer from a roaming vendor (COP$3,000) and wander the walls at your leisure.

COCKTAIL BARS

In an unassuming corner of the Plaza de San Pedro Claver, **El Barón** (Cra. 4 No. 31-7, tel. 5/664-3105, 5pm-1am Sun.-Mon., noon-1am Tues., noon-2am Wed.-Sat., no cover) is devoted to cocktail culture. The interior is all brass and rustic furnishings, but you can also sip the evening away out on the plaza, where the people-watching is fantastic. Allow the bartender to mix you a gin-basil smash—you can get a beer anytime. Tapas are also on offer.

If you're looking for atmosphere, head to **El Coro** (Cl. del Torno No. 39-29, tel. 5/650-4700, 5pm-2am Sun.-Thurs., 5pm-3am Fri.-Sat., no cover), at the Hotel Sofitel Legend Santa Clara. At this posh bar in a former 17th-century convent, crisply dressed bartenders serve Caribbean cocktails to hotel guests and others while Latin jazz plays in the background. Of the larger convent complex, El Coro is located in the chorus area from where the resident nuns sang while mass was celebrated in the adjacent chapel. Ask to see the crypt, which was an inspiration for Gabriel García Márquez as he wrote *Of Love and Other Demons.*

SALSA AND *SON CUBANO*

Donde Fidel (Plaza de los Coches, tel. 5/664-3127, noon-2am Sun.-Thurs., noon-3am Fri.-Sat., no cover) is a tiny salsa lovers' spot where the action spills out onto the plaza in front. Good times and cold beer can be found here.

La Esquina Sandiegana (corner of Cl. del Santísimo and Cl. de los Púntales, 5pm-2am Sun.-Thurs., 5pm-3am Fri.-Sat., no cover) is a locals' place, where the music is salsa and the drink is beer. Its walls are decorated with salsa posters, album covers, and photographs of salsa greats. It's a hole-in-the-wall bar in the San Diego neighborhood.

GAY CLUBS

Gay nightlife in Cartagena is not exactly thriving: There are only a couple of spots worth checking out. Crowds are friendly and the scene is mixed.

Brash **D8** (Cl. del Arsenal No. 8B-155, tel. 5/646-0657, 10pm-4am Fri.-Sat.) is the dance club of the moment in Cartagena. To take it down a notch, try **Le Petit Club** (Cl. del Candilejo No. 32-34, 5pm-2am Wed.-Sat.), which has a pub-like atmosphere, especially midweek.

Getsemaní

Wednesdays are the new Saturdays in Cartagena. In Getsemaní, **Visa por un Sueño** (Media Luna Hostel, Cl. de la Media Luna No. 10-46, tel. 5/664-0639, http://medialunahostel.com, 9pm-3am Wed., COP$10,000) is a weekly party held on the rooftop of the Media Luna Hostel. It has become Cartagena's most famous soiree, where international party people mix it up with Colombians. Get there early—this party gets seriously packed, and lines will be very long. Another option offered by the hostel is the **Media Luna Boat Party** (medialunaboatparty@gmail.com, usually 2pm-6pm Sun., COP$60,000), which leaves from the Muelle de los Pegasos every Sunday. To confirm the schedule, check the hostel's Facebook page or swing by the hostel in person to reserve your spot.

BARS

It's easy to like **Locombia Café Bar** (Cl. de la Media Luna No. 29-209, cell tel. 316/585-9172, noon-1am daily), with its unpretentious personality, cool music, and tiny location from which you can keep tabs on all the activity on happening Calle de la Media Luna.

SALSA AND *SON CUBANO*

Café Havana (intersection of Cl. de la Media Luna and Cl. del Guerrero, cell tel. 314/556-3905 or 310/610-2324, www.cafehavana-cartagena.com, 8:30pm-4am Thurs.-Sat., cover varies) famously got the endorsement of Hillary Clinton on her trip to Colombia in 2012, when she was Secretary of State. It's a place for rum drinks and dancing. Café Havana is open Sundays when the following Monday is a holiday.

CHAMPETA

Bazurto Social Club (Av. del Centenario No. 30-42, tel. 5/664-3124, www.bazurto-socialclub.com, 7pm-3am Thurs.-Sat., cover varies) is an always-lively restaurant-bar, popular with Colombians and international visitors alike. Get a taste for Afro-Colombian *champeta* beats, as live acts, including the Bazurto All Stars, often perform here. They also serve food, such as shrimp empanadas and paella. The house drink is the fruity rum *machacos*.

FESTIVALS AND EVENTS

Cartagena feels like a celebration all the time, but it's especially true from November to February, when an array of cultural events are featured. Pick up a copy of *Donde,* a free monthly newspaper with Cartagena event listings. You can find it at the airport and in big hotels.

Hay Festival

The **Hay Festival** (www.hayfestival.com) is an important international festival that began in Wales nearly 30 years ago. It celebrates literature, music, environmental awareness,

The Teatro Heredia is the site of the Hay Festival.

Internacional de Música (International Music Festival, www.cartagenamusicfestival.com, tickets www.tuboleta.com). Most concerts sell out far in advance, but if you can't get tickets, you might be able to catch a free performance in one of the churches or plazas in the Old City.

Festival Internacional de Cine de Cartagena de Indias

If you're in town during late February and are looking for an excuse to escape the heat, here it is: the **Festival Internacional de Cine de Cartagena de Indias** (International Film Festival, tel. 5/664-2345, www.ficcifestival.com). A tradition since the 1960s, this weeklong film festival has an interesting program of documentaries, Colombian films, and shorts; a series of roundtable discussions with prominent actors and directors; and educational activities in neighborhoods throughout the city. The venues include historic buildings and plazas.

and community and is held in various cities across the world, including in Cartagena in late January. Bill Clinton has called it the "Woodstock of the mind." In addition to talks and concerts, the festival holds educational programs for youth in the neighborhoods of Cartagena. It also provides free or discounted tickets to students. Most of the events take place in the **Teatro Heredia** (Cl. de la Chichería No. 38-10, tel. 5/664-6023 or 5/664-9631). While the festival's name is pronounced as the English "hay," in Colombia it's often pronounced as the Spanish *"hay"* ("ai"). Hay Festival is thus a double entendre: *hay festival* in Spanish means yes, there is a festival!

Festival Internacional de Música

Over the course of a week in early to mid-January, the churches, plazas, and theaters of the Walled City become the setting for classical music concerts by musicians from all over the world during the **Festival**

Concurso Nacional de Belleza

Beauty contests, and especially the **Concurso Nacional de Belleza** (Miss Colombia Pageant, tel. 5/660-0779, www.srtacolombia.org), are a big deal in Colombia. The coronation of Señorita Colombia takes place every November and is the highlight of Cartagena's Independence Day celebrations. Aspirers for the title represent each of the departments of the country, in addition to some cities. Ladies from the Valle del Cauca and Atlántico have won the most titles (10 each) since the pageant began in the 1930s. In 2001, the first Miss Colombia of Afro-Colombian heritage was chosen: Vanessa Mendoza, who represented the Chocó department. Tickets to the main events—the swimsuit competition at the Cartagena Hilton and the coronation at the Centro de Convenciones—are hard to come by but not impossible to purchase.

Electronic Music Festivals

In early January every year, especially on the first weekend after New Year's Day, one or two multiday beachside electronic music festivals take place. Drawing a hip and sexy crowd from Bogotá, Medellín, and Cali, as well as international visitors escaping cold winters, the festival of the moment is **Storyland** (www.storyland.com.co). Tickets and information can also be found at Tu Boleta (www.tuboleta.com). Buy your tickets well in advance.

Shopping

SHOPPING CENTERS AND MALLS

The bazaar-like **Centro Comercial Getsemaní** (Cl. 30 No. 8B-74, tel. 5/664-2508, hours vary daily) shopping center doesn't cater to tourists. It's made up of hundreds of small mom-and-pop kiosks that sell just about everything: computer supplies, notebooks, beauty supplies, handicrafts, and knickknacks. You can probably get your nails done here as well. This place is huge and oozing with personality.

You didn't come all this way to go to a mall. But if you want to browse upscale shops, have a meal, go to a movie, or just enjoy the air-conditioning, Cartagena has a pair of malls just for you. The newer of the two, the **Centro Comercial Bocagrande** (Cra. 1 No. 12-118, Bocagrande, 10am-9pm Mon.-Thurs., 10am-10pm Fri.-Sun.), is also the easier to access. It's located at the entrance of Bocagrande, along the water, and has a movie theater, gym, and a large food court, including a Ruby Tuesday's, where you can dine while you watch the sun set. **Centro Comercial Caribe Plaza** (Cl. 29D No. 22-108, Pie de la Popa, 10am-8pm Mon.-Thurs., 10am-9pm Fri.-Sun.) is an upscale modern mall near the Castillo de San Felipe with numerous clothing and shoe stores, a movie theater, and a food court. Traffic can be heavy getting to and from this mall.

ANTIQUES

Antiques shops provide a glimpse into aristocratic living from the Cartagena of yesteryear. **El Arcón Anticuario** (Cl. del Camposanto No. 9-46, tel. 5/664-1197) showcases Colombian furniture from both the colonial and Republican eras. This is the spot to pick up your very own whimsical Cartagenan doorknocker or chandelier.

HOUSEWARES AND FURNITURE

Casa Chiqui (Cl. de la Universidad No. 36-127, Centro, tel. 5/668-5429, www.casachiqui.com, 10am-6pm Mon.-Sat.) specializes in interesting interior design items, housewares, and furniture from around the world. While Asia, Africa, and the Middle East are represented, there are Colombian handicrafts, such as colorful Barranquillan Carnaval masks, woven handbags, and placemats made from palm leaves, on display as well.

HANDICRAFTS

The most historic place to pick up some Colombian handicrafts is at **Las Bóvedas** (San Diego, extreme northeastern corner of the wall, 9am-6pm daily). Once a military storehouse, today it's the place to buy multicolored hammocks and all kinds of Colombian *artesanías* (handicrafts) of varying quality.

For high-quality handicrafts, you're better off going to **Artesanías de Colombia** (Centro de Convenciones, Local 5, Getsemaní, tel. 5/660-9615, 10am-7pm Mon.-Sat.). This is a government entity whose mission it is to promote Colombian handicrafts and craftspeople. This store sells handicrafts from across the country but specializes in masks from the Carnaval de Barranquilla, woven *mochilas* (handbags) from indigenous groups in the Sierra Nevada, and the colorful embroidery of *molas* from indigenous groups in the Darién Gap region near Panama.

El Centavo Menos (Cl. Roma No. 5-08, Centro, tel. 5/664-7939, 9am-7pm Mon.-Sat.) has been around since 1933, and it keeps going strong, still managed by the same family. Once a general store, today you can pick up hammocks, hats, and pretty much anything else.

For brightly painted depictions of old Cartagena on recycled wood, check out the workshop Marquetería Mau (Cl. Quero No. 9-23, Centro, cell tel. 312/629-9153, 9am-5pm Mon.-Fri., 9am-1pm Sat.).

JEWELRY

L.A. Cano (Cl. Estanco del Tabaco No. 35-81, Centro, tel. 5/647-8704, www.lacano.co, 9am-9pm Mon.-Sat., 10am-9pm Sun.), a nationally recognized family jewelry business that has generations of experience, specializes in 24-karat gold-plated jewelry. Cano has another smaller location at the Hotel Santa Clara (Cl. del Torno No. 39-29, tel. 5/664-4434, 10am-6pm daily).

Colombian emeralds are considered to be some of the finest in the world, with the most acclaimed stones coming from the Buzo mines in the country's interior. Check out reasonably priced Lucy Joyería (Cl. Santo Domingo No. 3-19, Centro, tel. 5/664-4255, www.lucyjoyeriacartagena.com, 10am-8pm Mon.-Sat.), one of the best-known jewelers in the city. They specialize in emeralds and can accept custom orders, but expect a wait of several weeks.

CIGARS

In Cartagena, touches of Cuba are found everywhere: mojitos, music, and, too, the cigars. At La Cava del Puro (Cl. de las Damas No. 3-106, Centro, tel. 5/664-9482, www.lacavadelpuro.com, 9am-8pm Mon.-Sat., 10am-8pm Sun.) they don't sell just any old stogie; here the cigars come from Havana and are of the best quality. Smoking is not only permitted here, but in fact promoted. Sometimes a little whiskey is even served to perusing clients.

ART GALLERIES

NH Galería (Cra. 2 No. 33-36, tel. 5/664-0561, www.nhgaleria.com, 10am-6pm Mon.-Tues. and Thurs.-Sat., 4pm-8pm Sun., free) features contemporary Colombian artists and works in conjunction with the Nora Haime Gallery in New York City.

CLOTHING AND ACCESSORIES

For men, nothing says Cartagena chic like a crisp guayabera shirt. The typical linen or cotton guayabera has two vertical embroidered stripes and four pockets, and can be worn to a wedding or special event, or even out to dinner at one of the elegant restaurants of the Old City. Tailor Edgar Gómez of Ego (Cl. de Portobello No. 10-92, Centro, tel. 5/668-6016, 9am-5pm Mon.-Fri.) purportedly once made a guayabera for Bill Gates and the king of Spain. Guayaberas of all qualities and prices can be found throughout the city, from mom-and-pop shops in the San Diego neighborhood to department stores like Éxito (Cl. 38 No. 10-85, tel. 5/664-1066, 10am-9pm daily). Malls are a good bet too: Try PatPrimo (Centro Comercial San Felipe Local 1-22, Cl. 29B with Cra. 17, Pie de la Popa, tel. 5/693-0026, 10am-7pm Mon.-Sun.) in the Centro Comercial San Felipe, where you can pick up one for under US$40.

Along Calle Santo Domingo there are several boutiques of top Colombian designers. Bogotana Bettina Spitz (Cl. de la Mantilla No. 3-37, Centro, tel. 5/660-2160, www.bettinaspitz.com, 11am-1pm and 2pm-8pm daily) sells casual, beach, and formal clothes for women, as well as an array of accessories, shoes, and some men's items. Onda de Mar (Cl. de las Damas, Centro, tel. 5/668-5226, 9am-6pm daily) is a Colombian clothing brand that has everything you need for a day at the beach. St. Dom (Cl. de Santo Domingo No. 33-70, Centro, tel. 5/664-0197, 10am-8pm Mon.-Sat., noon-6pm Sun.) is a boutique that brings together Colombian designers of accessories, clothing, handbags, and jewelry.

Jon Sonen (Cl. Ricaurte No. 31-56, Centro, tel. 5/664-1092 or 5/660-4682, www. jonsonen.com, 10am-8pm Sun.-Thurs., 10am-9pm Fri.-Sat.) is a Colombian label specializing in menswear, with other stores throughout the country. Único (Cl. San Juan de Dios No. 3-121, tel. 5/664-4999, 11am-8pm, Mon.-Sat.) is a Colombian brand of underwear and swimsuits marketed to gay men and metrosexuals looking to make an impression.

BOOKS

The most atmospheric book-browsing experience in the city is on the northern edge of the Parque del Centenario in Getsemaní, home to several secondhand book stalls. You never know what you might find. Days and hours of operation are irregular, so just stroll by if you're in the area.

Abaco Libros (Cl. de la Mantilla, Centro, tel. 5/664-8290, 9am-9pm Mon.-Sat., 3pm-9pm Sun.) is a cozy bookshop and café with a variety of books on Cartagena, top Colombian novels, and a selection of magazines, classics, and best sellers in English. Librería Nacional (Cl. Segunda de Badillo No. 36-27, Centro, tel. 5/664-1448, 8:30am-12:30pm and 2pm-6:30pm Mon.-Fri., 8:30am-5pm Sat.) is a chain bookstore with shelves full of Colombian and Spanish-language books, and some books in English.

Sports and Recreation

BEACHES

Though Cartagena boasts a seaside location, it lacks the spectacular beaches that first-time visitors might be envisioning. Instead, the most popular beaches in Cartagena, located on the Caribbean side of the Bocagrande peninsula, feature gray-sand beaches packed with Colombian families and plied by vendors and masseuses. Umbrella rentals are expected, and usually cost around COP$20,000 for the afternoon. Near the jetties is a section of the beach where gay men tend to gather, called Playa Hollywood. Beyond this point, the beach hangs a sharp left and merges into the beaches of the Laguito neighborhood; there are some waterfront restaurants and wind-surfing rentals here. Bocagrande's beaches are just a 10-minute cab ride from the Old City and offer water that's good for swimming and splashing around—but don't expect the turquoise colors often associated with the Caribbean.

For those willing to travel farther afield, there are beaches at Marbella and Las Americas (neighborhoods just east of El Cabrero, northeast of the city) that attract fewer crowds and are fine destinations for swimming. Marbella, closest to the Old City, offers public beaches in front of the Ibis Hotel, but few services. The beaches of Las Americas are about 30 minutes outside of the Old City, and are lined with high-rise hotels and condos. Though these beaches are open to the public, the best way to enjoy them is to purchase a *pasadia* (day pass) at one of the hotels. A day pass typically allows you to access the hotel's beachfront as well as its pool, and may include lunch and a few beverages. To purchase a pass, just walk into any of the hotels—or buy one in advance from the COTELCO office (tel. 5/656-9200, www.cotelcoctg.org, open until late daily) in the baggage claim area at the airport, as they offer a 20 percent discount.

The top day-pass option is at the Hotel Karmairí (Km. 3 Vía Manzanillo, cell tel. 317/775-2097, www.karmairi.com), in the Manzanillo neighborhood, just beyond Las Americas. The hotel boasts a spa with numerous services, thatched-roof *cabañas,* and a pool. They play good music, too, especially on weekends. The Plan Karmairí (COP$180,000) includes drinks, lunch, towels, and use of the beach, pool, and deck. A massage costs another COP$35,000.

For postcard-perfect white-sand beaches and palm trees, book a day tour or multiday excursion to **Barú** or the **Islas del Rosario.**

BIKING

The best time to explore Cartagena by bike is early on a Sunday morning or on a Sunday or Monday evening when there is little activity and light traffic in the Old City. Many hostels and some hotels have bicycles for rent.

Bicitour Getsemaní (Cl. Don Sancho, Edificio Aqua Marina, cell tel. 300/357-1825, COP$5,000/2-hour rental) rents out bikes and offers guided tours of the Old City, Manga, and Bocagrande. **Velo Tours** (Cl. Gastelbondo, tel. 5/664-9714, www.velo-tours.com.co, COP$80,000/day) offers several bike tours of the city, including a three-hour nighttime tour (COP$80,000).

DIVING

Diving Planet (Cl. Estanco del Aguardiente No. 5-09, tel. 5/660-0450, www.divingplanet. org, 8am-7pm Mon.-Sat.) offers classes and diving excursions to some 25 locations throughout the Parque Nacional Natural Corales del Rosario y San Bernardo. A one-day course costs COP$305,000; a day trip for already-certified divers costs COP$290,000. Discounts are offered for paying in advance online or in cash. Multiday PADI certification courses are also available, some of which include an overnight on the white beaches of the Islas del Rosario. Snorkeling excursions are also available (COP$190,000).

KITESURFING

About half an hour's drive northeast of Cartagena, along the beaches of the Manzanillo neighborhood, the Swiss-run **Pure Kitesurf** (Manzanillo, cell tel. 321/521-5110, www.purekitesurf.com) offers kitesurfing classes, with instruction available in Spanish, English, and German. They also offer a six-day, all-inclusive tour of the Caribbean coast for US$750.

Cartagena Kitesurf School (Cra. 1B No. 1-52, El Laguito neighborhood, cell tel. 300/461-9947, www.kitesurfcarta-gena.com) offers a basic eight-hour course (COP$700,000) and a two-hour course (COP$200,000). If wind conditions are not good enough, the school will transport students to Puerto Velero, up the coast, where there's always a good breeze. While the school is located in the Laguito section of

The beaches in Bocagrande are popular with Colombian families.

Bocagrande, most classes take place on the beaches of Las Americas.

SAILING

It doesn't get much better than renting out a 43-foot catamaran with a captain and crew and sailing around Cartagena and its nearby islands. **Veleros Colombia** (cell tel. 316/528-2413, www.veleroscolombia.com, COP$2,900,000/4 hours) can make that happen. In addition, they offer sailing courses (COP$4,650,000/3-day course) along the Caribbean coast, and diving excursions in the Islas del Rosario and the Islas de San Bernardo.

SALSA CLASSES

With its salsa classes, the cultural center **Ciudad Móvil** (Cl. del Espíritu Santo No. 29-140, Getsemaní, cell tel. 311/652-0842, 10am-11pm daily) is a good stop for anyone hoping to make a splash on the dance floor. This funky spot is also home to the occasional Zumba and yoga class, and sometimes hosts art exhibits and film nights.

GOLF

The challenging 18-hole **TPC Cartagena at Karibana** (Manzanillo, cell tel. 317/516-1073, www.tpc.com/cartagena, greens fees US$180), about half an hour's drive east of the city, offers gorgeous views of the Caribbean—especially from the 13th hole, which is surrounded by the sea—and the Old City. This is the first Jack Nicklaus-designed course in South America. Karibana offers stay-and-play packages with several Cartagena-area hotels, in addition to being a resort hotel itself. Greens fees are discounted if you're a Karibana guest.

YOGA

Santuario del Yoga (Cl. El Estanco del Aguardiente No. 5, Centro, tel. 5/668-5338, cell tel. 313/649-3133 or 313/819-3114, 8am-5pm daily, COP$15,000) offers yoga classes in a small studio (that's also a shop/café) in the Centro. Some instructors are bilingual. On occasion they organize excursions (COP$120,000 pp) to the Volcán de Totumo that include canoeing through marshes, a yoga class, and a vegetarian lunch.

Vive Yoga (Cl. Ancha 44-10B, Getsemaní, cell tel. 304/528-9863) leads a free yoga class in the Parque de la Marina on Wednesdays and at the Media Luna Hostel every Tuesday. Check out their Facebook page for more information.

Food

Seafood reigns supreme in Cartagenan cuisine. Popular fish are *pargo rojo* (red snapper), *corvina* (sea bass), *dorado* (mahimahi), and *sierra* (swordfish). Shellfish include *langosta* (lobster), *langostinos* (prawns), and *chipi chipis* (tiny clams). These main dishes are often accompanied by delicious coconut rice and *patacones* (fried plantains).

On the street, especially in the Old City, there are food and drinks on practically every corner. There's no better refreshment than a cold *agua de coco* (coconut water), either straight from the fruit or out of a plastic bag. Street snacks, popular in the late morning or late afternoon, are called *fritos*. They include items like *arepa*

de huevo (fried eggs in a corn arepa), *carimañola* (fried yucca-flour pastry with cheese and meat), and seafood empanadas. Fresh fruit, particularly *mango biche* (green mango served with salt and hot spices), can be a good break from the heavier *fritos*. For a sweet bite, head to the Portal de las Dulces, a traditional sweets market near the Torre del Reloj.

Though many restaurants in the Walled City sport Manhattan prices, an inexpensive meal is not impossible to find. There are still a few mom-and-pop restaurants featuring set (cheap!) lunches for locals who would balk at paying over COP$10,000 for their midday meal.

CENTRO
Caribbean Cuisine

Popular ★ **Santísimo** (Cl. del Torno No. 39-62, tel. 5/660-1531, www.elsantisimo.com, noon-midnight daily, COP$40,000) has a religious theme, with candles and an austere interior design. The Plan Milagro ("Miracle Plan," COP$45,000) is a prix fixe meal that's recognized as the restaurant's best deal.

Malanga (Plaza de San Diego No. 8-19, tel. 5/660-1472, noon-midnight daily, COP$22,000) prides itself on serving only the freshest ingredients and regional recipes. Try the mango shrimp ceviche and relax with a glass of sangria. The space is welcoming and intimate, with soft lighting, but most patrons sit outside on the colorful Plaza de San Diego.

Some of the freshest ceviche in town is served at **La Cevichería** (Cl. Stuart No. 7-14, tel. 5/660-1492, noon-11pm Mon.-Sat., noon-10pm Sun., COP$28,000). The restaurant has a creative menu, featuring options with mango and coconut. Its location on a quiet street makes the outdoor seating especially welcoming. Get a little taste of everything by ordering the "Miss-Cellanea" ceviche sampler. You can also pick up a T-shirt at their little shop.

★ **La Mulata** (Cl. Quero No. 9-58, tel. 5/664-6222, noon-4pm Mon.-Sat., COP$18,000) specializes in Cartagenan cuisine. Their seafood dishes feature a perfect mound of coconut rice and a thin, crispy slice of fried plantain on top, to add some height to the presentation. Decorated with names of regional dishes, the restaurant walls provide a vocabulary lesson on Caribbean cuisine. Try the coconut lemonade.

Seafood and Steak

Don Juan (Cl. del Colegio No. 34-60, tel. 5/664-3857, www.donjuancartagena.com, noon-3pm and 7pm-11pm daily, COP$40,000) is a sophisticated bistro with high ceilings where you can order seafood, steak, and pasta in an elegant setting. Try the tangy grilled sea bass on lemon risotto.

Transport yourself to the Havana of yesteryear at ★ **La Vitrola** (Cl. Baloco No. 2-01, tel. 5/664-8243, noon-3pm and 7pm-midnight daily, COP$35,000), an always-elegant, always-packed restaurant that specializes in Caribbean seafood, such as their popular tuna steak with avocado and mango, as well as pasta dishes. Immaculately dressed bartenders are a blur of constant motion as they mix innumerable mojitos. La Vitrola is pricey, but the

Each night crowds flock to the Plaza de Santo Domingo for dinner and people-watching.

atmosphere, with live Cuban music in the evenings, makes it worthwhile. Reservations must be made well in advance.

Caribbean Fusion

Fabulous ★ **Carmen** (Hotel Ananda, Cl. del Cuartel No. 36-77, tel. 5/660-6795, www. carmenrestaurante.com.co, COP$159,000) blends Caribbean with Asian and Middle Eastern cuisine, offering a five-course tasting menu that includes wine. Impeccable service and an unforgettable meal await. Seating is indoors or out on the patio next to the pool. Reservations are necessary.

For pork ribs in hoisin sauce or a lobster sandwich, visit **María** (Cl. del Colegio No. 34-60, tel. 5/660-5380, www.maria-cartagena.com, noon-3pm and 6:30pm-11pm Mon.-Fri., 6:30pm-11:30pm Sat., COP$42,000), a restaurant with nods to Asian cuisine. It's a cheerful, bright space, and the only place in town where you can dine under the glow of a chandelier of ceramic pineapples.

1621 (Hotel Sofitel Legend Santa Clara, Cl. del Curato, tel. 5/650-4741, noon-11pm daily, COP$45,000) combines French and Caribbean cuisine in the elegant atmosphere of a classic hotel that was once a 17th-century convent. Desserts are sumptuous, a perfect match for the ambience. Don't miss their extensive wine collection.

El Gobernador by Rausch (Cl. del Sargento Mayor No. 6-87, tel. 5/642-4100, www.bastionluxuryhotel.com, noon-3pm and 7pm-11pm daily, COP$45,000) is a fancy Mediterranean-Caribbean fusion restaurant with serious chandeliers in the Bastion Luxury Hotel. Favorites on the menu include scallops with pork belly and duck in *corozo* sauce. For dessert, try the piña colada mousse.

Pacific and Caribbean cuisine unite at **La Comunión** (Cl. de las Bóvedas No. 39-116, tel. 5/645-5301, noon-10pm daily, COP$36,000), which is housed in a cheerfully decorated space. The menu features black tamales filled with octopus and squid.

Casual Dining

El Balcón (Cl. Tumbamuertos No. 38-85, cell tel. 300/336-3876, www.elbalconcartagena. com, noon-midnight daily, COP$22,000) is a friendly place with a view in Plaza de San Diego. Get here in the early evening and enjoy a sundowner cocktail as you listen to lounge music or have a light meal like a refreshing gazpacho or their shrimp "sexviche."

Casual and cute, **Collage Charladero** (Cl. Roman No. 5-47, tel. 5/660-7626, noon-midnight Mon.-Sat., COP$22,000) serves sandwiches, burgers, falafels, fresh juices (watermelon with lime and mint), and refreshing sangria in a clean and cool environment close to all the historic sites.

Simple (Hotel NH, Plaza de los Coches, tel. 5/645-5051, www.simplecartagena. com, 7am-10:30pm daily, COP$36,000) has Scandinavian interior design and an interesting menu with items like crab tacos and coconut prawns. They also serve fresh pastries at breakfast.

★ **Crepes & Waffles** (Cl. Baloco Edificio Piñeres, Local 1, tel. 5/664-6062, www.crepesywaffles.com.co, noon-10:30pm Mon.-Thurs., noon-11:30pm Fri.-Sat., 8am-10:30pm Sun.) is a wildly successful and reliable Colombian family-style chain that specializes in savory and sweet crepes and sweet waffles. It can also satisfy your health needs with its fresh salad bar. The restaurant has a progressive policy of hiring women who are heads of their households. Besides healthy and quick meals, Crepes makes delicious ice cream, perfect on those muggy Cartagena afternoons.

D'Alex (Plaza Fernandez de Madrid, cell tel. 312/883-5925, noon-10pm daily, COP$14,000) is a cheap spot that is popular with the backpacker crowd looking for a bargain on *pescado frito* (fried fish), the restaurant's specialty.

Cafés

One of the best bakery-cafés in town is ★ **Mila Pastelería** (Cl. de la Iglesia No. 35-76, tel. 5/664-4607, www.mila.com.co, 8am-10:30pm daily, COP$17,000), a bright place for sandwiches, tempting desserts, and a late breakfast (served until 11am) for those who slept in too late at the hotel.

Italian

Twinkling lights and fountains create ambience on the patio of **Enoteca** (Cl. San Juan de Dios No. 3-39, tel. 5/664-3806, www.enoteca. com.co, noon-11:30pm daily, COP$30,000), a Cartagena pizza and pasta institution. The pizzas are better than the pasta. If you want air-conditioning more than atmosphere, grab a table inside.

Greek

For a change of pace, bright and tiny **Grecia Café y Suvlaki** (Cl. de las Estrella No. 4-47, cell tel. 313/707-7827, noon-10pm Mon.-Sat., COP$15,000) is Greek-run and specializes in gyros and souvlaki.

Indian

For a little curry with your shrimp, try **Ganesha** (Cl. del Colegio, tel. 5/660-9165, www.ganesharestaurante.com, noon-3pm and 6:30pm-11pm Tues.-Sun., COP$24,000), an authentic Indian restaurant with an extensive menu and many vegetarian options.

Sweets

A homemade ice cream popsicle from ★ **La Paletería** (Cl. de Ayos, 11am-11pm daily, COP$10,000) makes a late-afternoon stroll around the steamy city much more enjoyable. At this ice cream stand, order one of the interesting flavors such as *mango biche* (green mango) or Tropical Paradise, a non-dairy option packed with fruit chunks.

Classic American

Satisfying comfort food such as burgers, chicken sandwiches, and corn bread are on the menu at **La Teibol** (Cl. Estanco del Aguardiente No. 5-94, tel. 5/660-6626, noon-11pm daily, COP$25,000), a small restaurant with a lot of heart. In addition to crafting the food, the chef also made the restaurant's gorgeous wooden tables.

Vegetarian

The inexpensive set lunches at vegetarian **Girasoles** (Cl. de los Puntales No. 37-01, tel. 5/660-2625, 11am-4pm daily, COP$12,000) are a salvation to many a vegetarian visitor. The usual lunch includes a vegetable soup to start, followed by a main protein dish accompanied by rice and vegetables. You won't leave hungry. This informal lunch counter has many regular customers. Girasoles usually publishes the day's menu on its Facebook page.

GETSEMANÍ
Caribbean

At ★ **La Cocina de Pepina** (Callejón Vargas, Cl. 25 No. 9A-06, Local 2, tel. 5/664-2944, noon-4pm and 6pm-10pm Tues.-Sat., noon-4pm Sun.-Mon., COP$25,000), typical dishes from across the Caribbean coast are thoughtfully reinvented. The *mote de queso*, a thick soup made of salty Costeño cheese and yams, gets rave reviews. It's a cozy place in an alley near Calle del Arsenal. Make a reservation for dinner.

Unpretentious **Casa de Socorro** (Cl. Larga No. 8B-112, cell tel. 315/718-6666, noon-3pm and 6pm-10pm Tues.-Sat., COP$28,000) may surprise you with its Cartagenan specialties, ceviche, and *limonada de coco* (coconut lemonade). The loyal clientele of locals speaks for itself.

Seafood

Marea by Rausch (Centro de Convenciones, Cl. 24 No. 8A-344, tel. 5/654-4205, www.mareabyrausch.com, noon-3pm and 7pm-10pm Tues.-Sat., 4pm-10pm Sun., COP$52,000) is an ultra-chic seafood restaurant that is the brainchild of the Rausches, two brother chefs from Bogotá. Specialties include tuna tartare and prawns in a coconut and saffron sauce. This restaurant has excellent views of the bay and the Torre del Reloj.

Tapas

The Plaza de la Trinidad is the beating heart of happening Getsemaní, and it's home to some swanky spots perfect for a small meal and a couple of drinks. Cool **Demente** (Plaza de la Trinidad, cell tel. 311/831-9839, www.demente.com.co, 4pm-2am Mon.-Sat., COP$22,000) specializes in cocktails and tapas. It's an open-air spot with a retractable roof, where the music is funky, the cocktails are chic, and the cigars are Cuban. On the back patio is a beer garden complete with twinkling lights, serving wood-oven pizza and craft beer. It's a fun place for an evening of small plates and drinks.

Italian

VIPs such as Colombian president Juan Manuel Santos have been known to sample the authentic Italian dishes at **I Balconi** (Cl. del Guerrero No. 29-146, cell tel. 311/392-0936, www.ibalconi.com, noon-10pm Sun.-Thurs., noon-midnight Fri.-Sat., COP$18,000). It gets boisterous here as the evening wears on and the wine flows. Ask for a table on one of the balconies so you can enjoy the street life from on high.

Dutch-Indonesian Fusion

Delightful **Saint Roque** (Cl. Espíritu Santo No. 29-214, cell tel. 317/226-8039, Mon.-Sat. 5pm-10:30pm, COP$24,000) serves Dutch-Indonesian cuisine in an up-and-coming area of Getsemaní. Try the *gado-gado* vegetarian salad with peanut sauce, and choose a candlelit table on the sidewalk.

Argentinian

Chef Rodrigo at ★ **Gaucha** (Cl. Espiritu Santo No. 29-207, cell tel. 310/648-7942, COP$38,000) knows his *bife de chorizo* (New York strip) from his *vacio* (flank), and it's no wonder this sophisticated restaurant with both sidewalk and indoor seating has become a Cartagena favorite. The waitstaff here is attentive.

French

Brasserie Montaigne (Cra. 8B No. 25-103, tel. 5/650-3030, noon-3pm and 6pm-11pm daily, COP$28,000) is a classic French restaurant in the Hotel Monterrey. Cordon bleu and crème brûlée are classics on the menu.

BOCAGRANDE

Elegant **Arabe Internacional** (Cra. 3 No. 8-83, tel. 5/665-4365, www.restaurantearabeinternacional.com, noon-3:30pm and 7pm-10pm Mon.-Fri., noon-10pm Sat.-Sun., COP$25,000) has been serving authentic Middle Eastern cuisine since 1965. It's a popular place for the Cartagena business crowd.

Tabetai (Av. San Martín No. 5-145, cell tel. 301/680-3680, noon-11pm daily, COP$22,000) specializes in Japanese cuisine, specifically sushi. They have fun happy hours most afternoons, often with DJs on the weekend.

Riquisimo BBQ (Cra. 1 No. 1A-148, tel. 5/6550-0861, 7:30am-midnight daily, COP$18,000) looks like an American-style coffee shop, but it serves typical Cartagenan fare in addition to sandwiches and fixed-price lunches. Their generously portioned breakfasts are a specialty.

MANGA

With a terrace that overlooks the bay, **Verona** (Cra. 20 No. 24-22, tel. 5/670-0416, noon-3pm and 6pm-11pm Mon.-Fri., 6pm-11pm Sat.-Sun., COP$24,000) serves delicious thin-crust pizzas, offers a salad bar, and caters to locals in the Manga neighborhood. After dinner, be sure to stroll the pleasant promenade along the water.

The **Club de Pesca** (Fuerte de San Sebastián del Pastelillo, tel. 5/660-4594, noon-11pm daily, COP$55,000) is a Cartagena classic in the old San Sebastián del Pastelillo fort, with magnificent views to the bay. It's a favorite spot for wedding banquets, and some guests arrive in yachts. Try the *jaiba gratinada* (crab au gratin).

Accommodations

As the top tourist destination in Colombia, Cartagena boasts a large and diverse hotel sector. The Centro and Getsemaní are the top neighborhoods for small, high-end boutique hotels, often occupying well-restored colonial-era homes; many featuring rooftop terraces. Being pampered at one of these luxury options—even for just a few nights—will be a highlight of your visit.

Hostels proliferate in the city, especially in Getsemaní. The vast majority offer private rooms with air-conditioning, but these tend to go fast, so plan to reserve at least a few weeks in advance. Some hostel dorm rooms don't have air-conditioning.

Bocagrande, with its high-rise hotels and condos, is more popular with Colombian families than with international visitors. Staying here means proximity to Bocagrande's beaches, cheaper food options, and more space for less money. For those interested in the higher-quality beaches of Las Americas, this area two kilometers (1.25 miles) past the airport is home to many beachfront hotels. You'll have to take a car to get to the Centro.

For a last-minute deal, visit **COTELCO** (Aeropuerto Rafael Nunez, tel. 5/656-9200, www.cartagena.cotelco.org, 7am-1:30am Mon.-Sat., 8am-5:30pm Sun.) at the Cartagena airport, which is generally open through the last arrival of the day. This association of hotels often has discounted prices for a variety of options in the Centro, Getsemaní, Bocagrande, and Las Americas. Look for them in the baggage arrival area.

For most international visitors, hotels should not charge IVA (sales tax). Inquire about IVA when you make your reservation, and again when you're checking in, to be sure you aren't improperly charged. (For more information on the regulations behind IVA, see the Essentials chapter.)

CENTRO
Under COP$70,000

Your stay at the ★ **Volunteer Hostel** (Calle del Quero No. 9-64, tel. 5/643-4185, www.volunteerhostel.org, COP$40,000 dorm, COP$130,000 d) supports an array of social projects in underserved communities in and around Cartagena. Accommodations are basic, but comfortable and clean. One of the other perks is the chance to meet like-minded people from across the globe.

In the Old City, the Uruguayan hostel chain **El Viajero** (Cl. Siete Infantes No. 9-45, tel. 5/660-2598, www.elviajerohostels.com, COP$60,000 dorm, COP$230,000 d) has air-conditioned dorm rooms of various sizes. A handful of private rooms are located across the street in a more subdued environment. A decent breakfast is included in the room rate. Guests enjoy socializing at the bar.

COP$70,000-200,000

★ **Casa Blue** (Plaza Fernández de Madrid, Cl. del Curato No. 38-08, tel. 5/668-6501, COP$200,000 d) is within the Walled City just a few blocks from the Plaza de Santo Domingo. Previously a hostel, the rooms are private and the hotel markets itself to a budget-conscious business crowd. Its location on a popular plaza means you should expect some noise in the evenings.

A midrange option with a guesthouse feel is **3 Banderas** (Cl. Cochera del Hobo No. 38-66, tel. 5/660-0160, www.hotel3banderas.com, COP$200,000 d). This hotel is housed in a 200-year-old building with two interior patios and a rooftop terrace with a tiny pool. Some of the 24 rooms are small, but it's generally a good value. Request one of the rooms with a small balcony.

Hotel Casa Real (Cl. del Caurtel No. 36-122, tel. 5/664-7089, www.casarealhotel.com.co, COP$180,000 d) has two rooftop terraces, adequate rooms with antiques from old Cartagena, and a central location.

COP$200,000-500,000

With just eight rooms, a pleasant rooftop terrace, and a delicious breakfast, **Hotel Boutique Santo Toribio** (Cl. Segunda del Badillo No. 36-87, cell tel. 317/893-6464, www.hotelsantotoribio.com, COP$350,000) checks off all the boxes for a comfortable stay in the city. Lounge music adds an air of chicness. Bikes are available for rent.

You can't really go wrong at the ★ **NH Urban Royal** (Plaza de los Coches No. 34-10, tel. 5/645-5050, www.nh-hotels.com, COP$443,000 d), one of two locations of the NH Hotels chain in the city. Rooms are equipped with basics and most offer nice views of the always-busy Plaza de los Coches. The rooftop pool is a welcome sight after a long day—the view is quite something, too—and the included breakfast is ample.

A friendly staff is what sets **Hotel Boutique Las Carretas** (Cl. de las Carretas No. 34-28, tel. 5/660-4853, COP$280,000 d) apart. Rooms are spacious and some have balconies with a street view. On the rooftop you'll find a small pool. The building itself is an architectural mishmash, and the interior design is more folksy than sophisticated.

Over COP$500,000

The two-story **Bóvedas de Santa Clara** (Cl. del Torno No. 39-114, tel. 5/650-4464, www.bovedasdesantaclara.com, COP$580,000 d) has only 18 rooms, some of which are extremely spacious, and some with views of the water. Guests can use the Hotel Sofitel Legend Santa Clara spa and facilities across the street. The hotel staff can organize day trips to the Hotel San Pedro Majagua in Islas del Rosario. There is no restaurant on-site, although breakfast is served.

The comfort and fabulous location of ★ **Hotel Movich** (Cl. Velez Danies No. 4-39, tel. 5/660-0133, www.movichhotels.com, COP$880,000) make it a good value, even though the rates are steep. Light floods its spacious rooms, and the rooftop terrace has a refreshing pool and a 360-degree view of the Old City. A 15-minute massage is included with your stay.

The two-story colonial-era **Casa la Cartujita** (Cl. del Curato No. 38-53, tel. 5/660-5248, www.casalacartujita.com, COP$725,000 d) has seven bright-white minimalist rooms and a lovely terrace, a Jacuzzi, a dipping pool, and a pleasant reading room. Rent the entire house and you'll have a personal chef at your service.

The result of a meticulous restoration of three adjacent 17th-century houses, the ★ **Casa San Agustín** (Cl. de la Universidad No. 36-44, tel. 5/681-0000, www.hotelcasasanagustin.com, COP$1,500,000 d) is easily one of the most luxurious addresses in Cartagena, if not all of Colombia. Among the amenities are an inviting pool on the main floor, complimentary afternoon tea in the library, a terrace with a fabulous view, spacious rooms with exposed wood-beamed ceilings, a cozy bar, and the original stone walls. This hotel is a member of Leading Hotels of the World.

Good taste reigns at **Anandá** (Cl. del Cuartel No. 36-77, tel. 5/664-4452, COP$960,000 d), whose name means "maximum state of happiness" in Hindi. It's certainly close to the truth at this gorgeous, meticulously restored 16th-century home. There are 23 rooms of three different styles and a pool, Jacuzzi, and daybeds on the rooftop. Anandá is home to the restaurant Carmen.

The 89-room ★ **Hotel Charleston Santa Teresa** (Plaza de Santa Teresa, tel. 5/664-9494, www.hotelcharlestonsantateresa.com, COP$740,000 d) is steps away from the wall. It was originally built in the 17th century as a convent for Carmelita nuns. In the 1980s it was converted into a hotel. There are two wings to this historic hotel, a colonial one and a Republican-era one dating from the early 20th century. Rooms are nothing short of luxurious, with accommodations in the colonial wing a notch above the more modern ones. The two inner courtyards are lovely, including the Iglesia de San Pedro Claver. This luxury hotel has seven spacious rooms and an "interactive" kitchen, where guests can participate in food preparation. Rooms are decorated with original artwork. Hotel LM is just around the corner from the Plaza de Santo Domingo.

Vacation Rentals

For an unforgettable experience, rent a fully furnished luxury apartment in a colonial house—or rent the whole house. The website of rental agency **This Is Cartagena** (Cl. Sargento Mayor No. 6-107, tel. 5/660-9128, www.ticartagena.com) makes it easy with a search engine, detailed descriptions and photos, and an easy reservation process. The staff at their office near Iglesia de Santo Toribio is attentive. Colonial houses in the Centro start at around US$1,250 per night, but they can also hook you up with a hotel room or an apartment.

GETSEMANÍ
Under COP$70,000

Australian-run ★ **Mamallena** (Cl. de la Media Luna No. 10-47, tel. 5/670-0499, www. hostelmamallenacartagena.com, COP$35,000 dorm, COP$100,000 d) is a small, attitude-free, friendly place where guests linger over beers at the small bar in front. Air-conditioning is available 24 hours a day, and pancakes are served for breakfast. Tours to area attractions can be arranged. There's a resident dog, cat, and a couple of tortoises.

Colorful and cheerful **Papaya** (Cl. del Pozo No. 28-36, tel. 5/643-7340, COP$40,000 dorm) only has dorm accommodations and is seconds away from the Plaza Trinidad scene.

The Shangri-la of backpacker accommodations in Cartagena is the famous ★ **Media Luna Hostel** (Cl. de la Media Luna No. 10-46, tel. 5/664-3423, www.medialunahostel.com, COP$35,000 dorm, COP$120,000 d). Located on the edge of Getsemaní, it's a high-energy kind of place with multicultural socializing (and flirting) centered on the small pool in the courtyard. If you're looking to break out

Hotel Sofitel Legend Santa Clara

with astounding and ever-changing floral displays. Concierges can arrange any excursion you'd like. The hotel's many amenities—four restaurants (one run by renowned chef Harry Sasson), a rooftop pool, a spa, and a gym—ensure a relaxing stay.

One Old City classic is in San Diego. The 122-room **Hotel Sofitel Legend Santa Clara** (Cl. del Torno No. 39-29, tel. 5/650-4700, www.sofitel.com, COP$780,000 d) is synonymous with class and luxury, though it once served as a convent. The stunning colonial courtyard features tropical plants, a fountain, and modern sculptures. The gorgeous chapel is available for weddings. Be sure to request a tour of the hotel from a staff member to see remnants of the convent. Make time for drinks at the on-site bar El Coro. The pool area is large; during low season, nonguests can obtain day passes.

From the rooftop terrace of ★ **Hotel LM** (Cl. de la Mantilla No. 3-56, tel. 5/664-9100, www.hotel-lm.com, COP$637,000 d), guests enjoy spectacular views of old Cartagena, of your shell, this may be the place. It has a capacity of over 100 guests with just a couple of private rooms (book early for those). Note that the vast majority of rooms don't have air-conditioning, which may be a challenge for those unused to the Cartagena heat. The staff organizes lots of activities and bikes are available to rent. There's also an attached burrito stand. Then there's the bar: On Wednesday nights, show up around 9pm for their famous Visa por un Sueño party.

COP$70,000-200,000

★ **Casa Relax** (Calle del Pozo No. 25-105, cell tel. 310/443-1505, www.cartagenarelax. com, COP$170,000 d) feels like a hostel for adults without the discomfort of dorm accommodations. Here you can make use of the kitchen, have a cocktail by the groovy pool, and socialize a bit. There are 12 rooms.

Low-key **Casa Villa Colonial** (Cl. de la Media Luna No. 10-89, tel. 5/664-5421, www. casavillacolonial.com.co, COP$185,000 d) is a midrange option for those interested in staying close to the Old City. The rooms are basic, with wood furniture and tiled floors. Its rooftop terrace has a pool.

COP$200,000-500,000

Style is the thing at ★ **Casa Lola** (Cl. del Guerrero No. 29-108, tel. 5/664-1538, www. casalola.com.co, COP$374,000 d), designed and managed by a Spanish couple who were some of the first hoteliers in Getsemaní. The hotel, spread over two buildings (one colonial and one Republican-era), has 10 rooms featuring furniture and art from all over the world. Its location near Café Havana means there may be street noise on weekend nights. Casa Lola also offers design-oriented apartments (US$250-450) for rent in the Centro that sleep 4-10 people.

Hotel Monterrey (Cra. 8B No. 25-100, tel. 5/650-3030, www.hotelmonterrey.com.co, COP$290,000) is a classic hotel with a huge rooftop terrace that houses a small pool, perfect for soaking up the views of the Old City. It's on a busy street across from the convention center, but traffic noise isn't an issue. Breakfast is served in a cute interior courtyard.

BOCAGRANDE
Under COP$70,000

Relaxed **Hostal Las Velas** (Cl. 1A No. 1-52, cell tel. 300/831-0159, www.hostallasvelas. com, COP$35,000 dorm, COP$230,000 d) opened in 2015. Its location just steps from the beach draws travelers who can't get enough kitesurfing, surfing, and windsurfing. This medium-sized house has one dorm room with eight beds and two private rooms (one with an en suite bathroom). The rooms don't have much flair, but this is a friendly spot in an area not frequented by tourists.

COP$70,000-200,000

Small **Barahona 446** (Cra. 2 No. 4-46, tel. 5/665-6144, www.hotelesbarahona.com, COP$180,000 d) is a bargain spot in the middle of Bocagrande, about a five-minute walk from the beach. The rooms are decent, but don't expect a view. Light sleepers may want to use earplugs, as noise from common areas can be a nuisance.

COP$200,000-500,000

The old classic in town is the **Hotel Caribe** (Cra. 1 No. 2-87, tel. 5/650-1160, www.hotel-caribe.com, COP$480,000 d). These swanky digs, comprising three large buildings, are next to the beach, and they even have a beach club exclusively for guests. The nicest feature here is the garden complete with resident parrots and deer. The 360 medium-sized rooms have views of the sea or the garden. Most visitors enjoy lounging by the pools and drinking a fruity cocktail.

For a no-surprises brand-name hotel experience, the **Hilton Cartagena** (Av. Almirante Brion, tel. 5/665-0660, www.hilton.com, COP$460,000 d) won't fail you. It's at the tip of Bocagrande, isolated from the crowds, and has multiple pools and tennis courts as well as a gym. Rooms feature all-marble bathrooms. President Obama stayed here during the 2012 Summit of the Americas.

Information and Services

TOURIST INFORMATION

In addition to locations at the airport and at the cruise ship terminal, there are city-run **tourist information kiosks** (no phone, 9am-noon and 1pm-6pm Mon.-Sat., 9am-5pm Sun.) near the Torre del Reloj and an air-conditioned main office in the historic **Casa de Marquez Plaza de la Aduana** (tel. 5/660-1583, 9am-noon and 1pm-6pm Mon.-Sat., 9am-5pm Sun.).

EMERGENCY AND MEDICAL SERVICES

In case of an emergency, call the **police** at 112. For medical emergencies, call an **ambulance** by dialing 125 or head to **Hospital Universitario** (Cl. 29 No. 50-50, tel. 5/669-7308, 24 hours daily).

POST OFFICE

The post office, **4-72,** has a branch in the Walled City (Cl. de la Moneda No. 7-94, tel. 5/670-0102, 8am-noon and 2pm-5:30pm Mon.-Fri., 9am-12:30pm Sat.). It costs COP$2,000 for postage to the United States and Canada. This branch has a small exhibition space with old postage stamps on display.

LAUNDRY

Beer & Laundry (Hotel Boutique La Artilleria, Cl. Pacoa No. 10-101, Local 2, Getsemaní, http://beerandlaundry.wix.com/beerandlaundry, 8am-7pm Mon.-Sat.) is a friendly full-service laundry service that will wash your clothes, and you can hang out and have a beer or slice of pizza while you wait.

LIBRARY

The public library, **Banco de la República Biblioteca Bartolome Calvo** (Cl. de la Inquisición No. 3-44, tel. 5/660-0777, 8:30am-6pm Mon.-Fri., 9am-1pm Sat.), is located in a grandiose building facing the Parque de Bolívar. It offers reading rooms and has an exhibition space.

LANGUAGE COURSES

Cartagena offers many opportunities to take group and individual Spanish classes. Many hostels have local Spanish tutors or can recommend a school or private teacher.

You may want to try out a class before committing to several days' instruction. One recommended school is **Lengua Nativa Spanish School** (cell tel. 304/573-1027, individual class US$15). **Nueva Lengua** (Calle del Pozo No. 25-95, Getsemaní, tel. 5/660-1736) has a solid track record, with locations in various cities. A 15-hour week of classes costs US$200.

Centro Catalina (Cl. Siete Infantes No. 9-21, San Diego, cell tel. 310/761-2157, www.centrocatalina.com) offers small-group classes in a house in the San Diego district.

VOLUNTEERING

The tourist sectors of the Old City and Bocagrande do not accurately portray the living conditions of the many Cartagenans who live in poverty. Wages are low for many in the service industry and some residential areas lack basic services, such as running water. Several private nonprofit organizations are working to break the cycle of poverty.

The **Fundación por la Educación Multidimensional** (FEM, Cl. del Quero No. 9-64, Centro, tel. 5/643-4185, www.femcolombia.org) strives to make an impact on budding entrepreneurs by pairing them with volunteers who have expertise in business, architecture, community development, and other vocations. FEM generally seeks longer commitments of multiple weeks from its volunteers, but some short-term opportunities are occasionally offered.

The **Fundación La Vecina** (La Boquilla, www.fundacionlavecina.com) helps low-income children living in La Boquilla. It was started by a Dutch woman, Nathalie Rietman. The foundation has short-term positions open during school vacations (January, July, and December), in addition to long-term (three months and up) opportunities.

The **Fundación Juan Felipe Gómez** (Cl. 31 No. 91-80, Ternera, tel. 5/661-0937, www. juanfe.org) is the brainchild of Catalina Escobar, a Colombian businesswoman who was nominated as CNN Hero of the Year in 2012 for her tireless efforts to help at-risk teenage mothers. Both short- and long-term volunteers are invited to share their skills with the young women at this impressive center. You can take a public bus or a taxi (20 minutes) from the Centro to the *fundación*.

Founded by Colombian pop singer Shakira in the late 1990s, the **Fundación Pies Descalzos** (Pie de la Popa, www.fundacionpiesdescalzos.com) builds schools, including the stunning Colegio Lomas del Peyé to the northeast of town, which it also operates. See their website for volunteer opportunities as well as fundraising needs.

Cartagena Paws (www.cartagenapaws. com) rescues abandoned dogs, and can always use kind dog walkers.

Transportation

GETTING THERE
Air
Cartagena's **Aeropuerto Internacional Rafael Núñez** (CTG, tel. 5/656-9202, www. sacsa.com.co) is located to the east of the city, about a 12-minute cab ride from Cartagena. Taxis from the airport to the Old City are reliable and regulated. The current fixed rate is COP$15,000.

Delta (www.delta.com) is the latest U.S. carrier to launch nonstop service to Cartagena, offering flights from Atlanta. **JetBlue** (www. jetblue.com) and **Avianca** (www.avianca. com) operate flights between New York-JFK and Cartagena. Nonstop flights from Florida are offered by **Spirit Airlines** (www.spirit. com) via Fort Lauderdale; Avianca has a nonstop out of Miami. **Copa** (www.copaair.com) serves Cartagena from its hub in Panama City, Panama. Charter carrier **Air Transat** (www. airtransat.com) flies nonstop from Montreal to Cartagena from December to March.

The main national carriers, Avianca and **LATAM Airlines** (www.latam.com), operate many flights each day to Cartagena from various Colombian cities. **VivaColombia** (www.vivacolombia.co) often offers inexpensive fares between Cartagena and Medellín, Bogotá, Cali, and Pereira. **ADA** (www. ada-aero.com) serves the city with flights from Medellín, Montería, and Cúcuta. **EasyFly** (www.easyfly.com.co) has a nonstop from Bucaramanga.

Bus
Regular bus service connects Cartagena with all major and coastal cities. The **Terminal de Transportes** (Diag. 56 No. 57-236, tel. 5/663-0454) is a 20- to 30-minute cab ride from the Centro. Expect to pay about COP$20,000 for the trip.

The Terminal de Transportes offers bus service to Bogotá, Medellín, Cali, and other interior cities. However, if you are making your way along the coast, it's quicker and easier to get to Santa Marta or Barranquilla by taking one of the fast *busetas* (large vans) that regularly serve the main Caribbean cities. **Marsol** (Cra. 2A No. 43-11, tel. 5/656-0302, www.transportesmarsol.net) and **Berlinas** (Cl. 46C No. 3-80, tel. 5/693-0006, www. berlinasdelfonce.com) are the top choices and have pickup sites near the Centro in the Marbella neighborhood. Marsol even offers door-to-door service (*puerta-puerta*). The last *buseta* leaves Cartagena around 8pm. It's a decent option to travel after dark—the roads are good and it's safe—as the roadside scenery isn't that impressive, there's less traffic, and you may as well spend the remaining daylight hours enjoying a mojito in the Old City.

Car or Motorcycle

Thanks to its narrow streets, scarce parking, and heavy traffic, Cartagena is not a particularly car-friendly city.

Consider renting a car or motorcycle for overland travel. Hertz and National, as well as local companies, have pickup and drop-off locations at the airport. This could be a good option if you are planning on taking your time getting to know the Caribbean coast or are continuing onward to Colombia's interior. The main road to Barranquilla is mostly four lanes, but shrinks to two lanes farther on to Santa Marta.

Cruise Ships

Cartagena is a major port of call for cruise ships from across the globe, bringing around 350,000 visitors each year. Entry into the Bahía de Cartagena is a dramatic one, as the ships pass through ruins of old Spanish forts.

The city is a living museum, and the best way to get to know it is by walking its narrow streets, getting lost, and finding one's way again. Be sure to bring some sun protection and water—the sticky midday heat can be sizzling. If you take an organized walking tour, you will likely be hounded by hawkers selling Colombian souvenirs.

Take a cab from the port to the Torre del Reloj, one of the main entrances to historic Cartagena. Pop into a museum and a grandiose colonial-era church, enjoy a delicious meal at one of the many fine restaurants, and cap it all off with a walk and a drink on the *muralla* (wall) facing the Caribbean Sea.

GETTING AROUND

Walking is the best way to get around the Old City, Getsemaní, and Bocagrande.

Taxis

For short hops between neighborhoods, cabs are quick and easy. Taxis here do not have meters, so it's possible you won't get the local rate. Before hopping in a cab, ask a local or two the standard rate. From the Old City to Bocagrande, expect to pay around COP$6,000. A ride to the airport will cost COP$15,000, and a trip to the beaches at Las Americas will be COP$12,000. Tipping is not customary. Ride-sharing services such as **Uber** (www.uber.com), **Easy Taxi** (www.easytaxi.com), and **Tappsi** (www.tappsi.co) have arrived in Cartagena, which may help minimize anxiety or confusion about taxi fares.

Buses

It may seem overwhelming at first, but taking a public bus is a cheap way to get around. To hop on a bus to Bocagrande from the Old City, walk down to Avenida Santander along the sea and flag down just about any bus you see (or look for a sign in the window that reads "Bocagrande"). The ride will set you back COP$1,800. There are a few options for getting off: As you board, tell the bus driver where you would like to be let off; belt out *"¡Parada!"* as you approach your destination; or discreetly exit behind someone else. On the main road (Carrera 11) just to the east of the walls, facing the Monumento India Catalina, is a nonstop parade of buses loading and unloading. From here you can get to the Castillo de San Felipe, the Mercado de Bazurto, or the bus terminal, for the same low price of COP$1,800.

TransCaribe

Launched in December 2015 after more than 10 years in development, the **TransCaribe bus system** (www.transcaribe.gov.co) employs organized stations (rather than standard bus stops). It caters mostly to residents, but may be useful for visitors interested in traveling out of the Centro to the city's southern neighborhoods. Some of the major stops are at Muelle de la Bodeguita, La Matuna, Chambacú (Castillo de San Felipe), and Mercado de Bazurto.

The bright-orange bus stations are located along Avenida Venezuela, a thoroughfare between the Centro and La Matuna that extends into the southern neighborhoods. Expect to pay under COP$2,000 for the comfortable ride.

Vicinity of Cartagena

BOCACHICA

Bocachica, which means "Small Mouth," is one of two entrances to the Bahía de Cartagena. It is at the southern end of the bay. The other, much wider entrance is Bocagrande ("Big Mouth"), more familiar as the peninsula southwest of the Old City. In 1640, when three galleons sank at Bocagrande and blocked that passage, the Spaniards decided to fortify the more easily defensible Bocachica.

The **Fuerte de San Fernando** (Isla Tierrabomba, tel. 5/655-0211 or 5/655-0277, www.patrimoniodecartagena.com, 8am-6pm daily, COP$9,000) and **Batería de San José** are two forts at either side of Bocachica, the first line of defense. The Fuerte de San Fernando, at the southern tip of the island of Tierrabomba, is a particularly impressive example of 18th-century military architecture. It is very well preserved and you can still see the barracks, kitchen, storerooms, and chapel enclosed within the massive fortifications. The low-lying Batería de San José is a much more modest affair, and can be visited with a ticket for Fuerte de San Fernando.

The only way to get to Bocachica is by one of the *lanchas* (fast boats, COP$7,000) that depart from the Muelle de los Pegasos, the tourist port in Cartagena near the Torre del Reloj. The 45-minute trip through the bay provides interesting views of Cartagena and the port. The waits between departures can be long, so bring sunscreen and something to do.

In Bocachica, there are a few small, informal restaurants where you can eat fried fish, coconut rice, and *patacones* (fried plantains) and drink a cold beer.

★ PLAYA BLANCA AND ISLAS DEL ROSARIO

South of Cartagena is the elongated island of **Barú,** which is separated from the mainland by the Canal del Dique, an artificial waterway built in 1650 to connect Cartagena with the Río Magdalena. On Barú lies **Playa Blanca,** a Caribbean paradise of idyllic, white-sand beaches bordering warm blue waters. West of Barú and about 25 kilometers (15.5 miles) southwest of Cartagena is the archipelago **Islas del Rosario,** part of the much larger **Parque Nacional Natural Corales del Rosario y San Bernardo.** On Barú and the Islas del Rosario, traditional Afro-Colombian communities with rich cultural heritages share space with the vacation houses of Colombia's rich and famous.

Barú is home to several beautiful beaches. With the exception of Playa Blanca, most of these are inaccessible to the general public. The 25 small coral islands of the Islas del Rosario are a marine wonderland. The once-spectacular coral reefs off of Barú and surrounding the archipelago have been badly damaged by the increased flow of freshwater from the Canal del Dique, which has been dredged in recent years.

Quiet **Isla Grande** in the Islas del Rosario has a handful of hotels and a community group, Nativos Activos, run by Afro-Colombian locals who rent bikes and equipment and can organize tours and other activities. They are always available at Hotel San Pedro de Majagua. Expect to pay COP$20,000 for a bike rental.

This Is Cartagena (Cl. Sargento Mayor No. 6-107, Oficina 104, Centro, tel. 5/660-9128, www.ticartagena.com, 9am-6pm Mon.-Fri.), based out of the Old City, offers fantastic tours to the islands. A standard day trip (US$70) features a day at a fab beach resort, lunch, and snorkeling or kayaking, and includes hotel pickup and drop-off. For an unforgettable time, upgrade to the Island Hopping in Style tour, which offers the same activities—from your own personal yacht. This option ranges US$600-6,000, depending on the yacht.

(Km. 3 past Pasacaballos Bridge, Barú, cell tel. 315/394-2374, www.elpescadordecolores.com, 11:30am-5:30pm Wed.-Mon., COP$40,000) is the place to be on Barú. This swanky beach lounge specializes in Euro-Caribbean cuisine, but the biggest attraction is hanging out on a beach bed.

Accommodations

Best known for its location in Cartagena, **Media Luna Hostel** (Playa Bobo, Isla Barú, cell tel. 313/536-3146, www.medialunahostel.com, COP$50,000 dorm) also owns a chill beachside hostel in Barú, which consists of five two-story thatched-roof *cabañas*. Each *cabaña* has four beds and a bathroom and can be either a private room or a dorm, depending on your preference. They will take care of round-trip transportation (COP$60,000) from their Getsemaní location, where pickup is at 9am daily.

Sport Barú (Ensenada del Cholón, Km. 26, Isla Barú, cell tel. 314/506-6520, www.sportbaru.com, COP$800,000 d) is a relaxing beach resort nestled among the mangroves on the quiet side of the Cholón lagoon. There are three cabins with multiple rooms each for rent; the older ones with thatched roofs have more charm. All of them are comfortable, but the Wi-Fi is iffy. A visit here usually includes lounging on the beach in front of the hotel or at Playa Azul, a quick boat ride away. For those staying more than a day, the food can get a little repetitive (lots of fried fish and coconut rice). You can also take a day trip here (COP$145,000), which includes transportation, lunch, and an excursion to Playa Azul.

In a quiet section on the north side of Isla Grande, **Eco Hotel Las Palmeras** (Isla Grande, cell tel. 314/584-7358, COP$75,000 d) is a laid-back and no-frills beachside hostel that has lots of charm, thanks mainly to the nice people who run it. Don't expect luxury here: A shower requires scooping water from a bucket with a coconut shell.

Isla Grande

If you are willing to pay more, there are more upscale day tours to the *islas*. One is a day trip to the luxurious beachside **Hotel San Pedro de Majagua** (Cartagena office: Cl. del Torno No. 39-114, tel. 5/650-4464, www.hotelmajagua.com, day trip COP$173,000) on Isla Grande. They take care of transportation from the Muelle de Marina Santa Cruz in Manga (boats leave at 9am, return at 3:30pm daily). The price also includes a seafood lunch and a visit to an aquarium. For an unforgettable sunset experience, try the Neon Sunset Tour on a paddleboard with LED lights, perfect for illuminating bioluminescent plankton. You can also spend the night at this comfortable hotel (COP$350,000 d including transportation).

Food

To enjoy fresh seafood and fabulous cocktails under the sun, **Pescador de Colores**

Mompox

Mompox was founded in 1540 on the eastern edge of a large island between two branches of the Río Magdalena (the Brazo de Loba and the Brazo Mompox). This lovely town was an opulent center of trade, connecting the interior of the country with Cartagena during the colonial era. But then the mighty river changed its course in the late 18th century and Mompox's importance steadily declined, never to return.

Mompox is what Cartagena looked like before it became a tourist destination, and it's hard to deny the melancholic charm this oppressively hot town retains even today. The attraction here is strolling the wide streets, admiring the whitewashed houses decorated with intricate iron latticework, and watching the river flow by. In 1995, due to its architectural importance, the town was declared a UNESCO World Heritage Site.

The town is spread out along the muddy Magdalena, and the river is its raison d'être. It does not have a central plaza, but rather three squares, each with a church, facing the river. It is believed that each of these squares is on the location of a former indigenous settlement. From south to north, they are **Plaza de Santa Bárbara, Plaza de la Concepción** (also known as Plaza Mayor), and **Plaza de San Francisco.** Three main streets run parallel to the river: Calle de la Albarrada (which corresponds to Carrera 1) facing the river; the Calle Real del Medio, Mompox's main street, one block west of the river; and the Calle de Atrás (literally, the "street behind").

SIGHTS

There are two historic churches worth visiting in Mompox. The riverfront **Iglesia de Santa Bárbara** (Cl. de la Albarrada and Cl. 14, mass 6pm Fri.-Sun.) was built in 1630. The facade is painted a striking yellow, with colorful floral decorations. It has an unusual baroque octagonal tower with a balcony wrapping around it. Inside is a magnificent gilded altar. The church extends from the Plaza de Santa Bárbara to the Plaza de San Francisco. The second noteworthy church is the **Iglesia de San Agustín**

Iglesia de Santa Bárbara

(Cl. Real del Medio and Cl. de la Albarrada, mass 4pm daily), which houses the Santo Sepulcro, a gilded reproduction of Christ's tomb. The churches are only open during mass times. Guests of the **Casa Amarilla** (Cl. de la Albarrada No. 13-59, tel. 5/685-6326 or cell tel. 301/362-7065, www.lacasaa-maraillamompos.com) can make a request with the hotel to take a quick peek inside the churches.

The only museum in town, which keeps irregular hours, is the **Museo Cultural de Arte Religioso** (Cl. Real del Medio No. 17-07, tel. 5/685-6074, 9am-noon and 3pm-4pm Tues. and Thurs.-Fri., 9am-noon Sat.-Mon., COP$2,000). It's home to displays of gold- and silverwork from the colonial era. Mompox silver- and goldsmiths made a name for themselves with their intricate filigree jewelry.

Another interesting sight is the **Piedra de Bolívar** (Cl. de la Albarrada and Cl. 17), a river-facing monument with a stone slab that lists all the visits Simón Bolívar made to Mompox.

Mompox's atmospheric 19th-century **Cementerio Municipal** (Cl. 18 and Cra. 4, 8am-noon and 2pm-5pm daily, free) is well worth a detour. The cemetery houses the tomb of Afro-Colombian poet Candelario Obeso and General Hermógenes Maza, who fought beside Simón Bolívar. The cemetery is also known for the resident cats that frolic among the graves.

FESTIVALS AND EVENTS

Semana Santa (Holy Week), which occurs during late March or April, is the most important celebration in Mompox. Visitors from all over Colombia converge on the town to watch its religious processions and attend concerts. You'll have to book months in advance to get a hotel room during that time.

The **Mompox Jazz Festival** (early Oct.) has become the biggest show in town, with performances by international artists such as Tito Puente selling out far in advance.

SHOPPING

Mompox is known in Colombia for its intricate gold filigree jewelry. Look for the **Joyería Filimompox** (Cl. 23 No. 3-23, tel. 5/685-6604 or cell tel. 313/548-2322, hours vary), where the staff will explain their craft to you during your visit to their workshop. They accept credit cards.

At the **Escuela Taller de Artes y Oficios de Santa Cruz de Mompox** (Claustro de San Agustín, Cl. 16 No. 1A-57, tel. 5/685-5204, hours vary), young people learn traditional handicrafts. Visitors are welcome to drop by and watch these artisans at work. Inside, there's an interior courtyard, an inviting place to linger for a while.

FOOD AND ACCOMMODATIONS

During low season, restaurant options in Mompox become scarce. With sufficient notice, most hotels will prepare meals. Belgian-run **El Fuerte** (Cra. 1 No. 12-163, tel. 5/685-6762, 6pm-9pm Fri.-Sun., COP$20,000) is the best dining option in town. It's mostly Italian cuisine, and the pizza and pasta are done right. The **Comedor Costeño** (Cl. de la Albarrada No. 18-45, tel. 5/685-5263, 7am-5pm daily, COP$12,000) serves *comida típica* (Colombian fare) overlooking the Magdalena.

On the Plaza de la Concepción, **Khalilieh** (Cra. 1A No. 17A-54, tel. 5/685-5978, noon-9pm daily, COP$14,000) serves Lebanese food and grilled meats.

For a drink, look for the **Cava de los Ángeles** (Cl. de la Albarrada, cell tel. 301/533-1780, 4pm-midnight daily).

During high season, inquire about the *planchon* **sunset cruise** (three hours, COP$30,000), where passengers enjoy a drink on the river, floating on a wooden barge. For more information, contact Carmen Garrido (cell tel. 310/606-4632) or ask at the Casa Amarilla.

Bioma Hotel Boutique (Cl. Real del Medio No. 18-59, tel. 5/685-6733 or cell tel. 315/308-6365, www.bioma.co, COP$190,000

d) may be one of the most comfortable options in town, as it offers 12 air-conditioned rooms, a dipping pool, and good food.

The ★ **Casa Amarilla** (Cl. de la Albarrada No. 13-59, tel. 5/685-6326 or cell tel. 301/362-7065, www.lacasaamarillamompos.com, COP$25,000 dorm, COP$100,000 d), owned by a British travel writer, is another excellent choice, with accommodations for backpackers as well as private rooms for those seeking more comfort. After a careful restoration, the Casa Amarilla added a luxurious colonial house, the Casa de la Concepción (COP$1,500,000), which has four bedrooms and two interior patio gardens; the second-story balcony provides a lovely view to the plaza below. Best of all, it has a pool.

Casa España (Cl. Real del Medio, tel. 5/685-5373 or cell tel. 313/513-6946, www.hotelcasaespanamompox.com, COP$180,000 d) is a guesthouse with 16 basic rooms, most with two double beds, and an interior courtyard with plenty of rocking chairs in which to relax.

GETTING THERE

Most visitors arrive in Mompox from Cartagena, and there are several ways to make the journey.

There is one direct bus that leaves from Cartagena's **Terminal de Transportes** (Diag. 57 No. 24-236, tel. 5/663-0454) at 6:30am daily. The ride takes eight hours and costs COP$50,000. More comfortable is a door-to-door service with a company like **Toto Express** (cell tel. 310/707-0838, COP$75,000), which takes six hours.

The fastest way involves a van, a boat, and a taxi: Take a van (COP$40,000 pp, 3.5 hours) from outside the Terminal de Transportes in Cartagena to Magangué, a port on the Magdalena; there hop on a *chalupa* boat that will take you to a spot called Bodega de Mompox (COP$7,000, 30 min.); and from there take a shared taxi or *mototaxi* (COP$15,000, 30 min.) to Mompox.

Satena (www.satena.com) offers seasonal flights, especially during Semana Santa, from Bogotá to Mompox's small airport. The flight takes less than an hour.

Santa Marta and La Guajira

Look for ★ to find recommended sights, activities, dining, and lodging.

Highlights

★ **Carnaval de Barranquilla:** Madcap and euphoric, this is Colombia's most famous celebration. Put on a costume and dance your way down the parade route (page 66).

★ **Taganga:** Relax at the beach in this laid-back fishing village (page 75).

★ **Minca:** Take a break from the beach and chill in this refreshing town set in the foothills of the spectacular Sierra Nevada de Santa Marta (page 77).

★ **Parque Nacional Natural Tayrona:** Mountains meet jungles meet beaches at this popular national park near Santa Marta (page 81).

★ **Ciudad Perdida Trek:** Climb the thousand-plus stone steps through the cloud forest to the mystical Lost City, the most important settlement of the Tayrona civilization (page 87).

★ **Santuario de Fauna y Flora Los Flamencos:** Spot flocks of flamingos and other aquatic birds at this park on the outskirts of Riohacha (page 97).

★ **Cabo de la Vela:** This Wayúu community on the edge of the Caribbean is known for its eerie desert scenery as well as excellent wind- and kitesurfing (page 99).

★ **Punta Gallinas:** Continental South America's northernmost point is where you'll find spectacular dunes that drop dramatically to the sea (page 101).

Northeast of Cartagena are some of Colombia's biggest draws and most hidden gems. Here the gold-sand beaches are set against a backdrop of jungle; beyond are the mountains of the Sierra Nevada de Santa Marta.

Santa Marta is one of the oldest cities on the continent; Barranquilla's bacchanalian Carnaval celebration is world-famous. The rugged jungle coastline is home to the country's most visited and well-known national park, Parque Nacional Natural Tayrona, and one of South America's most famous treks, the hike to the ruins of Ciudad Perdida. The sandy beaches from PNN Tayrona to coastal Palomino are lined with hostels and five-star eco-lodges where the emphasis is firmly on relaxation. Beyond these treasures lies the vast Guajira Peninsula, an arid, otherworldly landscape.

For many, the Sierra Nevada is synonymous with adventure, but it is also the sacred home to four indigenous groups: the Kogi, the Wiwa, the Arhuaco, and the Kankuamo, who are descendants of the Tayrona civilization.

La Guajira is home to the Wayúu indigenous people, who have maintained their independent way of life through centuries. Though many Wayúu now live in cities and towns, their traditional *rancherías* (settlements) still dot the sands of La Guajira.

PLANNING YOUR TIME

A couple of days in Santa Marta will suffice for most, especially if you're there over a weekend, when the city comes alive. Barranquilla is an easy day or overnight trip from Cartagena.

A visit to Parque Nacional Natural Tayrona (2-3 days) is often tacked onto the end of a Cartagena vacation. PNN Tayrona can also be visited as a day trip from Santa Marta, Taganga, or any of the beachside resorts along the coast. It's best to spend one or two nights in the park, otherwise a trip here is more work than relaxation. Avoid visiting the park between mid-December and mid-January and during Semana Santa (Holy Week), when it's very crowded.

Another popular addendum to a visit to Cartagena is the four- to six-day trek

Previous: *mochilas* made by the indigenous Arhuaco people; Parque Nacional Natural Tayrona. **Above:** Sierra Nevada de Santa Marta.

Santa Marta and La Guajira

CARIBBEAN SEA

Barranquilla
CARNAVAL DE BARRANQUILLA
Ciénaga Grande de Santa Marta
Ciénaga
Santa Marta
TAGANGA
PARQUE NACIONAL NATURAL TAYRONA
MINCA
Calabazo
Pueblito
Aracataca
PNN Sierra Nevada de Santa Marta
CIUDAD PERDIDA TREK
Guachaca
Burítaca
SANTUARIO DE FAUNA Y FLORA LOS FLAMENCOS
Valledupar
Palomino
Camarones
Riohacha
Mayapo
Distracción
Manaure
Albania
Uribia
CABO DE LA VELA
Bahía Portete
VENEZUELA
Maicao
Paraguachón
CERREJÓN RAIL LINE
Puerto Bolívar
Bahía Hondita
Bahía Honda
PUNTA GALLINAS
Lago de Maracaibo
Golfo de Venezuela
PNN Macuira
Nazareth

0
25 km
0
25 mi

© AVALON TRAVEL

to Ciudad Perdida in the Parque Nacional Natural Sierra Nevada de Santa Marta. The trek is usually organized out of Santa Marta or Taganga. After the sweaty (but rewarding) slog to these mystical ruins, give yourself a few days afterward to relax in a comfortable hotel in Santa Marta or Barranquilla. The best times for the trek are February-March, August-September, and late November-late December, when it's raining less and the crowds are fewer.

Travel along this stretch of coast is easy, as you'll generally be on the Troncal del Caribe, the main highway linking Cartagena to Riohacha. Public transportation is readily available, especially between Cartagena and Santa Marta, but less so after dark. Renting a car is an option, especially if you're planning on staying at one of the beachside lodges between PNN Tayrona and Palomino. The road is safe, even at night.

Most visitors to La Guajira join an organized tour from Riohacha. It's possible to visit Cabo de la Vela independently of a tour, but the trip takes several hours and requires multiple modes of transportation. Do not drive through the Guajira Peninsula without a guide: It is dangerous.

Santa Marta and Vicinity

With a charming historic district, great hotel and restaurant options, and proximity to popular natural attractions, Santa Marta is a major tourist destination. Steamy Barranquilla lies halfway between Cartagena and Santa Marta, and is home to the world-renown Carnaval de Barranquilla.

BARRANQUILLA

Colombia's fourth-largest city (pop. 1.6 million) is known for its busy port and for the bacchanalian Carnaval de Barranquilla, designated a World Masterpiece of the Oral and Intangible Heritage of Humanity by UNESCO. This, the most famous celebration in Colombia, is a time of music, dancing in the streets, and revelry. Usually occurring in February, it lasts only about four days, but the city pulses with anticipation for days (if not weeks) in advance.

During the rest of the year there's not a whole lot to lure the visitor to Barranquilla. It is not a colonial city, but vestiges of its early-20th-century importance can be seen in its El Prado district.

Barranquilla offers a handful of attractions, including the Museo del Caribe and the quirky Bocas de Ceniza, a jut of land that divides the Río Magdalena from the Caribbean Sea. A wealth of comfortable hotel and restaurant options may be the trick for weary travelers returning from the jungle or beach.

Sights

Two museums lend insight into Barranquilla's people and culture. The first, **Casa del Carnaval** (Cra. 54 No. 49B-39, tel. 5/319-7616, 9am-5pm Mon.-Sat., COP$5,000), is Carnaval headquarters, and its Sala Carnaval Elsa Caridi provides an interactive introduction to the annual event. After a visit here, you'll come to understand the many different components of the celebration, like the different musical styles: *cumbia, mapalé, chandé,* and *son.* While at first blush it may seem that the Carnaval de Barranquilla is just a big party, there is more to it than meets the eye. Behind every costume, parade, and dance there is a story. Knowledgeable guides will share this story and their genuine enthusiasm for the festival at this well-done museum.

The other top museum is **Museo del Caribe** (Cl. 36 No. 46-66, tel. 5/372-0582, www.culturacaribe.org, 8am-5pm Tues.-Fri., 9am-6pm Sat.-Sun., COP$10,000), one of the finest museums in the country, with a focus on Costeño (Caribbean coast) culture. There is a room dedicated to Gabriel García Márquez,

Santa Marta and Vicinity

in which characters from the author's books come alive; the exhibit may be hard to follow if your Spanish is less than fluent. There are slide shows on Caribbean ecosystems and exhibits on the people of the Caribbean, including a fascinating video series on the region's many different indigenous tribes. Of particular interest is a room that examines immigration to the coast, from African slaves to "Turcos," meaning those mostly coming from Syria, Lebanon, and Palestine. The museum has a small restaurant with reasonably priced meals on the plaza in front.

The **Banco de la República** (Cra. 54 No. 52-258, tel. 5/371-6690, 8am-noon and 2pm-6pm Mon.-Fri., free) is the address for culture in Barranquilla. Along with temporary art exhibitions, classical music concerts are

held on occasion at the on-site Teatro Amira de la Rosa. This modern theater is noted for the fantastic artwork by modern Colombian painter Alejandro Obregón (1920-1992); called *Se va el caiman*, it's a large and colorful piece that evokes the Caribbean legend of the alligator-man. Check in with a staff member to see it.

The **Paseo Bolívar** (Cl. 34 between Cras. 38-45) is the gritty main drag downtown. It's lined with discount shops and used-book stands, where you can often find Colombian classics—even in English—if you look hard enough. There's always a crowd at the newspaper kiosks, which seems like a scene from a different era. On the restored **Plaza San Nicolás** (between Clls. 32-33 and Cras. 41-42) is the neo-gothic **Iglesia San Nicolás**

Barranquilla

Tolentino (Cra. 42 No. 33-45, tel. 5/340-2247), which took about 300 years to build. It's usually open, with mass occurring several times a week. Be wary of pickpockets in this part of the city.

Not about roses and chocolates, the **Museo Romántico** (Cra. 54 No. 59-199, tel. 5/344-4591, 9am-11:30am and 2:30pm-5:30pm Mon.-Fri., COP$5,000) is really a history museum of Barranquilla with artwork, old Carnaval costumes, missives signed by Simón Bolívar, and a typewriter used by Gabriel García Márquez. The majestic building, in the posh El Prado neighborhood, was once the home of Jewish immigrants who arrived in Colombia at the turn of the 20th century.

BOCAS DE CENIZA

For an unusual excursion, visit **Bocas de Ceniza,** a narrow peninsula surrounded by the Caribbean on one side and the Río Magdalena on the other. The highlight is getting out to the edge: On old train tracks (used to transport goods on and off freight ships) a "train," which is more like a truck, travels back and forth ferrying passengers to the end of the peninsula. The 10-minute ride (COP$3,000) operates daily and is most popular on the weekends, when locals make the trip. It's also possible to follow the tracks on foot. From January to March, the winds whip the water into a fury, making it an atmospheric if wet experience to make one's way to the end.

To get to Bocas de Ceniza, take a cab along Carrera 40 through the industrial area to the fishing village of Las Flores. Las Flores boasts several open-air seafood restaurants that face the river and are very popular on weekends. From Las Flores, bici-taxis (COP$2,000) can take you to the departure point for the Bocas de Ceniza train. They'll also take you to the end of the tracks for another COP$3,000.

Nightlife

Salsa fans will want to visit **La Troja** (Cta. 44 No. 72-263, no phone, www.latroja.org, 11am-midnight daily, no cover), a Barranquilla classic that regularly features musicians from New York, Puerto Rico, and Cali on its stage.

The thumping gay club of the moment is **Lives Club** (Cra. 53 No. 70-191, tel. 5/385-5880, 9pm-3am Fri.-Sat., cover COP$15,000) where the music is a mix of crossover and house.

Festivals and Events

★ CARNAVAL DE BARRANQUILLA

For most Colombians, Barranquilla is synonymous with Carnaval, and they boast that the city's celebration is the world's biggest after that held in Rio (although folks from New Orleans may balk at this claim). During the four days prior to Ash Wednesday, in late February or early March, the **Carnaval de Barranquilla** (www.carnavaldebarranquilla. org) is full of Costeño pageantry, with costumes, music, dancing, parades, and drinking. This is the only place in Colombia where the bacchanal is fully celebrated, although some Caribbean cities make an effort.

Prior to the official festivities of Carnaval, there are *verbenas*, which are parties open to the public in different parts of the city. To get an invite to one, ask a local or two. Carnaval officially begins on a Saturday, but on the Friday night one week before, the celebration **La Guacherna** (Cra. 44 and Cl. 70) awakens the city with parades and concerts.

Saturday is the main event. That's the day of the **Batalla de las Flores** (Battle of the Flowers) parade. It's when floats carrying beauty queens, dancers, and members of the general public in *comparsas* (groups) in elaborate costumes make their way down Calle 40 under the sizzling Barranquilla sun. This event dates back to 1903, when it began as a celebration of the end of the Guerra de los Mil Días (Thousand Days' War). Participation in the parades is serious business here, involving planning, practice, money, and, sometimes, connections. However, there is one *comparsa* during the Batalla de las Flores in which just about anyone can participate, and it's one of the most popular: the "Disfrázate como Quieras"—go however you like. Anybody in a costume, from the silly to the sexy, can participate. Check out the Disfrázate como Quieras Facebook page to find out how you can join in the fun.

On Sunday, during the **Gran Parada de Tradición y Folclor,** groups of dancers perform on Calle 40 to the hypnotic music of Carnaval—a mix of African, indigenous, and European sounds. On Monday there is another parade, the **Gran Parada de Comparsas.** Starting in the late afternoon, a massive concert attracts more than 30 musical groups, who compete for the award of Congo del Oro.

On Tuesday, after four days of music and dancing, things wind down with the parade **Joselito Se Va con las Cenizas** (Cra. 54 and Cl. 59). This is when Joselito, a fictitious Barranquillero, "dies" after four days of rumba, and his "body" is carried through the streets as bystanders weep. Joselito is sometimes played by an actor, and other times is a mannequin.

Watch all the action of the parades from the *palcos* (bleachers) that line Calle 40, the only way to spectate. Keep in mind that the parades take place in the middle of the day, meaning lots of sun and heat. Tickets (COP$100,000-300,000) for the *palcos* can be ordered online at **Tu Boleta** (www.tuboleta. com), or your hotel may be able to assist in getting you a ticket.

With regard to Carnaval, it's said that *"Quien lo vive es quien lo goza"* ("Whoever experiences it is who enjoys it"). But to do that, it's crucial to get hotel and flight reservations early—ideally around six months in advance.

OTHER FESTIVALS

During the first or second week of March each year, the fledging **Festival Internacional de Cine de Barranquilla** (www.ficbaq.com, early Mar.) showcases regional and international films over a week at various locations across the city. Tickets are inexpensive, going for around COP$5,000 for each film showing.

A weeklong tribute to the city's Latin jazz roots, September's **Barranquijazz Festival** (www.barranquijazz.com, third week of Sept.) has been held annually since 1997, with Colombian and international artists performing at various venues throughout the city. Tickets for the main events are available at Tu Boleta (www.tuboleta.com), and there is always a selection of free concerts and workshops throughout the city.

Sports and Recreation

The national *fútbol* (soccer) team, known as La Selección, plays all of their World Cup qualifying matches at the **Estadio Metropolitano Roberto Meléndez** (Aves. Circunvalar Alberto Pumarejo and Murillo, box office hours vary) in Barranquilla, usually in the middle of the day when the sun is at its most potent. If you want to get the full-on experience, buy a bright-yellow team jersey and try to get a ticket (COP$200,000). If La Selección isn't playing, there's a good chance that the beloved local first-division professional team, Junior (www.juniorfc.co/boletas), is. Known as the *tiburones* (sharks), Junior made it to the national championship in 2015. Matches occur nearly year-round. At the stadium, be on the lookout for the statue of Colombian pop singer Shakira, Barranquilla's favorite daughter. Tickets to La Selección can be purchased at online ticket retailers like **Tu Boleta** (www.tuboleta.com) and **Ticketbis** (www.ticketbis.com.co) or at the stadium box office. Ticket information and schedules for Junior can be found on their website.

Lagos de Caujaral Club (Km. 9 via Puerto Colombia, tel. 5/359-8579, www.lagosdecaujaral.com, greens fees COP$80,000-120,000) is considered one of the top golf courses in Colombia. This 18-hole course is about 20 minutes from downtown. To play at this private facility, make reservations in advance.

Food

Regional standouts include *butifara soledena*, which is a beef and pork sausage normally served with *bollo de yuca*, a boiled ball of yucca. Another meaty dish, popular during Carnaval, is *sancocho de guandú*, a stew of beef, yucca, yams, plantains, and vegetables. For breakfast on the go, Barranquilleros grab an *arepa de huevo* (an egg in a cornmeal *arepa* that is then fried). Many restaurants are clustered around Carrera 52 between Calles 70-100.

The ★ **Restaurante Bar La Cueva** (Cra. 43 No. 59-03, tel. 5/340-9813, noon-3pm and 6pm-10pm Mon.-Thurs., noon-3pm and 6pm-1am Fri.-Sat., COP$30,000) has history and lots of character. It was the hangout of Gabriel García Márquez and artists such as Alejandro Obregón in the 1960s. Elephant tracks, memorabilia, and photos make it seem like a museum, but it is still a restaurant, and a popular one at that. The specialty here is seafood. There's live music on Friday and Saturday evenings. Be sure to check out the Obregón work *La Mulata de Obregón*, complete with a bullet hole thanks to a drunken friend of the artist. Reservations are essential on weekend evenings.

El Huerto (Cra. 52 No. 70-139, tel. 5/368-7171, 8am-7:30pm Mon.-Sat., 10am-3pm Sun., COP$12,000) offers an inexpensive and healthy all-vegetarian break from the norm with a set lunch menu every day. There is also a small store that sells baked goods and health food products such as quinoa and granola.

Barranquilla offers a few Middle Eastern restaurants to choose from. With its extensive menu, the best option is **Arabe Gourmet** (Cra. 49C No. 76-181, tel. 5/360-5930, 11am-10pm daily, COP$25,000).

Nena Lela Trattoría (Centro Comercial Buenavista, Cl. 99 No. 52-53, Local 414, tel. 5/537-5398, noon-10pm daily) is a local favorite for pasta, even though the mall location isn't exactly enchanting.

Varadero (Cra. 51B No. 79-907, cell tel. 316/269-8192, noon-midnight daily) serves great seafood (try the grilled seafood platter) on white tablecloths, making it one of Barranquilla's fanciest restaurants. There is live music on weekends.

For authentic coastal cuisine, Barranquilleros head to casual **Narcobollo** (Cra. 43 No. 84-188, tel. 5/359-5305, 7am-9pm daily, COP$12,000) where you can recharge with *arepa con huevo* (fried egg *arepa*) for breakfast and *chicharrón con bollo limpio* (pork rinds with boiled hominy corn rolls) for lunch, as well as fried snacks any time of day.

One of the top steak restaurants in town is **Chez Ernest Steak House** (Cra. 54 No. 70-69, Local 101, Edificio Prado 54, tel. 5/358-7103, noon-3pm Mon.-Fri., COP$35,000). Reservations are recommended, as this small place has its followers—and it's open only for lunch. The chateaubriand steak is a good choice.

Accommodations

Because of its status as a business destination, Barranquilla has a number of hotel options, although hostels are almost nonexistent. Rates at chain hotels can significantly drop on weekends. During Carnaval, prices skyrocket and hotels sell out months in advance.

Friendly and low-key, the **Meeting Point Hostel** (Cra. 61 No. 68-100, tel. 5/318-2599, www.themeetingpoint.hostel.com, COP$30,000 dorm, COP$100,000 d) is the only hostel catering to international backpackers in Barranquilla. This Italian-run spot has a pizzeria out front. The neighborhood is quiet and green, about a 15-minute walk from El Prado. You may suffer if you don't splurge on a room with air-conditioning.

Country International Hotel (Cra. 52 No. 75-30, tel. 5/369-5900, ext. 120, www.countryinthotel.com, COP$238,000 d) has a

nice pool and comfortable rooms. It's located in a good area.

★ **Hotel Estelar Alto Prado** (Cl. 76 No. 56-29, tel. 5/336-0000, COP$292,000 d) is a modern, comfortable, and stylish address in Barranquilla. This is where the Argentinian national soccer club stays when they face off against Colombia.

Transportation
GETTING THERE

Barranquilla's **Aeropuerto Internacional Ernesto Cortissoz** (Soledad, www.baq. aero) offers excellent connections with all major cities in Colombia and a handful of nonstop international flights as well. The airport is south of the city in Soledad. Taxi rides cost about COP$20,000 from the airport to downtown.

Avianca (www.avianca.com) flies nonstop to Barranquilla from Miami, Bogotá, Cali, and Medellín. **LATAM Airlines** (www.latam.com) has flights from Bogotá. On **Copa** (www.copaair.com) there are nonstop flights from San Andrés and Panama City.

VivaColombia (www.vivacolombia.co) flies from Medellín, **EasyFly** (www.easyfly.com.co) has nonstop flights from Bucaramanga and Valledupar, and **ADA** (www.ada-aero.com) flies from Montería.

There is regular bus service to all points in Colombia from the **Terminal Metropolitana de Transportes** (Km. 1.5 Prolongación Cl. Murillo, tel. 5/323-0034, www.ttbag.com.co), which is about 15 minutes from downtown. If you're traveling on to Santa Marta or Cartagena it's more convenient to take a fast van service directly from the city. From their terminals in town, both **Berlinastur** (Cl. 96 No. 46-36, tel. 5/385-0030, www.berlinastur.com) and **MarSol** (Cl. 93 No. 47-13 Local 4, tel. 5/357-6209) make the daily journey to Santa Marta (2 hours, COP$20,000) and Cartagena (1.5 hours, COP$20,000) from early in the morning until around 6pm. They are fast and reliable and usually take credit cards. There's no need to reserve a seat.

GETTING AROUND

Barranquilla is not a pedestrian-friendly city. Unmetered taxi cabs are the most convenient way to get around. Ask a local how much you should expect to pay before stepping into a cab. You should never pay more than COP$13,000 to get to in-town locations. Colombian apps such as Tappsi and Easy Taxi make getting a cab easier, and Uber is also available.

Transmetro (www.transmetro.gov. co, 5am-11pm Mon.-Sat., 6am-10pm Sun., COP$1,600) is the rapid bus system, which runs along two main avenues: Avenida Murillo (also known as Calle 45) and Avenida Olaya Herrera (also known as Carrera 46). There are stations in front of the Museo del Caribe, the cathedral, and the stadium.

SANTA MARTA

Santa Marta is the logical launching pad for visits to the nearby Sierra Nevada—including Parque Nacional Natural Tayrona and Ciudad Perdida—and is a convenient stop on the way to the Alta Guajira.

The **Centro Histórico** extends from the busy Calle 22 (Avenida Santa Rita) in the west to the Avenida del Ferrocarril in the east, toward the seaside village of Taganga.

The southern border ranges from the same Avenida del Ferrocarril in the south to the *malecón* (Carrera 1C/Avenida Rodrigo de Bastidas) in the north.

The focal point of the Centro is the Parque de los Novios (Carreras 2A-3 and Calles 19-20). This is a lovely park with pedestrian streets (Calle 19 and Carrera 3) intersecting on its eastern side. Most sights are within a smaller range of streets from Carrera 5 to the water and between Calles 20 and 14.

The **Rodadero district,** with condos and hotels lining the beach, is southwest of downtown Santa Marta, just around the bend on the main highway. Local buses continuously ply the stretch between the Centro Histórico and Rodadero.

SIGHTS
CENTRO HISTÓRICO

The compact Centro Histórico in Santa Marta feels like a living museum, with its mix of colonial and Republican-era architecture. All major sights, save for the Quinta de San Pedro Alejandrino, are located here and can be visited in one day.

The **Parque de los Novios** (Cras. 2A-3 and Clls. 19-20) is a symbol of the city's rejuvenation. The pedestrian streets (except for

sundown in Santa Marta

Santa Marta

one) around the park make a pleasant place for a stroll and a meal. Restaurants line the park's periphery and on the Calle 20 side of the park is the grandiose neoclassical **Palacio de Justicia,** Santa Marta's main courthouse.

The **Catedral de Santa Marta** or **Basílica Menor** (Cr. 5 No. 16-30, tel. 5/421-2434, masses at noon and 6pm Mon.-Sat., 7am, 10am, noon, and 6pm Sun.) took around 30 years to build and was completed in 1794, toward the end of Spanish reign in Nueva Granada, as colonial Colombia was called. It is one of the oldest cathedrals in Latin America. The city's founder, Rodrigo de Bastidas, is buried there, and Simón Bolívar laid in rest there before his body was moved to Caracas.

The **Plaza de Bolívar** (Cras. 1-2 and Clls. 14-15) has a statue of Simón Bolívar on

horseback, ready to destroy the oppressors. The **Banco de la República** (Cl. 14 No. 1C-37, tel. 5/421-0251, www.banrep.gov.co, 8:30am-6pm Mon.-Fri., 9am-1pm Sat., free) often has art exhibits and also has a peaceful public library on the third floor.

The **Museo del Oro Tairona** (Cl. 14 No. 1C-37, tel. 5/421-0251, www.banrepcultural. org, 9am-5pm Tues.-Sat., 10am-3pm Sat., free) is in the historic **Casa de la Aduana,** perhaps the oldest customs house in the Americas, dating back to 1531. A smaller version of the famous Museo del Oro in Bogotá, this focuses on the Tayrona people, who were the native settlers of the region and forebears of the Kogis, Arhuacos, Kankuamos, and Wiwas who live in the Sierra Nevada. There are ceramic and gold artifacts on display, and a description of the Ciudad Perdida archaeological site. A visit to this museum may enrich your hike up to the Lost City, as you'll have a better understanding of the people who once inhabited it.

Along the waterfront is the **Paseo de Bastidas** (Cra. 1) boardwalk. A sunset walk along the pier that extends from the boardwalk is a Santa Marta ritual. Check out the great views of the port, the sailboats moored at the Marina Santa Marta, and Isla Morro.

QUINTA DE SAN PEDRO ALEJANDRINO

Simón Jose Antonio de la Santísima Trinidad Bolívar y Palacios, better known as Simón Bolívar, was instrumental in bringing independence to several countries in Latin America, including Venezuela, Colombia, Ecuador, Peru, and Bolivia. While awaiting exile to Europe, he passed away at the age of 47 in Santa Marta at the **Quinta de San Pedro Alejandrino** (Mamatoco, tel. 5/433-2995, www.museobolivariano.org.co, 9am-4:30pm daily, COP$14,000). This country estate is now a museum where visitors can see the bedroom in which Bolívar died in 1830. A modern wing houses the Museo Bolivariano de Arte Contemporáneo.

Young guides will offer to take you around the complex for about COP$2,000, but you're probably better off on your own. The *quinta* is set in a manicured botanical garden. There is a small snack bar and gift shop on the grounds.

Nightlife

Chilled-out electronica, a gentle Caribbean breeze, harbor views, and expensive drinks await at **Miko** (Cra. 1 No. 22-93, cell tel. 322/529-9119, 5pm-1am Sun.-Thurs., 5pm-3am Fri.-Sat., COP$15,000) located on the pier near the Marina de Santa Marta. It's a trendy spot that draws both locals and visitors.

Supremely fun **La Puerta** (Cl. 17 No. 2-29, no phone, 7pm-3am Thurs.-Sat., COP$12,000) is a place in the Centro where locals and foreigners mingle as DJs spin an eclectic variety of music. On sultry Santa Marta weekends, the entire bar turns into a dance floor.

A popular nightspot, with guest DJs and euphoric dancers, is the terrace of **La Brisa Loca** (Cl. 14 No. 3-58, cell tel. 317/585-9598, 5pm-1am Sun.-Thurs., 5pm-3am Fri.-Sat., COP$15,000), the high-energy hostel in the Centro. On weekend nights, expect a line to get in. Other Centro hostels, such as **Mulata Hostel** (Cl. 19 No. 3-32, tel. 5/420-7305, 5pm-1am daily) and **Hostal Jackie** (Cl. 21 No.

Museo del Oro Tairona

3-40, tel. 5/420-6944, 5pm-midnight daily), also have rooftop bars, and are especially lively on weekends.

Voltage (Cl. 23 No. 4-34, Local 2, cell tel. 301/216-4146, 9pm-5am Fri.-Sat., COP$15,000) is the friendly late-night gay nightspot, with an open-air dance floor and music that alternates between crossover and house music.

Shopping

For funky gifts made by local designers, such as T-shirts and art, check out the small shop **Santa Marca** (Cl. 17 No. 2-45, Centro, tel. 5/423-5862, www.santamarca.co, 10am-7pm Mon.-Sat.).

El Amanuense (Cl. 16 No. 3-28, tel. 5/420-0993, Mon.-Sat. 9am-5pm) is a tiny bookshop that carries work mostly by Colombian authors. There's also a small café inside.

Go back in time in **Vejeces Casa de Antiguedades** (Cl. 18 No. 7A-64, cell tel. 300/305-3324, 9am-5pm Mon.-Sat.), a quaint Centro shop jam-packed with interesting stuff. While there are some pre-Columbian pieces for sale, note that it is illegal to take these abroad.

El Tiburón (Cra. 2 18-09, tel. 5/421-4301, 10am-6pm daily) makes shocking use of every square inch of its space in the Centro to display Colombian handicrafts and kitsch, and by no small miracle, shop employees seem to know where everything is.

Recreation

There are some terrific diving spots quite close to Santa Marta. **Santa Marta Dive and Adventure** (Cl. 17 No. 2-43, tel. 5/422-6370, www.santamartadiveandadventure.com) is a reputable agency that offers dive tours and courses with some English-speaking instructors. Dive sites are off the coast of Parque Nacional Natural Tayrona, at two shipwrecks near Santa Marta, and offshore from the town of Taganga. A three-day course goes for COP$650,000, a half-day course is COP$200,000, and a diving excursion for certified divers costs COP$160,000.

Food

Most of Santa Marta's finest restaurants can be found in the Centro Histórico, although the Rodadero area is known for its seafood joints. For a delightful ambience, seek out restaurants on pedestrianized streets in the Centro Histórico, such as Carretera 3 between Calles 15 and 16 (Callejón del Correo), Calle 19 between Carreteras 3 and 5, and on the Parque de los Novios.

CENTRO HISTÓRICO

One of the first restaurants to populate Callejón del Correo was ★ **La Casona/ Donde L'Italiano** (Cra. 3 No. 16-26, cell tel. 316/429-1131, 5pm-10pm Mon.-Sat., COP$30,000), a cheerful restaurant where even the standard pasta arrabiata tastes exquisite. The diverse menu offers Caribbean cuisine (with an Italian flair) in addition to traditional pasta dishes.

★ **Ouzo** (Cra. 3 No. 19-29, tel. 5/423-0658, 6pm-11pm Mon.-Sat., COP$25,000) consistently ranks as one of the top fine-dining restaurants in Santa Marta. Specializing in Mediterranean fare, Ouzo has brought some class to the Parque de los Novios. Order a plate of sizzling seafood or pasta accompanied by a glass of white wine. **El Balcón de Ouzo** serves tapas and pizza on the rooftop terrace of Ouzo. It's one of the best spots in Santa Marta for a sundowner.

An unassuming bistro, ★ **Ratatouille** (Cl. 21 No. 4-54, tel. 5/421-5356 or cell tel. 300/828-6966, noon-10pm Mon.-Sat., COP$22,000) is run by a recent arrival from France, serving traditional French cuisine with some Colombian touches. It's a smart choice for dessert and coffee, too. They hold occasional storytelling events with longtime Santa Marta residents.

For Peruvian food with a Caribbean twist, check out **Rocoto** (Cra. 2 No. 19-15, cell tel. 300/835-8604, noon-3pm and 6pm-10pm Tues.-Sun., COP$35,000), on an edgy street a couple of blocks from Parque de los Novios. The pisco sours (try the passion fruit version) and *causas* (traditional Peruvian potato dish) never disappoint, but there are also other tasty dishes to be tried, such as a steak served with polenta.

La Muzzería (Cra. 3 No. 16-02, tel. 5/422-1460, 6pm-midnight daily, COP$22,000) is at the end of a *callejón* (alley) that always feels like a street festival. The pizza and Colombian fare here earns mostly positive reviews, and the atmosphere is lovely.

On pedestrian Calle 19, **Ikaro** (Cl. 19 No. 3-60, tel. 5/430-5585, 8am-9pm Mon.-Sat., COP$15,000) specializes in vegetarian and vegan fare. This café and restaurant caters mostly to the international crowd, and it's an inviting place to nurse a cappuccino.

Facing the Parque Simón Bolívar and next to the gold museum, ★ **Juan Valdez** (Cl. 14 between Cras. 1 and 2, 8am-8:30pm Mon.-Sat., 9am-7:30pm Sun.) is an outdoor café where you can enjoy a coffee sitting under the shade of trees—and get a quick shoeshine if so inclined.

RODADERO

For delicious seafood, pasta, and wine in a minimalist setting, try **DiVino** (Cl. 6 No. 1-26, tel. 5/421-3735, noon-11pm daily, COP$30,000), one of the top restaurants in Rodadero.

★ **Donde Chucho** (Cl. 6 at Cra. 3, tel. 5/422-1752, 11:30am-10:30pm daily, COP$25,000) is the classic Santa Marta seafood joint. It's so popular it has even opened branches in Bogotá. The original restaurant (there is another location in the Centro) is a casual open-air place filled with photos of Chucho, the owner and chef, posing with Colombian beauty queens, sports stars, and politicians. It's hard to believe that Chucho began this seafood empire with a humble wooden ceviche stand in Rodadero in the 1990s.

The terrace of **Pepe Mar** (Cra. 1 No. 6-05, tel. 5/422-2503, noon-10pm Sun. and Tues.-Thurs., noon-midnight Fri.-Sat., COP$26,000) is the best place for people-watching in all of Rodadero. Try the fried red snapper with coconut rice and a *patacón* (fried plantain) or

two. Casual attire like tank tops and bathing suits are okay here.

Accommodations

The Centro Histórico offers posh boutique hotels and comfortable hostels. The Rodadero has plenty of high-rise hotels, many of which are all-inclusive. The relaxed beach village of Taganga is very close to the city; some prefer to stay there and visit Santa Marta for its restaurants in the evenings.

UNDER COP$70,000

Many hostels in Santa Marta vie for the title of "party hostel." **La Brisa Loca** (Cl. 14 No. 3-58, Centro Histórico, tel. 5/431-6121, www.labrisaloca.com, COP$45,000 dorm, COP$80,000 d) is a revamped mansion-turned-hostel that has earned its spot as a backpacker favorite. There's a small pool in the main courtyard surrounded by three floors of private rooms and large mixed dormitories (6-10 beds). On the top floor is an excellent bar that, thanks to its daily drink specials, gets jammed with backpackers and locals alike, especially on weekends. Don't expect peaceful sleep here.

Located in a quiet, tree-lined neighborhood about five kilometers (3.1 miles) east of the Centro, **The Dreamer** (Cra. 51 No. 26D-161, tel. 5/433-3264, www.thedreamerhostel.com, COP$40,000 dorm, COP$100,000 d) makes life easy for guests, offering tons of information on day trips and coordination of travel to other destinations (such as their location on the beach in Palomino). All the action here centers on the pool, where there is a bar and restaurant that serves burritos and huge lemonades.

Drop Bear Hostel (Cra. 21 No. 20-36, tel. 5/435-8034, www.dropbearhostel.com, COP$30,000 dorm, COP$60,000 d) is set in a huge house that was built by a drug trafficker in the 1980s. The hotel bar is aptly named the Cartel Bar. Rooms are massive. Perhaps the nicest feature at Drop Bear is the big pool, which is the main gathering area at this sociable place. Ask for a tour of the house, including its secret tunnels and oddities. The hostel is a 10- to 15-minute drive east of the Centro.

★ **Aluna** (Cl. 21 No. 5-27, Centro Histórico, tel. 5/432-4916, www.aluna-hotel.com, COP$30,000 dorm with fan, COP$100,000 d with a/c) is a small, quiet hostel with a mix of dorms and private rooms, all of which are immaculately maintained. Private rooms have their own bathrooms. The hostel's café serves breakfast and snacks.

Hostal Jackie (Cl. 21 No. 3-40, Centro Histórico, tel. 5/420-6944, www.elhostaldejackie.com, COP$36,000 dorm, COP$90,000 d) has dorms of different sizes and private rooms, most with just a fan. The rooftop is a friendly gathering place, and sometimes they have DJs playing at the bar. There is a small pool on the ground floor.

COP$70,000-200,000

The ★ **Hotel del Parque** (Cl. 19 No. 4-45, Centro Histórico, tel. 5/420-7508, COP$90,000 d) on the pleasant pedestrian Calle 19 is a gem. Supremely low-key, this hotel has just a handful of air-conditioned rooms but is very well maintained, and, best of all, it's fairly priced. There's complimentary coffee, but no free breakfast; however, there are many options within walking distance.

COP$200,000-500,000

La Casa del Farol (Cl. 18 No. 3-115, Centro Histórico, tel. 5/423-1572, www.lacasadelfarol.com, COP$317,000 d) was one of the first boutique hotels in the city. It's in an 18th-century house and has six rooms that are named for different cities of the world. From the tiny wading pool on the rooftop you get a nice view of the city. With the same owners and just across the street, **La Casa del Agua** (Cl. 18 No. 4-09, Centro Histórico, tel. 5/423-1572, www.lacasadelagua.com.co, COP$180,000 d) has four rooms of various sizes and styles. Try for one with a balcony. The small pool downstairs is a welcome sight after a day out in the heat.

The 10-room ★ **Casa de Isabella** (Callejón del Río, Cra. 2 No. 19-20, Centro Histórico, tel. 5/431-2082 or cell tel. 301/466-5656, www.casaisabella.com, COP$280,000 d) is a tastefully revamped Republican-era house with nods to both colonial and Republican styles, and it surrounds a tamarind tree that's over 200 years old. The suites on top have fantastic private terraces and hot tubs.

For a beachfront option, check out **Tamacá Beach Resort Hotel** (Cra. 2 No. 11A-98, Rodadero, tel. 5/422-7015, www.tamaca.com.co, COP$300,000 d). It has 81 rooms with all the usual amenities and a fantastic pool area that overlooks the water. The hotel has two towers, with the beachside tower preferred by most.

Information and Services

In addition to a stand at the airport, there is a **PIT** (Punto de Información Turística, Cra. 1 No. 10A-12, tel. 5/438-2587, 9am-noon and 2pm-6pm Mon.-Fri., 9am-1pm Sat.) tourist information booth along the waterfront.

Lavandería El Paraíso (Cl. 22 No. 2A-46, tel. 5/431-2466, cell tel. 315/681-1651, 9am-6pm Mon.-Fri., 9am-1pm Sat.) will wash your clothes and have them ready for pickup by the next day.

Transportation

Santa Marta is easily accessed by air and land from all major cities in Colombia.

The **Aeropuerto Internacional Simón Bolívar** (Km. 16.5 Troncal del Caribe) is 16 kilometers (10 miles) west of the Centro Histórico. Domestic carriers **Avianca** (www.avianca.com), **LATAM Airlines** (www.latam.com), **VivaColombia** (www.vivacolombia.co), and **EasyFly** (www.easyfly.com.co) connect Santa Marta with the major cities of Colombia. **Copa** (www.copaair.com) has nonstop flights from its hub in Panama City, Panama. Taxis to the Centro Histórico from the airport cost around COP$25,000.

There is hourly bus service to Cartagena, Barranquilla, and Riohacha. Many buses to nearby coastal destinations leave from the market area (Cra. 11 and Cl. 11) in the Centro Histórico. Long-haul buses for destinations such as Bogotá, Medellín, and Bucaramanga depart from the **Terminal de Transportes** (Cl. 41 No. 31-17, tel. 5/430-2040) outside of town.

Taxis to Taganga cost around COP$8,000 and *colectivo* buses are around COP$1,200. These can be found on the waterfront near Parque Simón Bolívar, along Carrera 5, or at the market at Carrera 11 and Calle 11.

The best way to get around the Centro Histórico is on foot. A recommended **walking tour** (cell tel. 301/485-9222, free) of historic Santa Marta is offered by local Eduardo Riveira. Tips are welcome, and the walks usually take place at 10am on most weekdays.

★ TAGANGA

This popular beachside community is only about a 20-minute ride northeast through the desert from Santa Marta and is actually considered part of the city. In the 1970s, this sleepy fishing village was discovered by hippie-types looking for an escape from urban life, and it soon evolved into a mecca for backpackers. On any given Saturday along the bayside promenade, you'll brush shoulders with Colombian families, diving fanatics, traveling musicians, and general sunseekers of all ages and nationalities. It's as close as Colombia gets to Venice Beach.

Recreation
DIVING AND SNORKELING
The warm waters (24-28°C/75-82°F) off of Taganga provide some good diving and snorkeling opportunities. Diving excursions take you into the waters off of Parque Nacional Natural Tayrona to the northeast, to Isla Morro off the coast of Santa Marta, or to a shipwreck near the beaches of Rodadero. The best months for diving here are between July and September.

Tayrona Dive Center (Cra. 1C No. 18A-22, tel. 5/421-5349, cell tel. 318/305-9589, 8am-noon and 2pm-6pm daily) is a very organized

agency that offers PADI certification courses (COP$650,000) over a period of three days with six dives each day, a one-day mini-course (COP$160,000), and diving excursions for those with experience. They also have a hotel (COP$70,000 d) at the same location with six rooms, five with views of the water. Rooms have a safe-deposit box and big refrigerators. The hotel is exclusively for divers during high season (mid-December to mid-January, Holy Week, and mid-June through mid-July).

Oceano Scuba (Cra. 2 No. 17-46, tel. 5/421-9004, cell tel. 316/534-1834, www. oceanoscuba.com.co, 8am-noon and 2pm-6pm daily) offers the whole array of diving activities, from one-day dives for certified divers (COP$110,000) to a one-day beginner's course (COP$180,000) to an open-water PADI certification course (COP$600,000) that lasts three days. Night dives (COP$80,000)—during which you might come across eels—and snorkeling (COP$50,000) are also on offer.

Poseidon Dive Center (Cl. 18 No 1-69, tel. 5/421-9224, www.poseidondivecenter. com, 9am-6pm daily) is a third well-established dive center that has English-speaking instructors. They offer dozens of courses, like an open-water diving class (COP$830,000) and tours, such as a 10-dive package (COP$860,000).

BEACHES
The gray, sandy beach in front of the boardwalk attracts hordes of locals, especially on weekends, but the best beaches are outside of town. **Playa Grande,** northwest of town, is the best of the bunch, and it is one of the closest to Taganga. It costs COP$10,000 roundtrip to get there by boat. To arrange for boat transportation, just head to the beach in front of the promenade or at La Ballena Azul. There are always boaters waiting for customers. There's a path to Playa Grande from Taganga, which takes 15 minutes to walk. Check with your hotel whether it's open and passable.

Boats can also take you to the beaches of the **Parque Nacional Natural Tayrona** for COP$40,000 round-trip, but you can negotiate that price, especially if you are in a group. Although all visitors to the park are supposed to pay an entrance fee (and it is steep for non-Colombians), some boat captains will take you to beaches without park employee supervision, which park officials rightly do not condone. During the windy months of December-February, boat transportation can be rough, bordering on dangerous.

Food

★ **Babaganoush Restaurante y Bar** (Cra. 1C No. 18-22, 3rd fl. above Taganga Dive Center, cell tel. 318/868-1476, 1pm-11:30pm Wed.-Mon., COP$20,000) is an excellent Dutch-run restaurant and bar with amazing views. It's a true crowd pleaser, with a diverse menu of falafel, seafood, steak, and even a shout-out to Southeast Asia. Go in the evening for the atmosphere, drinks, and sunset. The daily happy hour (5pm-7pm) is hard to pass up.

Tucked away on a side street a block or two from the beach, **Pachamama** (Cl. 16 No. 1C-18, tel. 5/421-9486 or cell tel. 318/393-9291, COP$24,000) has a sophisticated menu that includes Argentinian steaks, ceviche, pasta, and refreshing cocktails, all skillfully prepared by the French chef.

Direct from Atlanta comes ★ **Taco Beach Bar and Grille** (Cra. 1 No. 18-49, tel. 5/423-3912, www.tacotaganga.com, noon-8pm daily, COP$15,000). With Tex-Mex delights, happy hours, and sand beneath your feet, this spot is all that you need in a beach bar.

Café Bonsai (Cl. 13 No. 1-07, tel. 5/421-9495, www.cafebonsai.com, 8am-9:30pm daily, COP$18,000) is a cute place for coffee, freshly baked breads and pastries, and sandwiches and other lunch items.

Accommodations

It's not close to the beach, but **La Casa de Felipe** (Cra. 5A No. 19-13, tel. 5/421-9120, www.lacasadefelipe.com, COP$30,000 dorm, COP$70,000 d) is a spacious and comfortable choice. On the downside, it's in a neighborhood where music plays until the wee hours.

If you want backpacker prices without a backpacker scene, check out **Hostal Pelikan** (Cra. 2 No. 17-04, tel. 5/421-9057 or cell tel. 316/756-1312, www.hostalpelikan.com, COP$25,000 dorm, COP$65,000 d), a decent place to stay with a nice terrace for your morning coffee. Breakfast is an additional cost.

La Ballena Azul (Cra. 1 at Cl. 18, tel. 5/421-9009, www.hotelballenaazul.com, COP$173,000 d) is a classic Taganga hotel,

carefree Taganga

It Takes an Eco-Village

Visiting an eco-lodge in Colombia is one of the best experiences the country offers. In the jungle outside of Minca, there resides something even better—**Paso del Mango,** an eco-village comprising lodges and nature reserves that all share a commitment to preserving this beautiful land.

The best place to stay in Paso del Mango is the shockingly deluxe **Finca Carpe Diem** (tel. 5/420-9610, www.fincacarpediem.com, COP$17,000 hammocks, COP$35,000 dorm, COP$180,000 luxury cabin), which is perched on the cusp of the jungle. This Belgian-run lodge is also a working farm and a 50-hectare natural reserve, and is home to a tree-planting project. There's a refreshing natural pool, beekeeping classes, and a restaurant onsite, which offers a variety of options in a friendly atmosphere.

To get to Paso del Mango, take a taxi to the village of Bonda (COP$10,000) from Santa Marta. From the soccer field, take a *mototaxi* (COP$8,000) along the scenic road up to the mountains.

and from points east, such as the Parque Nacional Natural Tayrona and Palomino. Minibuses and buses ply both routes daily.

From Santa Marta's Centro Histórico, you can take a minibuses to Taganga for about COP$1,500. Taxis from Santa Marta cost around COP$12,000, more from the bus terminal or airport. Once in Taganga, you can walk everywhere you need to go.

★ MINCA

If you've had your fill of beaches or the seductive Caribbean cities, maybe it's time for an altitude adjustment. Artists, nature lovers, coffee farmers, and transplanted urbanites in the village of Minca (pop. 500) look down upon their neighbors in nearby Santa Marta—literally. At an elevation of 660 meters (2,165 ft.), midway up the Sierra, you get a bird's-eye view of Santa Marta, just 45 minutes away. You also get a great bird's-eye view of birds, especially higher up at the edge of the Parque Nacional Natural Sierra Nevada de Santa Marta. The blissful routine of mountain hikes, dips in invigorating swimming holes, and sunset ogling may make you want to linger here.

Recreation

In and around Minca there are no safety issues, and you can hike up the mountain on your own without a guide.

HIKING

Minca is a paradise for hikers. Nearby are several gentle hikes along tranquil mountain roads and paths to swimming holes of either freezing-cold or wonderfully refreshing pure water, depending on the thickness of your skin. Three popular swimming holes are within easy walking distance from Minca: Balneario Las Piedras (45 mins.), Pozo Azul (1 hr.), and the Cascadas Marinka (1 hr.).

The Sierra Nevada de Santa Marta is a renowned coffee-growing region. The **Finca La Victoria** (no phone, 9am-4pm daily, COP$10,000) is a family-run coffee farm that you can visit for a small fee. It is between

started by a Frenchwoman years ago. It's still in the family, and they still serve crepes in their restaurant. Ballena Azul is on the beach, with the best location in town—in the center of activity. Next door, the American-run ★ **Taganga Beach Hotel** (Cra. 1 No. 18-49, tel. 5/421-9058, www.tagangabeachhotel. com, COP$110,000 d) has seven comfortable rooms, with plans for more, and an awesome little bar in front. It's just steps from the beach.

Probably the most luxurious option in Taganga is the **Hotel Bahía Taganga** (Cl. 8 No. 1B-35, tel. 5/421-0653 or cell tel. 310/216-9120, www.hotelbahiataganga.com, COP$200,000 d). It's on the northern side of the bay. Head to the pool in the late afternoon and watch the sun slip behind the mountains.

Transportation

Taganga is easily reached from Santa Marta

Pozo Azul and Los Pinos, about a one-hour walk from town. The farm uses an astonishing hydroelectric system and machinery dating back over 100 years. After the tour, save room for lunch at the French-run bistro on the premises. Pick up some of Minca's homegrown beer, made by Happy Toucan, also on the farm's premises.

BIRD-WATCHING

High in the Sierra Nevada, at an elevation of around 2,400 meters (7,875 feet), the **Reserva El Dorado** (www.proaves.org) is one of the finest bird-watching reserves in the country. For reservations (COP$569,000 3 nights all-incl.), contact **EcoTurs** in Bogotá (Cra. 20 No. 36-61, tel. 1/287-6592, info@ecoturs.org) or **Aviatur** (tel. 1/587-5181, www.aviaturecoturismo.com) in Bogotá. The accommodations are excellent, with 10 spacious rooms, great food, and, crucially, hot showers. The area is home to 19 endemic species, including the Santa Marta antpitta, Santa Marta parakeet, Santa Marta bush tyrant, blossom crown, and screech owls. Anybody can stay at El Dorado, even the non-birding crowd.

TOURS

To go on a photo safari in the jungle and improve your skills, check out **Fototrails** (cell tel. 310/650-5200, www.foto-trails.com, COP$45,000-90,000). They offer unique one-day tours for all skill levels. Tours focus on wildlife and nature photography, or feature visits to a Kogi indigenous community or farming families. Tours are led by a native English speaker and professional photographer.

Food

There are a handful of good eateries in Minca, mostly catering to international travelers. Hotels and hostels are always a reliable and reasonably priced option for guests and non-guests alike. They are open every day with lunch hours generally noon-3pm and dinner 6pm-10pm. Main dishes rarely cost more than COP$20,000. Standouts include ★ **Hostal**

Casa Loma (50 m above the church, cell tel. 313/808-6134 or 321/224-6632, www.casalomaminca.com) and **El Mirador Hotel** (200 m from town entrance, cell tel. 311/671-3456 or 318/368-1611).

Dining at **Ei Mox Muica** (300 m from town entrance, cell tel. 311/699-6718, 10am-9pm daily, COP$18,000) is like being invited to a friend's house. They only have two tables, which overlook a lush garden. The menu includes a variety of pasta, salads, crepes, and wines. They are into locally produced chocolate here—it might even make an appearance in your pasta.

Tienda Café de Minca (diagonal from police station, cell tel. 312/638-5353, 8:30am-8pm daily) sells snacks (like empanadas), beer, and wine. There is sometimes live music on weekends. It's a good place to find out what's going on in town.

Lazy Cat (across from Tienda Julimar, cell tel. 313/506-5227, noon-9pm daily, COP$15,000) offers a filling meal of pasta or burgers, or just a fruit smoothie. It's in the center of town on the main street.

Accommodations
UNDER COP$70,000

★ **Hostal Casa Loma** (50 m uphill from a small church, cell tel. 313/808-6134, www.casalomaminca.com, COP$20,000 dorm, COP$80,000 d) is on a hilltop with an impressive vantage point over Santa Marta. It's a friendly place, where delicious food (often vegetarian) is served, and you can mingle with other travelers. Cabins such as the Casa Selva and Casa Luna farther up on the hillside are quieter than the rooms near the main social area, providing the ultimate jungle experience. Camping (COP$15,000) is also available. To get to Hostal Casa Loma, climb a winding path just behind the church. Casa Loma offers yoga classes (COP$20,000) and massages (COP$55,000), and shows two films a week in an outdoor setting.

Oscar's Hostal Finca La Fortuna (400 m from town entrance near casino area, cell tel. 313/534-4500, www.oscarsplace.com.co,

COP$20,000 hammock, COP$25,000 dorm, COP$40,000 d) consists of simple and luxurious cabins dramatically set on a bluff with extraordinary views of Santa Marta and the surrounding countryside. Oscar's is completely off the grid, with solar panels providing electricity and rainwater collection and a well accounting for all water. The sunsets here, particularly from mid-June until mid-December, are "living art," as owner Oscar puts it. At times Oscar's can have a party atmosphere.

Hostel Mirador (200 m from town entrance, cell tel. 311/671-3456 or 318/368-1611, http://miradorminca.wordpress.com, COP$25,000 dorm, COP$60,000 d) is an enchanting hostel with a great view, warm hosts, and delicious meals. The hostel has two private rooms and a dorm room with three beds. It's set in a lush garden, and the lovely dining area is open-air. The restaurant is open to the public nightly; meals cost around COP$20,000.

Casa Elemento (cell tel. 313/587-7677, www.casaelemento.com, COP$20,000 hammock, COP$35,000 dorm, COP$100,000 d) has a fantastic location far up the mountain, and is a sociable and fun place to spend a few days. There's lots of hanging out here, both at the bar and in the massive 10-person hammock, and it's so remote that there's nothing much going on. The countryside is inspiring, but a lot of guests are more interested in partying. To get there, hire a *mototaxi* from Minca (COP$20,000).

COP$70,000-200,000

Hotel Minca (near town entrance, cell tel. 321/204-1965, www.hotelminca.com, COP$120,000 d), once a convent, was one of the first hotels in Minca. There are 14 spacious yet basic rooms in this old-fashioned building that boasts broad verandas with hammocks. There's a nature path on the grounds, and numerous hummingbird feeders along the open-air dining area ensure that you'll have a breakfast-time show.

Information and Services

Bring plenty of cash with you to Minca: There are no ATMs here. There is a small **tourist information stand** (near police station, cell tel. 317/308-5270, 10am-6pm daily). It's run by the tour agency **Jungle Joe's** (www.junglejoeminca.com).

Transportation

Minca is easily reached from Santa Marta. *Taxis colectivos* (shared taxis) depart from Santa Marta on a regular basis from the market (Cra. 11 and Cl. 11). These cost COP$7,000; the ride takes about 45 minutes. Private taxis from the airport cost around COP$50,000, and taxis from Santa Marta's Centro Histórico to Minca cost COP$40,000.

Parque Nacional Natural Tayrona

Perhaps the best-known national park in Colombia, the **Parque Nacional Natural Tayrona** (PNN Tayrona, 34 km northeast of Santa Marta on the Troncal del Caribe highway, tel. 5/421-1732, www.aviaturecoturismo.com or www.parquesnacionales.gov.co, 8am-5pm daily, COP$37,500 non-Colombian, COP$14,000 Colombian resident, COP$7,500 children, COP$7,500 students under age 25 with a valid ID) encompasses gorgeous beaches, tropical rainforests, and archaeological sites.

The park covers 12,000 hectares (30,000 acres) of land from the edge of Taganga in the southwest to the Río Piedras in the east. The southern border of the park is the Troncal del Caribe highway and to the north is the Caribbean Sea. To the east and south of the PNN Tayrona is the PNN Sierra Nevada de Santa Marta, a much larger national park.

The frequently tempestuous waters of the PNN Tayrona provide dramatic scenery, with palms growing atop massive island boulders and waves crashing against them. More than 30 golden-sand beaches in the park are set dramatically against a seemingly vertical wall of jungle. Although you can't see them from the park, the snow-covered peaks of the Sierra Nevada de Santa Marta are only 42 kilometers (26 miles) from the coast.

The park includes significant tracts of critically endangered dry tropical forests, mostly in its western section; these forests are much less dense than the humid tropical forests. At higher elevations you will see magnificent cloud forests. In addition to beaches, the coast is home to marine estuaries and mangroves. The park is laced with streams fed by chilly waters that flow from high in the sierra. In the western part of the park, many of these run dry during the dry season, while in the eastern sector they have water year-round.

The forest in PNN Tayrona is alive with plant and animal life. Some 1,300 plant, 396 bird, and 99 mammal species have been identified here. Four species of monkeys live in the park, and they can often be spotted. Five species of wild cats have been identified in the park: the margay, jaguar, ocelot, panther, and jaguarundi. Their numbers are few and these great cats are expert at hiding in the jungle—don't count on stumbling across them during your visit. Other mammals include sloths, anteaters, armadillos, deer, and 40 types of bats. Birds include migratory and resident species, such as the rare blue-billed curassow (locally called El Paujíl), a threatened bird that lives in the cloud forest, as well as toucans, macaws (*guacamayas)*, and many hummingbirds.

Planning Your Time

The best months to visit the park are February, March, September, and October. There are two rainy seasons: April-June and September-November, with the latter being more intense.

During these times, trails can be extremely muddy.

If at all possible, avoid visiting PNN Tayrona during the high seasons of late December through mid-January, during Semana Santa (Holy Week), and, to a lesser extent, during summer school holidays from mid-June until mid-July. During these times, the park is swarmed with visitors. Long holiday weekends (*puentes*) are also quite busy here; a weekday visit is by far the best.

While many people visit the park on day trips from Santa Marta, spending one or two nights in the park is recommended, even though accommodations and food can be expensive.

Bring mosquito repellent (especially during rainy season), a flashlight or headlamp, hiking or athletic shoes if you will be hiking to El Pueblito, sunscreen, and cash. Darkness falls around 6pm year-round, and there is not much going on in the park, so bring playing cards and a book to read. Visitors are not permitted to bring alcohol into the park; your bags may be inspected upon entry. Passports are necessary for entry.

Orientation

The majority of visitors see just the extreme northeastern section of the park. This part of the park houses the main entrance, **El Zaino.** From El Zaino, visitors can access the **Cañaveral** area, which includes the Ecohab accommodations; campsites at **Castilletes;** and cabins and campsites at **Arrecifes.** Farther southwest are La Piscina and more campsites at **Cabo San Juan** (also called El Cabo). From Cabo San Juan, there is access to the archaeological site El Pueblito.

Closer to Santa Marta is the **Palangana** entrance, which provides access to Playa Neguanje and other remote beaches. No overnight stays are permitted in this part of the park.

For day-trippers, Bahía Concha and Playa Cristal are accessible by boat from Taganga.

taxi (COP$15,000 from Santa Marta) through the Palangana entrance (12 km northeast of Santa Marta). **Playa del Muerto** (Playa Cristal) is another recommended beach in the same area. It's more than 20 kilometers (12.5 miles) from the park entrance to the beach.

It's possible to visit some of the beaches at the western end of the park all the way to Cabo San Juan by boat from Taganga, but park staff prefer that visitors enter the park by land. The waters can also be quite rough, especially between December and February.

Hiking
CAÑAVERAL TO ARRECIFES

The best-maintained and most beautiful hike in the park is the underappreciated stretch between Cañaveral and Arrecifes (3 kilometers/1.9 miles, one hour). Upon arrival, most visitors take this path to reach campsites or cabins between Arrecifes and Cabo San Juan. Wooden bridges meander through the jungle as you follow the sound of the crashing waves until you reach a beach strewn with massive boulders. To best enjoy this hike, consider sending your luggage onward to Arrecifes by horse (COP$19,000). Be on the lookout for capuchin monkeys, snakes, and birds.

EL PUEBLITO

A highlight of any visit to PNN Tayrona is the trek up to **El Pueblito** (also called Chairama, 3 kilometers/1.9 miles, 1.5 hrs. one way from Cabo San Juan), which consists of ruins of what was an important Tayrona settlement. The site contains well-preserved remnants of terraces, and a small Kogi community still lives nearby. The challenging path through the tropical jungle is steep and the stone steps can be slippery, but it's well worth it. Hikers can go up to El Pueblito without a guide, but inquire when you enter the park if you'd like to hire one. El Pueblito is usually accessed from within Tayrona by walking west along the beach from Arrecifes and following the signs from Cabo San Juan.

A longer version of this hike can be started from the main highway, the Troncal del

golden sands on the beaches of Parque Nacional Natural Tayrona

★ EXPLORING THE PARK
Beaches

The beaches in Parque Nacional Natural Tayrona are spectacular, but though the water may appear inviting, currents are deceptively strong, and, despite the warnings posted on the beach, many people have drowned here. Of the park's 34 beaches, there are only 6 where swimming is permitted. There are no lifeguards on duty in the park, and no specific hours for swimming.

The best swimming beaches are around the Cabo San Juan area, including **Arenilla** and **La Piscina,** inviting coves of turquoise waters that are protected by natural rock barriers. It's a 20-minute walk from Arrecifes to both of those beaches. Cabo San Juan, with a large campground nearby, is a hub of activity in the park. Farther along is a clothing-optional beach, just past Playa Brava.

Some of the other beaches open to swimming are in the less-visited western part of the park. **Playa Neguanje** is accessed by car or

Caribe, at the Calabazo entrance to the park, around 24 kilometers (15 miles) northeast of Santa Marta. It's about a 2.5-hour trek from there. There's a good chance of spotting monkeys and birds on this longer hike.

FOOD AND ACCOMMODATIONS

The park has two surprisingly upscale restaurants. One is in Cañaveral, close to the Ecohabs, and the other is in Arrecifes, near the *cabañas*. They are open daily 7am-9pm, and the specialty at each is fresh seafood. Expect to pay around COP$30,000 for a lunch or dinner entrée. Both restaurants accept credit cards. There are some snack bars in the park concentrated around the popular beach and campsites, serving fried fish, empanadas, and fresh fruit. The snack bars are usually open during daylight hours (9am-6pm daily).

There are numerous lodging options in PNN Tayrona for every budget: high-end Ecohabs, mid-level *cabañas,* and camping. The travel agency **Aviatur** (Bogotá office Av. 19 No. 4-62, tel. 1/587-5181 or 1/587-5182, www.aviaturecoturismo.com) manages most of the lodging facilities in the park. Neither the Ecohabs nor the *cabañas* could

be considered a bargain, but the Ecohabs, where you can awake to a beautiful view of the sea, are indeed special, and worth one or two nights. The *cabañas* are set back from the beach but are quite comfortable. Safety boxes are included in all rooms, and can be provided to campers as well. Some visitors prefer to leave a bag or valuables at a trusted hotel in Santa Marta.

The **Ecohabs** (COP$712,000 pp all meals incl.), in the Cañaveral sector, consist of 14 private *bohíos* (thatched-roof cabins) that sleep 2-4 people. From a distance they look like giant nests amid the trees, but in reality they are modeled after the thatched-roof houses of the Tayrona people. There are two floors to the Ecohabs: On the first floor is the bathroom and an open-air social area. On the second floor is the bedroom. A flashlight is necessary if you need to go to the bathroom in the middle of the night, as you have to go outside and downstairs. This is inconvenient for some.

In nearby Arrecifes, there are six two-story *cabañas* (12 rooms, COP$476,300 pp all meals incl.) with a capacity of four persons each. These are like jungle duplexes, with the two units divided by thin walls. There is also a **hammock area** (COP$32,000 pp) in

Ecohabs at Parque Nacional Natural Tayrona

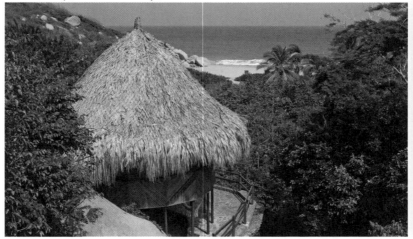

Arrecifes with a capacity of 60 hammocks. Those choosing this option have access to lockers and the safety box at the lobby area.

There are **campgrounds** (COP$20,000 pp) in both Cañaveral and Arrecifes and also at Cabo San Juan, which is a 15-minute walk to the west from the beach at La Piscina. Cabo tends to get very crowded, bordering on unpleasant (thanks to not enough sanitary facilities), during long weekends and holidays. A better camping option is low-key Castilletes, which is just before the entrance to Cañaveral.

TRANSPORTATION

From Santa Marta you can take any bus eastbound along the Troncal del Caribe to the main entrance (El Zaino). *Colectivo* buses can be caught at the intersection of Carrera 11 and Calle 11 (the market) in Santa Marta, and the trip takes about an hour and costs under COP$5,000. You can also take a cab for about COP$60,000.

Expect a thorough inspection of backpacks and bags upon entering the park. Visitors are not allowed to bring in plastic bags (to protect sea turtles), and no alcohol is permitted (although beer is served at restaurants and snack bars in the park). Be sure to bring bug repellent, a flashlight, and good hiking boots.

Visitors pay the entrance fee at the administrative offices. These fees are not included in the Aviatur package prices. Although technically park visitors are supposed to carry proof of a yellow fever vaccination, this is rarely, if ever, checked.

It's about four kilometers (2.5 miles) from the offices to Cañaveral, and vans travel this route on an ongoing basis (COP$3,000). From there it is 45 sweaty minutes on foot through the jungle to Arrecifes. Mules can be hired to carry your bags, or you can rent a horse for COP$20,000.

PNN TAYRONA TO PALOMINO

If you prefer less civilization and more tranquility, the coast between PNN Tayrona and Palomino has some interesting places to hang

your *sombrero vueltiao* (Colombian hat) for a few days. Between these two very popular tourist destinations are beaches that are rather overlooked by the masses. Day trips to PNN Tayrona can be easily coordinated from this area.

Accommodations

Impossibly placed atop giant beach boulders, the guesthouse **Finca Barlovento** (Playa Los Naranjos, 40 km east of Santa Marta, Bogotá tel. 1/325-6998, www.fincabarloventosantamarta.com, COP$400,000 d incl. 2 meals) is located between the sea and the Río Piedras. It's an amazing place to stay, and the food's good, too. There are just three rooms and one luxurious cabin here. Jungle excursions can be arranged by the hotel, but be sure to enjoy some beachside afternoons. You'll have the sand mostly to yourself.

The waves are the main draw at ★ **Costeño Beach Surf Camp and Ecolodge** (Playa Los Naranjos, 45 km east of Santa Marta, cell tel. 310/368-1191, www.costenosurf.com, COP$30,000 dorm, COP$80,000 d), but the property also gets exceptionally high marks from its guests for its laid-back atmosphere. Costeño Beach has both dorm and private accommodations on a former coconut farm. It's also solar powered. Rent a board (COP$30,000 per day) or take a class (COP$25,000) to make like the surfers do.

La Brisa Tranquila (45 km east of Santa Marta, Buritaca, cell tel. 321/599-5966, www.labrisatranquila.com, COP$30,000 dorm, COP$140,000 d) is the tamer version of La Brisa Loca in Santa Marta. This beachside hostel is only five kilometers (3.1 miles) from PNN Tayrona. It comprises six private rooms, beach huts, and dorms.

Playa Koralia (50 km east of Santa Marta, cell tel. 310/642-2574 or 317/510-2289, www.koralia.com, COP$209,000 d) is a beach-chic hotel on the water just east of PNN Tayrona. Accommodations are simple but comfortable, meals are healthy, and there's a spa and a bar. It's a popular place for weddings and celebrations for groups from Bogotá. Excursions to Tayrona and other sights can be arranged.

The recipe for pure relaxation, ★ **Gitana del Mar** (50 km east of Santa Marta, Buritaca, cell tel. 312/293-7053, www.gitanadelmar.com.co, COP$600,000 d with all meals) has six eco-chic bungalows, a stunning beachside location, and a spa and restaurant. There's no air-conditioning and the hotel strives to be as environmentally responsible as possible without sacrificing luxury. The hotel offers a calendar of wellness retreats and regular beachside yoga classes.

The environmentally conscious ★ **Quebrada del Plátano** (60 km east of Santa Marta, Buritaca, info@quebradadelplatano.com, cell tel. 312/338-4348, COP$80,000 camping, COP$140,000 pp with meals) is a nature reserve and working farm with organic fruit, herbs, coffee, and vegetables. The water here comes from mountain springs, and all electricity is solar powered. Waterfalls and swimming holes are a short walk away. The reserve is located between the Río Buritaca and a smaller creek. There is just one private room, one shared room, and an area for hammocks.

Palomino

Swaying coconut palms and uncrowded beaches: That's what the Caribbean is all about, isn't it? And at Palomino that's exactly what you get. This town has become quite a popular destination, particularly with backpackers. Caribbean currents can be frustratingly strong here, but the cool waters of the nearby Río Palomino flowing down from the Sierra Nevada de Santa Marta are always refreshing and much more hospitable. Palomino is a good stop to make between Santa Marta and desert adventures in the Alta Guajira.

Palomino extends out from either side of the main highway, Troncal del Caribe. There are no street names in Palomino; the main points of reference are The Dreamer hostel, the highway, and the gas stations Terpel and Mobil.

a beach in Palomino

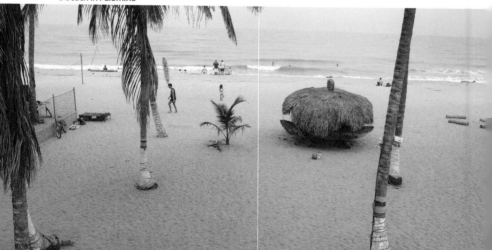

RECREATION

Recreational activities in and around Palomino include easy walks to the **Río Palomino,** about an hour away, where there is also tubing. Tubing down the river usually takes about 2.5 hours and costs around COP$25,000. Also in the area are the fantastic jungle waterfalls at private nature reserve **Quebrada Valencia** (village of Buritaca, no phone, COP$3,000). All hotels and hostels organize these easy excursions. On the weekends, families from Santa Marta take over the area—it's more peaceful during the week.

Chajaka (office on the south side of the main coastal highway, cell tel. 313/583-3288, calixtoteheran@gmail.com) offers interesting day trips or multiday hiking trips (COP$120,000) into the Sierra Nevada to visit Kogi communities and experience the jungle. Ask for Calixto Teheran, a longtime guide with Chajaka and a friendly expert who knows the Sierra well.

La Sirena Yoga (La Sirena hostel, cell tel. 312/861-4850, COP$18,000) offers 1.5-hour yoga sessions on the beach in front of the hostel of the same name. Class frequency depends on the number of participants, so stop by in advance to inquire about times.

To rent a surfboard, visit **Chill and Surf** (The Dreamer hostel, cell tel. 315/610-9561, www.chillandsurfcolombia.com, 9am-4pm daily). They have a stand on the beach in front of The Dreamer. They also offer classes.

FOOD AND ACCOMMODATIONS

Palomino is well on its way to dethroning Taganga as the deluxe backpacker resort. That's thanks largely to one famous hostel: ★ **The Dreamer** (cell tel. 300/609-7229, www.thedreamerhostel.com, COP$29,000 dorm, COP$110,000 d). This is by far the most social option this side of Santa Marta. Dorm and private accommodations are in *malokas* (cabins) surrounding an always-happening pool area and outdoor snack bar. The Dreamer is not just for partiers: You can always retreat to your cabin for some peace.

There are dozens of hostels that have sprung up in Palomino, all striving to compete with The Dreamer. If The Dreamer is booked, **The Tiki Hut** (cell tel. 314/794-2970, www.tikihutpalomino.co, COP$35,000 dorm, COP$135,000 d) is a suitable second choice, and it's just next door.

★ **La Sirena Eco Hostel** (cell tel. 310/718-4644, www.ecosirena.com, COP$190,000 d) provides a contrast to the neighboring The Dreamer. Here it's vegetarian food, yoga, reiki, massages, and quiet. The six beachside *cabañas* are simple and gorgeous, and the toilets are dry "eco" models. The restaurant serves delicious healthy breakfasts.

At the **Hotel Hukumeizi** (cell tel. 315/354-7871 or 317/566-7922, www.turismoguajira.com, info@hukumeizi.com, COP$250,000 pp with meals) there are 16 cute, round *bohíos* (bungalows) with a restaurant in the center. If you go during the week, you'll probably have the place to yourself. From here it's about a 15-minute walk along the beach to the Río San Salvador and about an hour to the Río Palomino.

★ **El Matuy (Donde Tuchi)** (Palomino, cell tel. 315/751-8456, www.elmatuy.com, COP$180,000 pp with meals) is a privately owned nature reserve with 12 cabins, each with a hammock out front, set amid palm trees and with no electricity (this means candlelit evenings and no credit card machine). Hotel staff can help organize horseback riding or other activities. Surprisingly, there's Wi-Fi available in the reception area (making it a popular place).

On the southern side of the highway, called La Sierrita, there are a number of options for those who prefer mountains to beaches. **Casa Campestre Ameli** (La Sierrita, cell tel. 311/232-0034, COP$15,000 camping, COP$25,000 private room) is surrounded by beautiful gardens and offers budget-conscious accommodations. ★ **Mamatukua Hostel** (La Sierrita, cell tel. 320/354-8791, www.lasierrita.co, COP$135,000 d) is a sweet, relaxing hostel managed by a pair of Bogotanos. Set amid the trees of the Sierra, the hostel has three rooms (with a shared bath) and a cabin. You'll wake to the sounds of birds chirping. **Jaguar Azul** (La Sierrita, cell tel. 313/800-9925, www.jaguarazulpalomino.com, COP$25,000 dorm, COP$60,000 d) has a couple of dorms as well as private rooms. This hostel is set among fruit trees, about a 15-minute walk to the beach. It's closer to the beach than Mamatukua. There's parking available.

TRANSPORTATION

There is regular bus transportation along the Troncal del Caribe between Santa Marta and Riohacha. From Santa Marta, at the market on Carrera 11 and Calle 11, take a bus bound for Palomino. It's about a two-hour trip and costs COP$10,000. On the highway where the bus drops you off, there are young men on motorbikes who will take you to your hotel for about COP$3,000.

Parque Nacional Natural Sierra Nevada de Santa Marta

Parque Nacional Natural Sierra Nevada de Santa Marta (www.parquesnacionales. gov.co) has a total area of 383,000 hectares (945,000 acres), making it one of the largest parks in Colombia.

The main attraction is the **Ciudad Perdida (Lost City)**, the most important archaeological site of the Tayrona, the pre-Columbian civilization that inhabited the Sierra Nevada. The Tayrona had a highly urbanized society, with towns that included temples and ceremonial plazas built on stone terraces. There are an estimated 200 Tayrona sites, but Ciudad Perdida is the largest and best known. Many of these towns, including Pueblito (in the Parque Nacional Natural Tayrona), were occupied at the time of the Spanish conquest. Today, an estimated 30,000 indigenous people who are descendants of the Tayronas, including the Kogis, Arhuacos, Kankuamos, and Wiwas, live on the slopes and valleys of the Sierra Nevada de Santa Marta. These people believe that the Sierra Nevada is the center of the universe and that the mountain's health controls the entire Earth's well-being. Many areas of the Sierra are sacred sites to these people and are barred to outsiders.

The Sierra Nevada de Santa Marta is best described as a giant pyramid, which is bordered on the north by the Caribbean and on the southeast and southwest by the plains of northern Colombia. Although some believe that the range is a distant extension of the Cordillera Oriental (Eastern Mountain Range) of the Andes, most geologists believe it is a completely independent mountain system.

It is the world's highest coastal mountain range, with the twin peaks of **Pico Cristóbal Colón** and **Pico Bolívar** (the two are called Chinundúa by indigenous groups in the area) reaching 5,776 meters (18,950 feet; Colón is said to be slightly higher than Bolívar) but located only 42 kilometers (26 miles) from the sea. Pico Cristóbal Colón is the world's fifth-most prominent mountain after Mount Everest (Nepal/Tibet, China), Mount Aconcagua (Argentina), Denali (United States), and Mount Kilimanjaro (Tanzania). The range includes seven other snow-covered peaks that surpass 5,000 meters (16,400 feet): Simonds, La Reina, Ojeda, Los Nevaditos, El Guardián, Tulio Ospina, and Codazzi. Treks to these peaks used to be possible from the northern side of the mountains, starting at the Arhuaco indigenous village of Nabusímake (Cesar), but are no longer permitted by the indigenous communities.

The PNN Sierra Nevada de Santa Marta encompasses the entire mountain range above 600 meters (16,400 feet). In addition, a small segment of the park east of the PNN Tayrona, from the Río Don Diego to the Río Palomino, extends to sea level. This means that the park encompasses the entire range of tropical ecosystems in Colombia: low-lying tropical forests (sea level to 1,000 meters), cloud forests (1,000-2,300 meters), high mountain Andean forest (2,300-3,500 meters), *páramo* (highland moor, 3,500-4,500 meters), super *páramo* (4,500-5,000 meters), and glaciers (above 5,000 meters). However, because access to the upper reaches of the park is limited, what visitors will most be able to appreciate is low-lying tropical and cloud forest.

The isolation of the range has made it an island of biodiversity, and it hosts many plant and animal species that are found nowhere else. The Sierra Nevada de Santa Marta is home to 187 mammal species, including giant anteaters, spider monkeys, peccaries, tree rats, jaguars, and pumas. There are 46 species of amphibians and reptiles, including several that live above 3,000 meters (9,840 feet) that are found nowhere else on the planet. There are an astonishing 628 bird species, including the Andean condor, blue-knobbed curassow, sapphire-bellied hummingbird, and black solitary eagle, as well as many endemic species. There are at least 71 species of migratory birds that travel between Colombia and North America.

★ CIUDAD PERDIDA TREK

A highlight for many visitors to Colombia is the four- to six-day, 52-kilometer (32-mile) round-trip trek to the **Ciudad Perdida (Lost City)** in the Sierra Nevada. The Ciudad Perdida is within the confines of the Parque Nacional Natural Sierra Nevada de Santa Marta.

The Ciudad Perdida, called Teyuna by local indigenous tribes and Buritaca 200 by archaeologists, was a settlement of the Tayrona, forebears of the people who inhabit the Sierra Nevada today. It was probably built starting around AD 700, at least 600 years before Machu Picchu. There is some disagreement as to when it was abandoned, although there is evidence of human settlement until the 16th century. The discovery of the site in 1976 marked one of the most important archaeological events of recent years. From 1976 to 1982, archaeologists from the Colombian National Institute of History and Anthropology painstakingly restored the site.

Spread over some 35 hectares (86 acres), the settlement consists of 169 circular terraces atop a mountain in the middle of dense cloud forest. Archaeologists believe that this sophisticated terrace system was created in

Ciudad Perdida, the remnants of the ancient Tayrona civilization part to control the flow of water in this area, which receives torrential rainfall for much of the year.

Plazas, temples, and dwellings for tribal leaders were built on the terraces in addition to an estimated 1,000 *bohíos* (traditional thatched-roof huts), which housed between 1,400 and 3,000 people. Surrounding the Ciudad Perdida were farms of coca, tobacco, pumpkins, and fruit trees. The city was connected to other settlements via an intricate system of mostly stone paths.

Planning Your Trek

The somewhat challenging hike to the Ciudad Perdida requires no special preparation. Booking your tour a few weeks in advance is necessary if you're planning to travel between mid-December and mid-January, during Semana Santa, or in June and July.

The trek is mostly uphill, starting at an elevation of around 150 meters (490 feet) and ascending to an elevation of 1,100 meters (3,600 feet). The out-and-back trek takes four to six days. Most people opt to make the trek in four days, but talk to your guide if you change your mind mid-trek and want to slow your pace and extend for one more day.

There is one set fee (COP$600,000) for the trek. This does not change, no matter if you're making the trek in four, five, or six days. If you are in very good shape and prefer to go fast, the trek can be done in three nights and four days. This requires six hours of hiking per day and rising early, with daily hiking distances varying from 7.5 kilometers (4.7 miles) to 15 kilometers (9.3 miles).

Thousands of people of all ages traverse the path each year. Each group is usually between 8 and 12 people, the majority being Europeans. Numerous groups populate different parts of the trails at any one time, and campsites can get crowded at night.

Frequent rain showers mean the trail can be muddy, and the weather is extremely humid. There are numerous river crossings to be made, some more thrilling than others, but all manageable. To reach the spectacular terraces of Ciudad Perdida, you will climb about 1,200 often-slippery stone steps. In case of an emergency on the mountain, a burro or helicopter will be sent to retrieve hikers in distress for a fee.

SEASONS AND CLIMATE

From mid-December through mid-January you'll have plenty of company on the way to the Ciudad Perdida: It's high tourist season. Other high seasons are during Semana Santa and when schools are on summer break, from June through July.

The wettest times tend to be April to May and September to November. Expect a daily downpour and doable, but sometimes treacherous, river crossings. Rainy weather makes the trek more challenging. On the plus side, there are usually fewer crowds on the mountain at that time.

WHAT TO PACK

Bring a small to medium backpack, enough to carry a few days of clothes; good hiking boots with strong ankle support; sandals for stream crossings; long pants; mosquito repellent; sunscreen; cash for refreshments to purchase along the way; a small towel; toilet paper; hand sanitizer; a flashlight (preferably a headlamp); sealable bags to keep things dry; a light rain jacket; and a water container.

Assume that everything in your backpack will get wet, but bring along extra plastic bags to minimize damage. If you have them, trekking poles are a nice addition, although it's easy to find a trusty walking stick along the way. There are beds with sheets and blankets provided, but a lightweight sleeping bag or sheet is a good idea, as the cleanliness of the provided bedding is questionable. Consider earplugs and sleeping pills—widely available at Colombian pharmacies. To limit carrying along wet clothes, consider wearing "disposable" T-shirts that can be left behind at the camps (they will be washed and used by locals).

Don't worry about bringing snacks—all meals are provided by your tour operator.

Ciudad Perdida Tour Outfitters

The tour companies who lead Ciudad Perdida treks are all roughly the same. The exception is **Wiwa Tours** (Cra. 3 No. 18-49, Santa Marta, tel. 5/420-3413, www.wiwatour.com), which employs indigenous guides who tend to be more reserved than the guides with other outfits. Other tour companies are listed below.

- **Magic Tour** (Cl. 16 No. 4-41, Santa Marta, tel. 5/421-5820; Cl. 14 No. 1B-50, Taganga, tel. 5/421-9429, www.magic-tourcolombia.com)
- **TurCol** (Centro Comercial San Francisco Plaza, Cl. 13 No. 3-13, Local 115, Santa Marta; Cl. 19 No. 5-40, Taganga, tel. 5/421-2556, www.turcoltravel.com)
- **Baquianos Tour** (Cl. 10C No. 1C-59, Santa Marta, tel. 5/431-9667, www.guiasybaquianos.com)
- **Expotur** (Santa Marta Cra. 3 No. 17-27, tel. 5/420-7739, Taganga Cl. 18 No. 2A-07, www.expotur-eco.com)

Bring a small amount of cash, as some snack breaks at coffee or fruit stands run by local families are not included in the tour price.

To keep you occupied at night, a small paperback and a deck of cards are good to have handy.

CAMPING

The campsites along the way seem to turn into backpacker villages during high season, with upwards of 60 people there every night, but they are never rowdy. Upon arrival the routine is fairly standard. You'll be able to cool off in the pristine waters of nearby swimming holes, have dinner, and hit the hammocks. Sleeping in hammocks can be uncomfortable for those not used to them, but bunk beds are also available.

The Trek

On the first morning, you will rendezvous with your tour operator either in Santa Marta or in Taganga, meet your fellow trekkers and guides, and take a 1.5-hour minibus ride to the villages of Mamey and Machete, at the edge of the park, where a generous lunch at a small restaurant will be served before setting off.

The first day of hiking, about 3-4 hours, will take you through cleared farmland, not jungle, so be prepared for extensive sun exposure. You'll take a break along the way for coffee or fruit at a stall run by a *campesino* family. At your campsite, you will have the opportunity to plunge into a natural swimming hole of cool, crystalline waters.

The second day of the trek is the longest one, and most groups aim for an early start. Under the canopy of the Sierra Nevada, the trail hugs the Río Buritaca for much of the time. There are multiple river crossings, including a swinging bridge. Before arrival at camp, you'll pass by the thatched roofs of the Kogi indigenous settlement Mutanyí. (Your guide will instruct you on photography etiquette.) Kogi children may ask you for *dulces* (candy), but otherwise interaction with the people that live here is unlikely. Your group will arrive at camp after noon. The rest of the day includes lots of downtime.

On the third day, the various groups on the trail jockey to be the first to arrive at the Ciudad Perdida. A 5:30am start is worth it to experience a sense of discovery as you climb the steps to the ancient terraces. Mosquitoes may be out in full force, so apply insect repellent. Leave your pack at camp; just carry your camera, walking stick, and bottle of water. The sun can be quite potent at the ruins, so bring sunscreen as well. After a final water crossing, the famed 1,200 stone steps dramatically appear, a silent invitation to this sacred lost city.

Take your time going up the steps. At the first series of grassy circular terraces, all that remains of the community's commercial center, your guide will give an introduction to the site. From there, climb the Queen's Path to the main site. Colombian soldiers guard the site and are always glad to chat up visitors. Take care when descending the steps on your way back, as they can become slippery.

Valledupar

To the south of the Sierra Nevada, Valledupar is Colombia's *vallenato* capital. This musical genre of cowboy love songs is most famously enjoyed at the Festival Vallenato, during which aficionados from Colombia and beyond converge on Valledupar for days filled with music and rumba.

Many sights in the city have a *vallenato* theme: Valledupar hosts the Museo del Accordeón and several music schools, while the city's plazas and parks contain tributes to beloved musicians. Outside of town are swimming holes and indigenous villages such as Nabusímake, the capital of the Arhuaco nation.

SIGHTS

The main point of reference in Valledupar's charming Centro is the **Plaza Alonso López Michelson** (Clls. 15-16 and Cras. 5-6). Carrera 5 is pedestrians-only. Carrera 9 has many restaurant options.

The charming **Museo del Acordeón/ Casa Beto Murgas** (Cra. 17 No. 9-18, Barrio San Juan, cell tel. 300/836-8877, www.museodelacordeon.com, COP$5,000) is in the home of musician and *vallenato* aficionado Jose Alberto Murgas, whose enthusiasm for the accordion and *vallenato* culture is infectious. On display are more accordions that you can imagine. Jose Alberto himself will provide some background on the instrument and the roots of *vallenato* music during the included guided tour.

Valledupar's children become musicians at the **Escuela Vallenato El Turco Gil** (Cl. 31 No. 4-265). The children who study here come from disadvantaged backgrounds and receive scholarships to be able to attend. Visitors are invited to drop by on weekday afternoons and on Saturday mornings, when the classrooms are humming with children learning how to make *vallenato* magic with their accordions. After a tour of the classrooms, you might be invited to an impromptu performance.

Worth a browse is the gallery at the **Banco de la República** (Cra. 9 No. 16-13, tel. 5/574-3055, www.banrepcultural.org/valledupar, 8:30am-6pm Mon.-Fri., 8:30am-1pm Sat., free), where temporary art exhibitions are always on display. This is also the place to find out about upcoming performing arts events.

ENTERTAINMENT AND EVENTS
Nightlife

Facing the Parque Alfonso López is **Tlön** (Cl. 15 No. 6-54, cell tel. 314/632-1325, 5pm-1am Sun.-Thurs., 5pm-late Fri.-Sat.), a popular watering hole that serves beer and whiskey. It's also a venue for a variety of cultural events.

At **Palenke** (Cra. 5 No. 13C-52, 5pm-1am daily), sit at the funky outdoor patio and down their signature orange (rather than lime) *micheladas* as you listen to non-*vallenato* music.

Festival Vallenato

Valledupar is known for its **Festival Vallenato** (www.festivalvallenato.com, Apr.), which attracts thousands of fans from all over Colombia every April. The four days of activities include a series of concerts, parades, and competitions. Much speculation centers on which musician will be crowned *rey* (king). Leading up to the big finale at the Parque de la Leyenda Vallenata Consuelo Araujo Noguera (Av. Hurtado and Cra. 12) are *parrandas*—evening concerts held in the patios of homes throughout the city. Ask a local for more information on attending a *parranda*.

RECREATION

The main recreational activity in Valledupar can be summed up in one phrase: Find me a river! For most that means a quick jaunt to nearby **Balneario Hurtado,** just north of the a *vallenato* musician at the Festival Vallenato

SHOPPING

Check out the **Calle Grande market** (Cl. 16 No. 7-18, 10am-6pm daily), where vendors sell wares like handwoven *mochilas* (shoulder bags), musical instruments, jewelry, and paintings celebrating *vallenato* culture at a number of different stands.

FOOD

Though it is often thought of as a meat-and-potatoes kind of place, Valledupar offers a surprising number of food options.

For all your shawarma needs, check out fast-food **Arab King** (Cra. 9 No. 13-53, cell tel. 300/769-1403, 5pm-11pm daily). An excellent and authentic Lebanese restaurant, ★ **Jerusalem Express** (Cra 9 No. 7C-29, tel. 5/573-7217, 4pm-10pm daily, COP$23,000) has an extensive menu, so come with an appetite. There is ample outdoor seating as well as a pleasant (air-conditioned) indoor dining room.

Across from the Parque Novalito in a lovely tree-lined barrio, ★ **ArteSano** (Cl. 13 No. 6-81, cell tel. 300/321-9814, 7:30am-10pm daily, COP$14,000) is three things in one: a vegetarian restaurant, a fruit and juice stand, and a bakery. ArteSano has quite a following, with an ever-present crowd enjoying the Valledupar evenings at the tables out front.

Under the shade of a mango tree is the delightful ★ **Compai Chipuco** (Cl. 16 No. 6-05, tel. 5/674-7711, 8am-8pm daily), an excellent place for a hearty and inexpensive lunch of fried fish or grilled chicken, or a refreshing juice or beer in the early evening.

Looking for coffee? Try **Café Arhuaco** (Cra. 9 No. 14-50, tel. 5/584-9290, 9am-9pm Mon.-Sat., 2pm-9pm Sun.) downtown or seek out the always-reliable **Juan Valdez** at the Guatapurí (Dg. 10 No. 6N-15, 9am-9pm daily) or Mayales (Av. Salguero with Cl. 31, 9am-10pm daily) malls.

Buffalo Grill (Cra. 9 No. 12-2, Orbe Plaza, tel. 5/585-3535, noon-10pm daily, COP$16,000) is a burgers-and-steak chain that has many followers in this beef-loving city. This casual restaurant offers outdoor

city along Carrera 19. Here you can get wet in the Río Guatapurí, dry off in the sunshine, and enjoy a drink or quick bite.

La Mina, a swimming hole in the Río Badillo about an hour away from town, makes for a satisfying day trip. It's a scenic spot, with giant white rocks, some miniscule beaches, and wonderful chilly water. On weekends it's a party spot, with music and drinking. There are deceptively dangerous currents, so take care. Local public transportation (COP$8,000 pp) departs from the Galería area downtown, four blocks from Provincia Hostel. Alternatively, the folks at Provincia are happy to organize a day trip for their guests with some advance notice.

For a gorgeous jog or bike ride beneath a tunnel of trees, with deep-green rice patties lining the road, head to the **Ruta del Arroz,** a little-used country road toward the village of Guacoche. To get to this road, follow Carrera 19 past the Balneario Hurtado. It's the first road on the right after crossing the river. This is about a two-hour bike ride.

seating and is popular for its late afternoon happy hour drink specials.

The classic Italian place in town is **Ferrini Trattoria** (Cra. 11 No. 9D-5, tel. 5/570-5589, noon-10pm Mon.-Sat., COP$22,000), while **Varadero** (Cl. 12 No. 6-56, tel. 5/570-6157, noon-10pm daily, COP$24,000) is a popular Cuban seafood restaurant.

ACCOMMODATIONS

With the exception of the Festival Vallenato, there is always a plethora of solid, reasonably priced accommodations options in Valledupar.

Within blocks of the Parque Alonso López in the walkable Centro are several excellent options. ★ **Provincia** (Cl. 16A No 5-25, tel. 5/580-0558, www.provinciavalledupar. com, COP$30,000 dorm, COP$94,000 d) is the only true hostel in Valledupar, with both shared and private rooms. Staff are attentive and can provide ideas on things to see and do. A kitchen is available for guest use; a simple breakfast can be ordered for an additional cost. In the back are hammocks and a reading area. The same friendly owners have converted an old house into the rather posh boutique-style ★ **Casa de los Reyes Santos** (Cl. 13C No. 4A-90, cell tel. 313/530-8269, www.hotelboutiquevalledupar.com, COP$180,000). On a pedestrian street, this lovely hotel has five spacious rooms, a small dipping pool, and an outdoor bar area, and there are often temporary photography exhibits in the common spaces. Rooms are tastefully decorated.

★ **Rosalía** (Cl. Grande 16 No. 10-10, cell tel. 320/566-2556, www.acasarosalia.com COP$210,000 d) is a fantastic boutique option that comprises a handful of rooms in a busier part of the Centro. You'll want to linger by the pool after a day of walking. *Vallenato* lyrics by musician Rafael Escalon are painted on the walls.

With sweeping views of the Sierra, the ★ **Sonesta Hotel** (Diag. 10 No. 6N-15, tel. 5/574-8686, www.sonesta.com/valledupar, COP$200,000 d) is Valledupar's high-end,

full-service hotel, with an attractive lobby decorated with local touches, a superb restaurant, a pool and deck, well-appointed rooms with comfortable beds, and excellent customer service. Request a room with a view of the mountains. The hotel is located near the stadium where the Festival Vallenato is held, and adjoins a shopping mall. Nonguests can visit the restaurant and pool for a fee.

The **Posada Mariangola** (Cra. 5 No. 5-50, village of Mariangola, cell tel. 310/887-4319) is an off-the-beaten-path choice for visitors interested in community tourism. Mariangola was severely affected by violence from both left-wing guerrillas and right-wing paramilitaries from the late 1980s through the early 2000s. This guesthouse, the town's first and only, is a resident's attempt to generate a sense of civic culture through tourism. Some rooms, many with funky details, have private baths and air-conditioning, while some just have a fan and a shared bath. The open-air kitchen is available for guest use and sits next to a lush backyard patio. Activities in the area include walks to the Río Mariangola and in the gorgeous countryside, visits to avocado and coffee farms, riding bikes, and visits to indigenous villages and pueblos. There are *busetas* that regularly ply the Valledupar-Mariangola route, departing from the Galería area. It's about 50 kilometers (31 miles) southwest of Valledupar.

INFORMATION AND SERVICES

Valledupar has all the standard city services. Medical assistance is available at the **Clínica Valledupar** (Cl. 16 No. 15-15, tel. 5/574-8550, www.clinicavalledupar.com.co, 24 hours daily).

TRANSPORTATION

The **Alfonso López Pumarejo Airport** (VUP, Km. 4 Vía a la Paz, tel. 5/571-6861) is south of town. **Avianca** (www.avianca.com) and **LATAM Airlines** (www.latam.com) offer several daily flights here from Bogotá (1.5 hours). **EasyFly** (www.easyfly.com.co) has connections from Barranquilla to Valledupar (30 minutes). The 20-minute cab ride from the airport to downtown Valledupar will cost around COP$25,000.

There is regular bus transportation to all major Colombian cities, including Riohacha (COP$22,000) and Santa Marta (COP$24,00). The **bus station** (Cra. 7 No. 44-156, tel. 5/571-7553) is located in the southern part of the city. As you arrive, touts will pursue you, barking out city names. You have two options: Ignore them and continue into the terminal to purchase your ticket, or follow one. The touts aren't trying to rip people off—they are working for commissions from bus drivers by steering passengers their way. This can be a stressful environment for some, but there's no reason to be alarmed.

Walking is a good way to get around Valledupar, but avoid walking in the Centro late at night. The smartphone app **Easy Taxi** (www.easytaxi.com) has service in Valledupar.

ATANQUEZ

This small agricultural town of sloping stone streets is located at the foot of the Sierra Nevada, about 50 kilometers (31 miles) north of Valledupar. It's known for being the home of the indigenous Kankuamo people. Woven *mochilas* (purses), made with wool and *fique* (reed), are a typical handicraft here.

The people of Atanquez suffered greatly during the worst years of the armed conflict, and for much of that time, the residents could not safely leave the town to tend to their farms or visit sacred areas in the mountains. Around 200 residents were killed by guerrillas or paramilitary forces vying for control of drug crops between 1986 and 2003. In light of this situation, men took up weaving, a productive activity that could be carried out in their homes. Today, the town is a peaceful place.

Look for the *tienda* (store) of **Aura Rosa Montero,** which, in addition to selling woven handicrafts and sweets made from *panela* (raw brown sugar), also functions as a cultural center where you can observe how locals make yarn out of recently sheared sheep's wool. The store is on the right side of the main street as you walk toward the mountains.

To get to Atanquez, you can take a shared car from the Galería area (Cra. 6 and Cl. 18) of Valledupar. Cars depart about every 30 minutes starting at 6am daily. The trip costs about COP$10,000.

La Guajira

The vast Guajira Peninsula has some of the most rugged, beautiful landscapes in Colombia. It is home to the Wayúu indigenous people, who have maintained their independent way of life through centuries. Though many Wayúu now live in cities and towns, their traditional *rancherías* (settlements) dot the desert. With the growth of tourism, many have set up lodging using traditional *ranchería* houses made out of *yotojoro,* the dried hearts of cactus plants.

The Colombian side of the peninsula (Venezuela claims the other part) can be divided into three sections. The Baja Guajira (Lower Guajira), near the Sierra Nevada de Santa Marta, is fertile agricultural and cattle-ranching land. The arid middle swath, with the departmental capital of Riohacha and the unlovely towns of Uribia and Maicao, is home to the majority of the peninsula's population. The Alta Guajira (Upper Guajira), from Cabo de la Vela to Punta Gallinas, is sparsely populated and has some otherworldly landscapes. Focus your visit on this last part.

Lack of infrastructure, especially in the north, makes visiting La Guajira a challenge, so most people opt for organized tours. Though it is possible to get to Cabo de la Vela on public transportation, do not travel elsewhere in the Alta Guajira without a dependable local guide. The roads are un-marked tracks in the sand, and getting lost is inevitable.

During the rainy months, September to November, it can be difficult to travel through the desert, which can become muddy to the point of impassability.

History

Spanish navigator Juan de la Cosa, who was a member of Columbus's first three voyages, disembarked in Cabo de la Vela in 1499, making the Guajira Peninsula one of the first places visited by Europeans in South America. It was not until 1535 that explorer Fernando de Enciso founded a settlement near Cabo de la Vela, which became a center of pearl extraction. This early settlement was relocated to Riohacha, which was founded in 1544. The traditional Wayúu inhabitants of the peninsula put up strong resistance to Spanish advances. During the 19th and 20th centuries, the peninsula was used primarily as a smuggling route.

For better or for worse, the fortunes of the Guajira changed in 1975 when the Colombian government entered into an agreement with oil giant Exxon to develop the Cerrejón open-pit coal mine 80 kilometers (50 miles) southeast of Riohacha. This project involved the construction of Puerto Bolívar, a coal port located in Bahía Portete, and of a railway to transport the coal. Production started in 1985. Coal has since become one of Colombia's main exports. The mine has generated more than US$2 billion in royalties for the Colombian government. Little of this wealth has trickled down to the people of La Guajira. The region is the fourth-poorest department in Colombia.

RIOHACHA

Called Süchiimma in the Wayúu language, meaning "city of the river," Riohacha (pop. 231,000), bordered on the east by the Río Ranchería, is La Guajira's slow-paced departmental capital. It is one of the oldest cities in Colombia, but there are few remnants of its colonial past on display.

While it's not a tourist destination in itself, Riohacha is an excellent base from which to launch tours of Alta Guajira or visit the flamingos of the Santuario de Fauna y Flora Los Flamencos. Visitors enjoy strolling the city's boardwalk in the evenings and perusing the colorful *mochilas* (shoulder bags) made and sold by Wayúu women.

Sights

Parallel to Calle 1, also known as Avenida Marina, is the **Paseo de la Playa boardwalk** (0.8 kilometers/0.5 miles long), where locals and tourists take their evening strolls and enjoy the sea air. Along the way are kiosks where vendors sell ceviche and Wayúu women display brightly colored *mochilas* (traditional woven handbags) on the sidewalk, nonchalantly waiting for customers. The kilometer-long pier known as the **Muelle Turístico** that extends from the midpoint of the boardwalk is another favorite place for a walk, especially in the evening, with the sea breeze providing relief from the heat of the day.

With its striking murals depicting Wayúu culture, it's hard to miss the large **Centro Cultural de la Guajira** (Cra. 15 No. 1-40, tel. 5/727-0990, www.banrepcultural.org/riohacha, 8am-11:30am and 2pm-5:30pm Mon.-Fri., 9am-1pm Sat., free). Inside, the cultural center has a permanent exhibition space that tells the history of the area, from Spaniard pearl harvesters to modern times, when multinationals arrived to extract natural gas and coal. A good portion of the museum discusses Wayúu culture, and includes an exhibit on the area's traditions for Carnaval. The content of the exhibition is quite interesting and is a must-visit for anyone mildly interested in this unusual place. Unfortunately, there are few English-language explanations of the exhibits. The center also houses a small public library.

Parque Padilla (Cl. 2 and Cra. 7), Riohacha's main plaza, is named after favorite son Admiral José Prudencio Padilla, who was the most prominent Afro-Colombian commander in the revolutionary wars. To one side of the plaza is the only remnant of colonial

Riohacha

Riohacha, the reconstructed **Catedral de Nuestra Señora de los Remedios** (Cl. 2 No. 7-13, tel. 5/727-2442, mass 6:30am and 7pm Mon.-Sat., 7am, 11am, and 7pm Sun.). This cathedral was erected in the 16th century, but completely rebuilt in the 1800s. The remains of Padilla repose here. The church is open to the public during mass, and occasionally at other times of the day. In the evening, the plaza buzzes with locals relaxing and catching up with friends and children playing.

Food

Enjoy a drink while relishing the sea breeze at the luxe rooftop terrace bar at the **Taroa Lifestyle Hotel** (Cl. 1 No. 4-77, tel. 5/729-1122, 5pm-11pm daily).

There are several seafood restaurants along Avenida Marina/Calle 1. A perennial favorite is **Casa del Marisco** (Cl. 1 4-43, tel. 5/728-3445, 10am-10pm daily, COP$25,000), a restaurant that serves an array of fresh seafood dishes and pastas.

With a modern design, a menu to please most anyone (sandwiches, pizza, crepes, and salads), and outdoor seating, **Lima** (Cl. 13 No. 11-33, tel. 5/728-1313, 10am-10pm Mon.-Sat., COP$15,000) is a crowd pleaser.

The first thing to do at ★ **Yotojoro** (Cl. 7 No. 15-81, cell tel. 315/754-0176, 11am-10pm daily, COP$22,000), a well-known favorite among Riohacha's upper crust, is order a *limonada de coco* (coconut lemonade). Their specialty is seafood, so go for either the hearty *cazuela de mariscos* (seafood stew) or the signature dish, the *pargo monsenor* (grilled red snapper stuffed with shrimp in a tomato-coconut milk sauce).

★ **Mantequilla** (Cl. 7 No. 11-183, tel. 5/729-1148, cell tel. 301/622-0442, lunch Mon., lunch and dinner Tues.-Sat., COP$15,000) is somewhat fancy by Riohacha standards, and it's a departure from the seafood-centric places that populate the main drag. The options are legion here: Order pasta, goat stew (a Wayúu specialty), or one of the many other menu items. Arrive early to take advantage of the set lunch menu.

The city's best Middle Eastern food can be found at ★ **Al Arz** (Cl. 7 No. 10-115, tel. 5/728-3760, noon-9pm Tues.-Sun., COP$13,000), an authentic, cheerful, and popular place for locals and visitors alike on Calle Ancha. If you've been out and about, get a table close to the air-conditioning unit.

Accommodations

Most visitors stay in Riohacha for only a night or two before heading onward. The options covered in this section are all centrally located, within walking distance of the city's attractions.

The 46-room ★ **Taroa Lifestyle Hotel** (Cl. 1 No. 4-77, tel. 5/729-1122, www.taroahotel.com, COP$260,000) is the swanky option in town, and it's not that expensive. Go for a room with a view of the boardwalk and sea, where you can swing in a hammock to your heart's content. Sip a cocktail on the top-floor terrace and feel the breeze.

Solera (Cra. 15 No. 9-29, tel. 5/728-1108 or cell tel. 310/713-4438, COP$140,000 d) is a small, modern hotel with an on-site travel agency. It's an adequate midrange option, but the rooms lack charm.

Close to downtown, the long-standing **Hotel Arimaca** (Cl. 1 Av. La Marina No. 8-75, tel. 5/727-3515, www.hotelarimaca.com, COP$185,000 d) is a standard Colombian business hotel with 50 rooms. It has a pool.

The helpful and friendly staff at **Happiness Hostel** (Cra. 15 No. 14-51, tel. 5/727-3828, COP$40,000 dorm, COP$140,000 d) make it the top choice of budget travelers. The building is spic-and-span and cheerfully decorated with fluorescent colors and whimsical signs. There are two private rooms; the three dorm rooms can sleep six people apiece. Guests can cook in the outdoor kitchen on the back patio, take a Spanish lesson, or order at drink at the small bar. Staff can assist with travel arrangements

mural depicting a Wayúu woman at the Centro Cultural de la Guajira to Alta Guajira and the Santuario de Fauna y Flora Los Flamencos.

The **Hotel Castillo del Mar** (Cra. 9A No. 16-150, cell tel. 315/792-4743, castillodelmarsuites@hotmail.com, COP$30,000 dorm, COP$110,000 d, discount for multiple nights) is about a 10-minute walk from the boardwalk in a quiet residential area. There are 11 rooms, some with air-conditioning. Private rooms are spacious and, as the name implies, the building really does resemble a castle.

Information and Services

At discount supermarket **Metro** (tel. 5/728-9670, 8am-10pm Mon.-Sat., 8am-9pm Sun.) in the modern **Centro Comercial Suchiimma** (Cl. 15 No. 8-56, 10am-9pm daily), you can pick up all the provisions you need for a long ride through the desert.

Transportation

Aeropuerto Almirante Padilla (RCH, Cl. 29B No. 15-217, tel. 5/727-3854) is five minutes north of town. There are only one or two flights per day from Bogotá to Riohacha on **Avianca** (www.avianca.com).

The **bus station** (Av. El Progreso and Cl. 11) has frequent service to Albania, Maicao, Santa Marta, and Barranquilla. There is also service to Valledupar, Cartagena, and Bogotá. **Shared taxis** to Uribia (where you can pick up trucks to Cabo de la Vela) leave from the market area (Cl. 15 and Cra. 1) in town. A cab to the bus station from downtown Riohacha will cost only about COP$6,000.

The atmosphere at the bus station is rushed and harried; do your best to not let it stress you out. Standard buses take longer, but are more comfortable. *Busetas* are faster minivans. Then there are shared taxis, which are more uncomfortable but much faster. If you're westbound (to Palomino, Santa Marta, or beyond), the frantic bus station experience can be avoided by turning up at the **Francisco El Hombre traffic circle.** You'll see folks hanging out waiting for transportation here; just ask them which *buseta* is going your way.

Getting around town is easy, and the best way to do so is on foot. Taxis are also considered safe. Popular taxi and ride-sharing apps have yet to arrive in Riohacha.

CROSSING INTO VENEZUELA

For stays less than 90 days, U.S., Canadian, and most European citizens do not require a visa to enter Venezuela. You may be required to show proof of a hotel reservation and proof of an air ticket departing from Venezuela, and your passport must not expire within six months of entry into Venezuela. There is a Venezuelan consulate in Riohacha for further queries: **Consulado de Venezuela** (Cra. 7 No. 3-08, Edificio El Ejecutivo, Piso 2, tel. 5/727-4076, 8am-noon and 2pm-5pm Mon.-Thurs., 8am-1pm Fri.). There is an entry point to Venezuela at the town of Maicao, but diplomatic tensions sometimes result in border closings.

★ Santuario de Fauna y Flora Los Flamencos

Spotting flamingos is the order of the day at the **Santuario de Fauna y Flora Los Flamencos** (Camarones settlement, www.parquesnacionales.gov.co, 7am-5pm daily, free). This park, 25 kilometers (15.5 miles) southwest of Riohacha, includes the Laguna Navio Quebradado and the larger Laguna Grande, with the fishing settlement of Camarones on the park's eastern side and the Caribbean Sea just beyond the mangroves and tropical dry forests on the north.

The park is home to thousands of American flamingos and up to 180 other species of migratory and resident aquatic birds, such as ibis and storks. Sea turtles also arrive at the lonely beach here, where conservation efforts help keep the threatened animals safe. The 7,000-hectare sanctuary (17,300 acres), which is part of the national park system, encompasses a coastal estuary where the flamingos fish for tiny shrimp in the shallow waters (from whom the birds obtain their gorgeous rose-colored plumage).

The flamingos are migratory, and are most often observed during rainy seasons such as

October-November, when their numbers reach into the thousands. During the rest of the year smaller flocks often reside in the park.

To see the flamingos up close, take an hour-long *chalupa* (wooden boat) excursion (COP$15,000 pp), captained by a local, onto one of the lagoons. The price of the excursion is negotiable, and the more people there are in a group, the lower the cost. To protect your skin from the powerful sun and glare off the water, visit the park early in the morning. Ample sun protection and drinking water are essential no matter the time of day.

TRANSPORTATION

The easiest way to get to the park is to arrange a taxi from Riohacha (COP$15,000 each way). Either request for the driver to wait while you visit the park (additional COP$50,000), or, after finishing your tour of the park, take a *mototaxi* (COP$3,000) to the main road, where buses (COP$2,000) back to Riohacha regularly pass.

To take public transportation both ways, take a bus from Riohacha going toward Camarones for a trip of about 20 kilometers on the main road toward Santa Marta. From Camarones take a *mototaxi* (COP$3,000) to the entrance of the park, or walk the 3.5 kilometers to the park entrance.

To have someone else do the organizing and coordinating, contact **Expedición Guajira** (Cl. 2 No. 5-06, Riohacha, tel. 5/727-2336, cell tel. 311/439-4677 or 301/485-2837, franklin_penalver@yahoo.com), which will take you on an organized tour of the park for COP$80,000 per person. Insist on an early start.

ALTA GUAJIRA

The sparsely populated Alta Guajira (Upper Guajira) comprises the peninsula east of Cabo de la Vela and Uribia. The area's three largest settlements, where most of the tourism infrastructure is located, are Cabo de la Vela, Punta Gallinas at the very northern tip, and Nazareth, in the northeast.

The terrain has a striking ochre color, with rocky and sandy patches. The vegetation is mostly shrubs and cacti. The Caribbean coast here is broken by three large bays with stunning turquoise and aquamarine waters: Bahía Portete, Bahía Honda, and Bahía Hondita. The last of these is easily accessible as a day trip from Punta Gallinas. There are a few low mountain ranges, including the Serranía de la Macuira (864 meters/2,835 feet), located in the extreme northeast of the peninsula, but overall the terrain is low and slightly undulated.

The only destination in the Alta Guajira that is accessible by public transportation is Cabo de la Vela. Though it is possible to contract transportation by land or sea to Punta Gallinas, most visitors choose to visit the region via organized tour, an easy option.

The sands of Alta Guajira are a favorite location for raucous 4x4 races and competitions.

Tours

A typical Alta Guajira tour (COP$380,000 pp, including food and lodging) lasts three days, spending a day each in Cabo de la Vela (with a stop at the now-abandoned salt mines of the Salinas de Manaure) and Punta Gallinas. A longer option (COP$800,000-880,000 pp, including food and lodging) adds two nights in Nazareth to visit the Parque Nacional Natural Macuira. Tours operate out of Riohacha and include SUV transportation.

Inquire before booking how many people will be in your SUV, as tour operators often try to cram seven people into a vehicle, making for an uncomfortable ride. Drivers generally have a limited grasp of English. If you'd like some background information about the region and the Wayúu people before setting off, check out the Centro Cultural de la Guajira in Riohacha first.

The desert countryside seems endless and is beautiful in its own desolate way. You'll be amazed at how these drivers know which way to go, as there are no road signs, only cacti and the occasional goat. Every once in a while, you will have to pay "tolls" to Wayúu children who have set up quasi roadblocks. To gain their permission to cross, drivers hand over crackers, cookies, or candy.

TOUR COMPANIES

Most tour companies are based in Riohacha, but some will take care of transporting you from other origin points, like Palomino, PNN Tayrona, or Santa Marta. Many companies don't regularly accept credit cards for payment; to avoid carrying a lot of cash around, consider making a *consignacion* (bank deposit), which can be done anywhere in Colombia. Get the tour company's bank account information and go in person to a branch of their bank, then make a cash deposit of the full trip amount. There are no ATMs in Cabo de la Vela or Punta Gallinas.

Franklin Peñalver and the Wayúu guides of **Expedición Guajira** (Cl. 2 No. 5-06, Riohacha, tel. 5/727-2336, cell tel. 311/439-4677 or 301/485-2837, franklin_penalver@yahoo.com) know the desert like the backs of their hands. A three-day tour that includes stops in Cabo de la Vela and Punta Gallinas costs COP$550,000 per person. A two-day tour of Cabo de la Vela costs COP$230,000. Tours include food and lodging. It's also possible to craft a custom private tour. A two-person personalized tour will tend to be priced at the standard four-person rate.

Kai Eco Travel (Cra. 9A 16-150, Riohacha, cell tel. 311/436-2830, www.kaiecotravel.com) has a range of tours for those who don't mind a group setting (maximum 6-8 people per group). A quick two-day jaunt to Cabo de la Vela costs around COP$220,000, with an extra night in Punta Gallinas bumping that up to COP$500,000. If you're up for the real Guajira experience of sleeping in a *chinchorro* (hammock), the rates decrease slightly. Get details from Francisco at the Hotel Castillo del Mar in Riohacha.

Kaishi (Av. La Marina No. 5-71, Uribia, cell tel. 311/429-6315, www.kaishitravel.com, adelgadorozco@yahoo.com) is another agency with a very good reputation. They only offer private tours. The per-person price decreases as the passenger list expands, so it behooves

you to go with a larger group of friends. A five-day private tour for two people that includes Cabo de la Vela and Punta Gallinas costs COP$2,000,000 per person. The shorter three-day tour to Punta Gallinas with a brief stop in Cabo de la Vela costs COP$1,300,000 per person.

★ Cabo de La Vela

Cabo de la Vela (known as Jepira in the Wayúu language), 180 kilometers (111 miles) north of Riohacha, is a small Wayúu fishing village spread along the Caribbean Sea. It comes as a pleasant shock to finally arrive at the waters of the Caribbean after several hours driving through the Guajira's arid landscape. Here the beaches are nice, the views otherworldly, and the atmosphere peaceful. Cabo de la Vela is a destination for windsurfers and kiteboarders, thanks to its smooth waters and ample winds that provide near-perfect conditions.

There are several excursions around Cabo; organized package tours should include all of them in the price. One is to **El Faro**, a lighthouse on a high promontory with nearly 360-degree views of the surrounding ocean. Another is to the **Ojo del Agua**, a small but pleasant beach near a freshwater spring. Farther afield is the **Pilón de Azúcar**, a high hill that affords incredible views to the surrounding region. Nearby is the **Playa de Pilón**, a beautiful ochre-colored beach. To the west is the **Jepirachi Wind Farm**, the first of its kind in Colombia; the turbines make for a somewhat surreal sight in the midst of this barren territory. For travelers not on an organized tour, any Cabo hotel can arrange an SUV tour to these sights for around COP$20,000 per site, per person.

RECREATION

Cabo de la Vela is an excellent place to learn how to kiteboard or windsurf, as there's a good breeze here most of the year (the exception being September through November).

There are two excellent schools offering courses and equipment rental. **Eoletto**

(10-min. walk from Rancheria Utta, cell tel. 321/468-0105 or 314/851-6216, www.windsurfingcolombia.com) is a windsurfing and kitesurfing school that also offers accommodations in hammocks (COP$22,000) in a quiet spot facing the water. An eight-hour windsurfing course costs COP$380,000; kitesurfing is COP$900,000. Rentals are available for COP$50,000 per hour.

Kite Addict Colombia (www.kiteaddictcolombia.com) offers a 10-hour, three- to four-day basic course for COP$800,000, has *chinchorro* accommodations (COP$10,000 pp), and does kitesurfing excursions to Punta Gallinas. Kite Addict is located between the Mana shop and Posada Pujurú. It's the only hut with a second story.

ACCOMMODATIONS

Family-run guesthouses are plentiful in Cabo de la Vela, and are quite rudimentary. Freshwater is scarce here in the desert, so long showers are not an option. Floors are usually sandy, and electricity is limited. The street in Cabo de la Vela along the sea is lined with about 15 guesthouses. There are a few lodgings outside of town toward El Faro, such as Rancheria Utta.

The ★ **Rancheria Utta** (300 m northwest of town, Vía al Faro, cell tel. 312/687-8237 or 313/817-8076, www.rancheriautta.com, COP$15,000 hammock, COP$35,000 bed pp) is a nice place to stay. It is just far enough from Cabo de la Vela that you can experience the magic of being far away from civilization. Cabins are simple, with walls made from the hearts of *yotojoro* (cacti), a traditional form of construction in the desert. There are 11 *cabañas* with a total of 35 beds and plenty of inviting *chinchorros* (hammocks) for lazing about. Being on the beach at night, looking up at the stars, and listening to the sound of gentle waves breaking nearby is unforgettable. A pleasant restaurant at the hotel serves breakfast (COP$7,000), lunch (COP$18,000), and dinner (COP$20,000). The fare is mostly seafood (lobster is a favorite but will cost extra), but they can accommodate vegetarians.

Hospedaje Jarrinapi (cell tel. 312/600-2884, 321/831-7850, or 310/643-2786 www.hospedajejarrinapi.com, COP$12,000 hammock, COP$35,000 bed pp) is a large hotel with 19 *yotojoro* (cactus) cabins for a total capacity of 60 people. This hotel has electricity from the afternoon until dawn and has an orderly kitchen and restaurant.

Posada Pujurú (cell tel. 300/279-5048, http://posadapujuru.blogspot.com,

beach near Cabo de la Vela

COP$20,000 hammock, COP$50,000 bed) has 14 rooms and a space for hammocks. Pujurú is adjacent to Kite Addict Colombia kitesurfing school.

TRANSPORTATION

Shared taxis (COP$15,000) ply the hourlong route from Riohacha to Uribia. Catch one in Riohacha at the intersection of Calle 15 and Carrera 5. Ask the driver to drop you off at the spot where passenger trucks depart for Cabo de la Vela and intermediate *rancherías*. Once your taxi drops you off, take one of the **passenger trucks** (COP$20,000) from Uribia to Cabo de la Vela. The trucks depart until 2pm every day. The uncomfortable ride, on a bench in the back of the truck, can take two or more hours, depending on how many stops are made, but this may be the quintessential Guajira experience.

★ Punta Gallinas

Punta Gallinas is a settlement on a small peninsula jutting into the Caribbean at the very northernmost tip of the South American continent. It is home to about 100 Wayúu who claim this beautiful spot as their ancestral land. The landscape here is a symphony of oranges, ochres, and browns, dotted with cactus and shrubs. The peninsula is hemmed in to the south by Bahía Hondita, a large bay with bright aquamarine waters and thin clusters of mangroves, and to the north by the deepblue Caribbean.

Sights in and around Punta Gallinas include the *faro* (lighthouse), which marks the northernmost tip of South America; **Bahía Hondita,** which is home to flamingos and mangroves; and the remote and unspoiled beaches at **Dunas de Taroa** (Taroa Dunes), where windswept and towering sand dunes drop abruptly some 30 meters (100 feet) into the sea, and at **Punta Aguja,** at the southwest tip of the peninsula of Punta Gallinas. These excursions are included in tour prices. If you are on your own, hotels charge around COP$20,000 per person to see the dunes (five-person minimum), COP$150,000 for a group boat ride on the Bahía Hondita to spot flamingos, and COP$20,000 per person to go to Punta Aguja (five-person minimum).

There are two good lodging options in Punta Gallinas, both with splendid views of Bahía Hondita. ★ **Hospedaje Luzmila** (Punta Gallinas, cell tel. 312/626-8121 or 312/647-9881, luzmilita10@gmail.com, COP$20,000 hammock, COP$30,000 bed pp) has 10 *cabañas* with 20 beds and is spread out alongside the bay. Breakfast (COP$5,000), lunch (COP$15,000), and dinner (COP$15,000) are served in the restaurant. Lobster dishes cost extra.

★ **Donde Alexandra** (Punta Gallinas, cell tel. 315/538-2718 or 318/500-6942, alexandra@hotmail.com, COP$15,000 hammock, COP$30,000 bed pp) has 10 rooms and 25 beds. Meals are not included in the prices but are usually around COP$6,000 for breakfast, COP$15,000 for lunch, and COP$15,000 for dinner, unless you order lobster (COP$45,000). Donde Alexandra has sweeping vistas of the bay and beyond from the restaurant area.

TRANSPORTATION

Although most travelers visit Punta Gallinas on an organized tour, it is possible to travel on your own from the Puerto de Pescadores at Puerto Bolívar on a *lancha* (boat) arranged by Hospedaje Luzmila or Donde Alexandra (COP$120,000 pp round-trip, minimum 5 passengers). In the rainy season, from September to November, this may be the only option, as overland tour companies may not be operating.

Parque Nacional Natural Macuira

The remote **Parque Nacional Natural Macuira** (PNN Macuira, 260 km northeast of Riohacha, cell tel. 311/688-2362, macuira@parquesnacionales.gov.co, 8am-6pm daily, free) covers an area of 25,000 hectares (61,780 acres) and encompasses the entire Serranía de la Macuira (Macuira mountain range), an isolated mountainous outcrop at the northeastern tip of the Guajira Peninsula. These mountains are a biological island in the middle of the surrounding desert. The Macuira range, which is 35 kilometers (22 miles) long and 864 meters (2,835 feet) in elevation at Cerro Palua, its highest point, captures moisture-laden winds from the sea that nourish a unique low-elevation tropical cloud forest teeming with ferns, orchids, bromeliads, and moss. At lower elevations, there are tropical dry forests.

The park includes 350 species of plants, 140 species of birds (17 endemic), and more than 20 species of mammals. The park is within the large Alta Guajira Wayúu Reservation. In the lower parts of the range, within the park, live many Wayúu families who raise goats and grow corn and other subsistence crops.

The gateway to the park is the Wayúu town of **Nazareth.** Visitors are required to register and participate in a brief presentation at the PNN Macuira park office, where they must also hire an authorized Wayúu guide. A few of the official independent guides are Ricardo Brito (cell tel. 312/654-5328), Pedro Quintero (cell tel. 313/648-8060), and María Eulalia Quintero (cell tel. 322/664-1319).

There are multiple hikes varying 1.5-6 hours; the cost of a guided walk ranges COP$35,000-45,000 per eight-person group. Day hikes meander along riverbeds through tropical dry forest. One leads to the **Arewolü Sand Dunes** (two hours, 1.5 kilometers/1 mile, COP$45,000), which are, surprisingly, located in the midst of the forest. Another hike takes you to the **Shipanoü pools.** A third hike goes to **Cerro Tojoro** (2.5 hours, COP$25,000), which affords beautiful views of

the coast and the mountain range. The most challenging hike, **Nazareth-Siapana** (seven hours, 12 kilometers/7.5 miles, COP$120,000) traverses the entire length of the park. Plan to hike early in the morning to increase your chances of seeing birds and other wildlife. Hiking to the Macuira's unusual cloud forest is not permitted by the Wayúu.

There are only a few lodging options in Nazareth, the town closest to the park. One suitable choice is **Hospedaje Vía Manaure** (entrance to Nazareth, cell tel. 320/310-3783 or 314/552-5513, evelasiosuarez@msn.com, COP$20,000 hammock, COP$30,000 bed pp), which can accommodate 40 people and offers Wi-Fi. It has an on-site restaurant (breakfast COP$10,000, lunch COP$15,000, dinner COP$10,000) serving regional dishes. Make arrangements in advance for meals. Another choice is **Villa Inmaculada** (cell tel. 320/504-8519, COP$20,000 pp), offering the same services as Hospedaje Vía Manuare.

TRANSPORTATION

Getting to Nazareth and PNN Macuira requires patience, money, time, and determination. If you are touring the Alta Guajira, PNN Macuira can be added to your itinerary after Punta Gallinas. Otherwise, hire a car out of Riohacha for the day (about COP$500,000, negotiable). Another option is to take public transportation from Uribia to Nazareth (Sun. only, 5-6 hours, COP$60,000). Before visiting, contact the **PNN Macuira park office** (cell tel. 311/688-2362, macuira@parquesnacionales.gov.co) for more transportation options, road conditions, and updated park information.

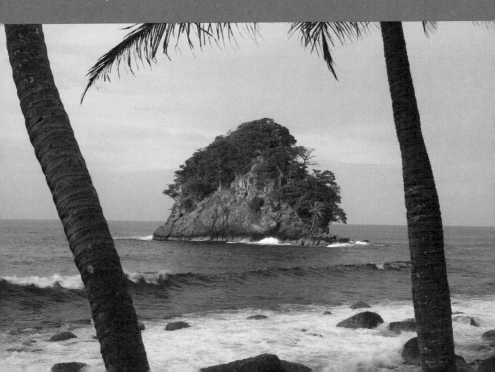

Western Caribbean Coast

Highlights

★ **Islas de San Bernardo:** This little-known archipelago is the perfect island getaway (page 106).

★ **Bahía de Cispatá:** Get your reptile fix at this nature preserve, which houses iguanas and American crocodiles (page 108).

★ **Río Cedro:** Enjoy the peace at this remote coastal hamlet, where sloths inhabit the nearby tropical dry forest (page 109).

★ **Capurganá and Sapzurro:** Explore lonely beaches, trek through the rainforest among colorful frogs and howler monkeys, and cool off in crystalline brooks in the remote Darién region (page 112).

Threbe portion of the Caribbean coast that stretches west from Cartagena is less visited and familiar than the region to the east. That may be just the ticket for those yearning to explore the undiscovered and escape the crowds.

From Cartagena, this area extends west to the Golfo de Urabá and then juts north through the Darién Gap and the border with Panama. The Golfo de Morrosquillo is home to the beach towns of Tolú and San Antero, as well as the inland city of Montería. Across the Golfo de Urabá, the tropical rainforests of the Darién provide an exuberant backdrop to the seaside towns of Capurganá and Sapzurro, which are accessible only by boat or plane. The diving off the coast here is superb.

What most visitors remember and cherish about a visit to this remote part of Colombia is being immersed in truly wild nature.

PLANNING YOUR TIME

Most of the destinations in this region can be visited in one or two days. The exception is the Islas de San Bernardo, where 2-3 days is ideal, and the Darién villages of Capurganá and Sapzurro, where it's better to give yourself 3-4 days, thanks to the plethora of hiking and diving opportunities.

Tolú and Coveñas are easily accessed by bus from Cartagena. To get to the Darién, consider flying at least one way (into Acandí or Capurganá), to maximize your travel time, as reaching this area by bus and boat takes a while. Flights into the area originate out of Medellín only.

Getting around in this region requires patience and time. Expect fewer buses, limited air connections, and weather-delayed boat departures. From December to February, the coastal waters are at their choppiest, so boat delays are inevitable.

SAFETY

This region was greatly affected by violence during the worst years of the armed conflict between paramilitaries, guerrillas, and the military, with civilians often caught in the middle. This was especially so in the remote

---

Previous: boat near Capurganá; island off the coast of Capurganá. **Above:** three-toed sloth near Río Cedro.

areas of the Darién, which was a major drug-trafficking route. Although drug smuggling and related skirmishes in inland areas continue to this day, the places covered in this guide are safe. It's never a bad idea to ask locals about the security of an area, especially if you venture to parts not described in this guide.

Golfo de Morrosquillo

South of Cartagena, the Golfo de Morrosquillo is a broad, 50-kilometer-wide (31-mile-wide) inlet. Largely unknown to international visitors, the gulf's easternmost shore is home to the beach community of Tolú, which is popular with vacationing Colombian families. Off its shores are the Islas de San Bernardo, with beautiful coral reefs and the world's most densely populated island, tiny Santa Cruz del Islote.

On the southern edge of the gulf is the town of San Antero, which is home to a crocodile preserve on Bahía de Cispatá. Outside of San Antero is peaceful Río Cedro, a place to truly disconnect from the world. Inland from San Antero is the region's major city, Montería, in the heart of Colombia's cattle country.

TOLÚ

Balmy beachside Tolú, 160 kilometers (100 miles) southwest of Cartagena, is best described as sleepy. Here, locals get around on foot or *bici-taxi* (bicycle cab), and it's hot and humid year-round. The beaches off the mainland are pleasant, but many visitors come here in order to catch a boat to the Islas de San Bernardo.

In the evening, when the mercury has dropped a few degrees, locals congregate in the main plaza to exchange gossip and people-watch. On weekends, the town becomes more lively, with a steady influx of weekend warriors. Along the boardwalk that parallels the beach, vendors sell ceviche, bars blast music, and kids splash around in the warm water.

Tolú is home to a few decent beaches, perfect for lazing in the sun. Check out laid-back **Playa El Francés,** five kilometers (three miles) north of Tolú. Another option is **Punta Bolívar,** nearly 30 kilometers (17 miles) southwest of Tolú.

Accommodations

★ **Villa Babilla** (Cl. 20 No. 3-40, Tolú, tel. 5/288-6124, www.villababillahostel.com, COP$45,000 s, COP$90,000 d) is the best place to stay in Tolú by a long shot, with its garden courtyard and serene atmosphere. Rooms have no TV or air-conditioning. A kitchen is available for guest use and there is an Olímpica grocery store a couple of blocks away. Nearby roosters may disturb your sleep.

Catering mostly to Colombian families and groups, **Camino Verde** (Playa El Francés, Tolú, tel. 5/288-5132 or 5/249-9464, www.vacacionescaminoverde.com, COP$270,000 d) is six kilometers (3.7 miles) east of Tolú, and is a peaceful (but not fancy) spot to relax during the week, despite its sprawling size. Room are generally set up family-style, with a double and a twin bed. Most visitors drive here.

Transportation

There is frequent bus service from Tolú to Cartagena (3 hours, COP$30,000) and Montería (2.5 hours, COP$25,000). Buses to Cartagena and Montería are at Calle 15 where it intersects Carreteras 2A and 3A.

ADA (www.ada-aero.com) flies from Medellín to Tolú, making this a quick, easy, and often inexpensive beach destination.

To get around Tolú, take a *bici-taxi* (bicycle cab).

★ ISLAS DE SAN BERNARDO

The easiest and least expensive way to spend some time on the turquoise waters of the

Western Caribbean Coast

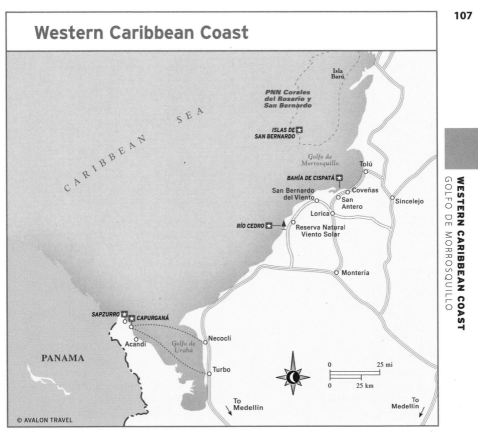

© AVALON TRAVEL

Golfo de Morrosquillo and relax on a tropical white-sand beach is to visit the **Islas de San Bernardo.** These islands, located about 16 kilometers (10 miles) offshore, are part of the Parque Nacional Natural Corales del Rosario y San Bernardo, although the islands have been privately developed.

A day tour is a good way to see the islands, and generally includes a stop for a seafood lunch, snorkeling at **Isla Múcura,** and passing by a handful of the other islands, including **Santa Cruz del Islote,** the most densely populated island in the world, with one person for every 10 square meters. Book a tour of the islands with **Mundo Mar** (Av. 1 No. 14-40, Tolú, tel. 5/288-4431, www.mundomar.com.co, COP$60,000 pp), a reputable tour agency. Other tour agencies are located

in the hotels that line Tolú's boardwalk. Most day tours depart at 8:30am and return to Tolú by about 4:30pm each day.

Food and Accommodations

★ **Punta Norte** (Isla Tintipán, cell tel. 310/707-4005, www.hotelpuntanorte.com, COP$195,000 pp), on Isla Tintipán in the Islas de San Bernardo, is run by a friendly Uruguayan and is most often referred to as Donde El Uruguayo, or "The Uruguayan's Place." Bring plenty of insect repellent to this remote island paradise. Accommodations are not luxurious, but it's a relaxed place. The restaurant includes all meals, and fresh lobster is part of the deal! It takes about an hour to get to the hotel from Tolú by boat (COP$40,000). When you make your reservation, inquire about transportation timing and availability.

For white-sand beaches, warm aquamarine waters, and the occasional calorie-loaded cocktail, go to the resort of **Punta Faro** (Isla Múcura, cell tel. 317/435-9594, www.puntafaro.com, COP$1,190,000 d), an island resort in the Islas de San Bernardo. There are 45 simple rooms with no hot water in the showers and unreliable Wi-Fi. All meals (included) are served buffet-style. Spend your time here lounging on the beach, discovering nearby islands, participating in various water activities, riding bikes, and taking short hikes. It's a good place to bring kids. Round-trip fast boat service from Cartagena (two hours) costs an additional COP$175,000 per person. You can also depart from Tolú. Punta Faro can assist with transportation to and from the island; inquire when you make your reservation.

For great Caribbean vibes on a floating piece of paradise, head to the ★ **Casa en el Agua** (Isla Tintipán, cell tel. 312/756-3439, www.casaenelagua.com, COP$39,000 hammocks, COP$150,000 d), a floating solar-powered hostel near Isla Tintipán. There is a restaurant here, which serves all meals family-style. Activities include diving, island tours, and spearfishing. At night, it's

possible to observe bioluminescent plankton. On nights where there's a full moon, Casa en el Agua hosts "reef raves." The quickest and easiest way to get here is via Casa en el Agua's boat service (1pm Mon., Wed., and Fri., COP$90,000 pp) from Cartagena. You must reserve a spot and confirm departure details in advance. It's also possible to get here overland, though it requires taking multiple modes of transportation. From Cartagena, take a bus to San Onofre (COP$25,000), a *mototaxi* to Rincón del Mar (COP$10,000), then a boat (COP$150,000 for four passengers) to the hostel. Or, from Tolú, it's a 45-minute trip if you hop aboard the island tour boat (8am daily, COP$35,000 pp). Check Casa en el Agua's website for specific transportation instructions.

★ BAHÍA DE CISPATÁ

The most interesting part of this region can be found along the coastline of **Bahía de Cispatá,** a serene bay lined with undisturbed mangrove forests, near the town of San Antero. Here, an interesting project by **Asocaiman** (cell tel. 300/810-1161, www. asocaiman.org, caimanmiranda@hotmail. com) helps in the protection and propagation of American crocodiles and turtles. These

Casa en el Agua in the Islas de San Bernardo

creatures were once hunted for their meat and eggs, but today, locals are trained on the importance of protecting these species. A visit to the small bayside refuge, where many species of crocodiles and turtles reside before being released back into the wild, consists of a tour led by a former hunter. There is no set price for the tour, but guides can accept tips. Asocaiman also offers boat tours (COP$15,000-50,000 pp, depending on group size) of the mangroves, during which you'll have the chance to see animals in their natural habitat. Call Asocaiman in advance to coordinate your visit.

Food and Accommodations

Go eat at ★ **Pesecar** (Bahía de Cispatá, cell tel. 312/651-2651, 7am-9pm daily). It's worth the trip to San Antero just for lunch here—very fresh seafood with an unbeatable bayside location.

San Antero borders the water and has some nice beaches at Playa Blanca. There is a long string of waterfront hotels popular with weekenders from Montería and Medellín. During the week, it's very quiet. The **Cispatá Marina Hotel** (tel. 4/811-0197 or 4/811-0887, www.cispata.com, COP$123,000 pp) has an enviable location overlooking Bahía de Cispatá and, on the other side, the beaches of Playa Blanca. The hotel comprises 16 cute red-roofed *cabañas* as well as smaller apartments. The hotel also has a large pool.

A locally run and quite friendly hotel, the **Mangle Colora'o** (Vereda Amaya, tel. 4/811-0722, cell tel. 301/203-7071, COP$35,000 pp), is just across the street from Bahía de Cispatá.

Transportation

San Antero and Bahía de Cispatá are about 30 kilometers (18.6 miles) southwest of Tolú, on the Coveñas-Lorica highway. Regular public transportation is available for under COP$8,000 from the bus terminal along the main highway.

★ Río Cedro

It's hard to find a place more tranquil than Río Cedro. This community of banana and plantain farmers on a mostly undeveloped coastline in Córdoba, near San Antero, is set amid an unusual tropical dry forest that is home to sloths, howler monkeys, iguanas, and many species of birds. The gray-sand beaches are strewn with driftwood, and pelicans routinely glide by in formation above the usually calm waters.

In peaceful Río Cedro, there are paths

a young crocodile at the Asocaiman conservation center in Bahía de Cispatá galore that wind through the forest and excellent swimming and kayaking opportunities. But perhaps the best activity of all is lazing in a hammock, enjoying the view. Take mosquito repellent.

There are only two accommodations options here. The first, **Río Cedro Paraíso Natural** (cell tel. 313/718-4015, www.riocedro.com, COP$230,000 pp d, three-night min.) is a single thatched roof *cabaña* with a 12-person capacity. There are no individual rooms available—the whole cabin is rented at once. A kitchen is available for use, but meal service is also provided.

The second option is the **Reserva Natural Viento Solar** (cell tel. 317/377-6244, www.vientosolar.org, COP$145,000 pp, all meals included), a private nature reserve with a variety of private and shared rooms. Viento Solar often hosts yoga, meditation, and indigenous healing retreats. Vegetarian meals are provided to guests.

Río Cedro is accessible from the town of Lorica, on the banks of the Río Sinú. To get to Lorica from San Antero, take one of the *busetas* (30 minutes, COP$8,000) that passes through town. From the Tolú-Montería highway in Lorica, take a shared taxi (one hour, COP$8,000) through San Bernardo del Viento to Moñitos—ask a local where to flag one down. From there, both lodges can arrange for a motorbike (45 minutes, COP$10,000) to collect you. Río Cedro Paraíso Natural will arrange from Lorica or Montería for its guests.

MONTERÍA

Montería, Colombia's cattle-ranching capital, is a place of urban renewal and civic pride. Despite being 80 kilometers (50 miles) from the coast, it's a gateway to coastal towns like San Antero, offering the services and comforts of a modern Colombian city. It is not a tourist magnet by any stretch of the imagination; however, this city by the Río Sinú has its charms.

The downtown area is a pleasant place to explore on foot. The **Plaza de Bolívar,** the city's main square, is beautiful. Facing it is the

Reserva Natural Viento Solar

prominent white **Catedral de San Jeronimo** (Cl. 27 No. 2-52). Nearby, the **Banco de la República** (Cl. 29 No. 2-32, second floor, tel. 4/782-3129, 8am-11am and 2pm-5pm Mon.-Sat.) hosts occasional art exhibits.

For a pleasant walk or jog, head to the **Parque Lineal Ronda del Sinú** (between Clls. 21 and 38) along the muddy Río Sinú and Avenida Primera. This lovely park under the shade of tall trees and with a view to the river has bike and jogging paths, playgrounds, workout stations, an amphitheater, and juice stalls. This is one of the nicest urban parks in the country.

One of the coolest things about Montería is its ingenious (and ecofriendly) system for crossing the Río Sinú: the *planchones.* These are small ferries attached to a cable that crosses the river as the captain rows passengers across. This transportation system has been around since 1915. Even though it takes less than five minutes to cross, and there's not much on the other side, the *planchones* themselves almost make Montería worth a trip. This simple pleasure costs a whopping COP$500 (under US$0.30).

To get a different perspective on the savanna surrounding Montería, **Helicop Aero Tours** (cell tel. 315/850-2610, www.helicop.co) offers an array of helicopter tours for all budgets, with some starting as low as COP$185,000 per person.

Food

Along Avenida Primera are several bars and outdoor restaurants where the volume kicks up a notch or two on Saturday nights.

In Montería, the focus is on beef. Many of the town's popular restaurants are near-sacred tributes to cowboy culture. **Bonga del Sinú** (Km. 5 Vía Cereté, tel. 4/786-0085, www.labongadelsinu.co, noon-11pm Mon.-Sat., noon-9pm Sun., COP$22,000) is a large restaurant under a thatched roof on the outskirts of the city. To eat like a true cowboy, order the Lomita Bonga Magnum, which is 600 grams (21 ounces) of grilled beef from a variety of cuts. The traditional *mote de queso,* a hearty cheese soup with *ñame* (a type of yam) and coconut milk, is a popular choice.

In a nod to the early-20th-century Arab immigration to the area, Montería has a couple of spots where kibbe (ground lamb and bulgur) trumps steaks. A couple of blocks from the river, on a tree-lined street, is **Farah Delicias Arabes** (Cra. 6 No. 60-42, tel. 4/789-9680, www.farahdeliciasarabes.com, 4:30pm-10:30pm daily, COP$15,000), an authentic Lebanese restaurant. Another option is **Baalbeck** (Cl. 61 No. 7-16, tel. 4/789-9713,

11am-10pm daily, COP$25,000), where portions are generous and the outdoor seating allows patrons to enjoy the night air.

There is a **Juan Valdez Café** (Cl. 44 No. 10-139, tel. 4/785-1607, 9am-10pm Mon.-Sat., 10am-9pm Sun.) at the Centro Comerical Alamedas. Get your macchiato fix here—you're a long way from another decent cup of joe.

Accommodations

Hotels tend to be overpriced in Montería. The **Hotel Casa Real** (Cl. 29 No. 6-26, tel. 4/782-4004, COP$120,000 d) is a few blocks from Avenida Primera and is also close to a police station. Many rooms are tiny with no windows, but the hotel is within walking distance of the Plaza de Bolívar.

A reliable national chain and recent arrival is the **GHL Hotel Montería** (Cl. 44 No. 8-43, tel. 4/789-2999, www.ghlhoteles.com, COP$210,000 d), located north of town and adjacent to the Centro Comercial Alamedas shopping mall. There's a small pool on the rooftop and the hotel is smartly designed with a wink to Caribbean cowboy culture.

Transportation

A bus ride from Cartagena to Montería's **bus station** (Terminal de Transportes de Montería, Cl. 41 No. 20-11, tel. 4/784-9000, www.terminaldemonteria.com) will cost around COP$50,000 and take about five hours. From the bus station, there are easy connections to all nearby coastal towns, such as San Antero (one hour, COP$15,000).

The Colombian Darién

The Darién Gap (Tapón del Darién) is a sparsely populated swath of land, roughly 160 kilometers (100 miles) long and 50 kilometers (30 miles) wide that straddles the border between Colombia and Panama. Its name comes from its interruption of the 48,000-kilometer (30,000-mile) Pan-American Highway, a storied road that extends from Prudhoe Bay, Alaska, to Ushuaia in Patagonia. The highway picks up again in the Colombian port town of Turbo.

The Colombian Darién is bookended by the delta of the Río Atrato that flows into the Golfo de Urabá on the east and the Serranía de Baudó mountain range on the west. This land of rivers, swamps, and rainforest-covered mountains is one of the most ecologically diverse regions of the world. Ecotourism is widely viewed as the future for this area.

The rainforests here are particularly rich in palm trees, of which 120 species have been identified, as well as cycads, ancient plants that look like palms. Notable too are more than 40 species of brightly colored poisonous frogs, known locally as *ranas kokois*. Some of these small frogs are covered with a deadly poison and have evolved stunning coloring of bright orange, red, gold, and blue. They are active in the day and therefore relatively easy to spot. Of Colombia's 1,800 species of birds, more than 1,000 have been identified in this region, including a large number of hummingbirds.

Safety

The absence of roads, abundance of navigable rivers, and the cover provided by the jungle's canopy have made this region into a major corridor for the trafficking of illegal drugs, which has also meant that there has been a heavy presence of both guerrillas and paramilitaries. The Colombian Darién is populated mostly by Afro-Colombian and indigenous communities that have been hard hit by violence fueled by trafficking.

Today, it is safe to visit the twin villages of Capurganá and Sapzurro, perched on idyllic crescent-shaped bays near the Panamanian border.

★ CAPURGANÁ AND SAPZURRO

While much of the Colombian Darién is lowland and swamp, as it is part of the Río Atrato basin, near the border with Panama, the terrain is mountainous and covered in tropical jungle. Here you'll find the twin towns of Capurganá and Sapzurro.

Capurganá is the larger village of the two, with a population of about 2,000. Many residents make their living by fishing. Tourism has increased in recent years, resulting in more guesthouses, hotels, and restaurants, many of which are run by Europeans.

Capurganá's *muelle* (port) bustles with activity during the day, with boats constantly bringing in passengers and supplies. In the evening, ramshackle bars, particularly around the town's soccer field, blast music for beer-drinking patrons. Nature is abundant here: Within minutes of leaving your hotel you'll be surrounded by the sounds of the jungle, accompanied only by the occasional green-and-black-speckled toad and maybe a band of howler monkeys.

Sapzurro is even more laid-back than Capurganá. This village is reachable only by foot or boat. Walking here means crossing a jungle path over a mountain, which is the attraction of coming here, though it can be a strenuous journey. For a few thousand pesos, you can opt to take a boat to Sapzurro, a short 10-minute ride.

Prepare yourself for the weather here: Rain and humidity mean mud and mosquitoes, so you'll want durable shoes and layered clothing. Bring a flashlight or headlamp for walking at night. There are no cars in either village. Get around on foot, by bike, or by boat.

Recreation
HIKING

There are several jungle walks to make around Capurganá. These take you through dense jungle overflowing with tropical vegetation populated by howler monkeys, birds, colorful frogs, and snakes. While the walks are short and fairly straightforward, you may want to ask at your hotel or hostel for a guide, especially for the walk between Capurganá and Sapzurro. Guides cost about COP$10,000. Wear hiking boots (waterproof if possible) and a swimsuit underneath your clothes for dips in the water off of Sapzurro or in freshwater swimming holes, and set off in the morning hours to give yourself plenty of time to get back.

An easy walk to make, without the need of a guide, is to **La Coquerita** (20-minute walk north from town, cell tel. 311/824-8022, COP$2,000), a delightfully ramshackle waterside hangout where you can have a refreshing coco-lemonade or maybe some guacamole and *patacones* (fried plantains) and take a dip in the refreshing freshwater or saltwater pools.

There are also some handicrafts on sale here. To get there, walk along the Playa Caleta just north of the port, passing in front of the Hotel Almar. Continue along the jungle path that hugs the coastline. La Coquerita is less than one kilometer (0.5 mile) from town, and the path is well marked. Look out for the black and fluorescent-green frogs along the way, but don't touch them; they're poisonous.

El Cielo waterfall is a 50-minute walk (about 3 kilometers/1.8 miles) through the jungle from Capurganá. The path is flat and easy, although you'll have to make about a dozen crossings of shallow streams. Bring a bathing suit to cool off in the swimming holes you'll encounter. To get to heavenly El Cielo, set out on the road that runs parallel to the airstrip and then ask locals for directions. On the way to El Cielo, look for **El Trébol Piscina,** a pool where you can take a dip in cool waters and have lunch.

The **path to Sapzurro** leads you through the exuberant rainforest to a lookout point and then down directly to the beach. The hike takes two hours. Start at the soccer field, on the southern end of Capurganá, and ask the way. Midway up the uphill path is a shack that is the home of a man who claims to protect the jungle. Once you find him, you know you're

swimming hole on the way to the El Cielo waterfall

on the right track. He expects those who pass through to pay him about COP$1,000. At the top of the mountain there is a nice overlook with views of Capurganá and the coastline. The hike is not difficult, but the path can get muddy and slippery in places. Wear hiking boots and pick up a walking stick along the way to help you manage the steep parts.

Once in Sapzurro, you're a short hike (15 minutes) from the border with **Panama** and the village of **La Miel.** This easy walk begins on the same street as Cabañas Uvali and the Reserva Natural Tacarcuná. The border crossing is at the top of a steep hill embedded with steps. You'll need to show a passport to cross over to Panama. There is not much to the community of La Miel. It has a small military outpost, many young children running around, and a pleasant beach where you can swim and have a seafood lunch or a drink.

DIVING AND SNORKELING

As you'd expect, the warm, turquoise waters off the coast of Capurganá, all the way up to San Blas in Panama, make for fantastic diving, and there are over 30 diving sites to choose from. The best time for underwater exploration is from May to November. During those months, visibility is exceptional with hardly any waves. There are coral walls, reef rocks, and caves to explore.

Dive and Green Diving Center (facing the port, cell tel. 311/578-4021 or 316/781-6255, www.diveandgreen.com, 7:30am-12:30pm and 2pm-6pm daily) is the best place to organize a diving trip (certified diver excursion COP$190,000) or to take a five-day PADI certification course (COP$820,000) with a bilingual instructor. For these packages it is best to pay in cash, as credit card transactions have an additional fee. For those interested in snorkeling, Dive and Green can make arrangements for you, though they don't themselves lead snorkeling trips. Dive and Green offers all the equipment you need. If you are on the fence about whether diving is for you, they offer a Discover Scuba Diving day for COP$150,000. Dive and Green has

accommodations, comprising four rooms in a house adjacent to their offices. These cost COP$25,000 per person. The house faces the water, guaranteeing a pleasant evening breeze.

TOURS
Sol del Darién (cell tel. 318/633-3994) is a recommended tour agency run by a French couple. It offers an interesting menu of excursions in the region, including canoe trips, guided nature walks, and multiday adventures in the San Blas Islands. The owners also operate the hostel La Bohemia.

Food
CAPURGANÁ
Hotels are usually the best options for food in both villages. **Donde Josefina** (Playa Caleta, cell tel. 316/779-7760, noon-9pm daily, COP$30,000) remains the top restaurant for a delicious, gourmet seafood dinner, right on the beach in the heart of Capurganá. Dining on lobster in a coconut-and-garlic sauce under the swaying branches of a palm tree: That sounds like a vacation!

Hernan Patacón (no phone, hours vary, COP$18,000) is a food stand serving fresh fish and shrimp. They are located in front of the town clinic. A decent **bakery** overlooking the soccer field in the center of town serves breakfast, and is open daily.

SAPZURRO
In Sapzurro, the best places for a meal are **Doña Triny** (Hostal Doña Triny, cell tel. 312/751-8626 or 313/725-8362, noon-10pm daily, COP$20,000), a two-story brick house facing the water, and the **Gata Negra** (cell tel. 314/725-0325, www.lagatanegra.net, open daily) for authentic home-style Italian dishes. Call in advance to let either restaurant know you're coming.

Accommodations
There are a surprising number of excellent and inexpensive accommodations options in both Capurganá and Sapzurro. While there are a few large, all-inclusive hotels with

welcome drinks and the works, the most interesting and comfortable options are the smaller guesthouses and hostels. Nearly all hotels are owned and operated by out-of-towners.

CAPURGANÁ

In Capurganá, many hotels and hostels are near the *muelle* (port), the hub of activity. Many visitors stay at one of the few all-inclusive hotels in Capurganá, but those options lack charm.

One of the best "urban" lodging options in Capurganá is **Posada del Gecko** (in town, cell tel. 314/525-6037, www.posadadelgecko.com, posadadelgecko@hotmail.com, COP$20,000 dorm, COP$35,000 d), which is run by an Italian-Colombian couple and offers both dorms and private rooms spread over two houses, with a capacity of 28 people. In between the buildings is a spacious garden ideal for lounging in a hammock or the hot tub. Enjoy a good Italian dinner by candlelight at the restaurant (7:30pm-11pm daily); it's open to nonguests as well, but it's best to stop by in advance and make a reservation. The hotel can arrange three-day excursions to the San Blas Islands (Panama), in which you visit a Kuna indigenous community, frolic on pristine white-sand beaches, and snorkel.

Several excellent guesthouses reside amid the trees in the Playa Roca area, about a 15-minute walk or horse ride from Capurganá. At night you'll need no air-conditioner, and in the morning you may awake to birdsong. This is more pleasant than staying in the Centro. Some of the perks of staying at welcoming ★ **Cabañas El Tucán** (Playa Roca, www.cabanatucancapurgana.com, COP$65,000), run by a friendly Bogotana-Italian couple, are that the owners make their own pasta and are good cooks. This house in the jungle is clean and comfortable, and the prices of the four spacious rooms are reasonable.

Right across the path from El Tucán is ★ **Cabañas Darius** (Playa Roca, cell tel. 314/622-5638, www.cdarius.blogspot.com, capurga05@gmail.com, COP$85,000 pp incl. 2 meals), a very nice guesthouse among the trees. Rooms are spacious and clean, and it's cool enough at night that you won't miss air-conditioning. Balconies and hammocks provide lounging space, but the top selling point is the warm hospitality and the good food.

A third option in the same area is **Hotel Los Robles** (Playa Roca, cell tel. 314/632-8408 or 314/632-8428, COP$120,000 d incl. 2 meals). This lodge has quite the entrance—a winding path lined by bright fuchsia ginger flowers. *Caracolí* and *higuerón* trees provide shade and a home for birds. There are 12 rooms in two houses.

The most low-key place to stay in the Capurganá area is Playa Aguacate. The German owner of the ★ **Bahía Lodge** (Playa Aguacate, cell tel. 314/812-2727, www.bahia-lodge.com, COP$190,000 pp incl. 2 meals) has carved a little paradise out of the jungle—once there you won't want to leave. Its simple and comfortable cabins, each with a sea view, are popular with honeymooners and those celebrating special occasions. Over the hill from Bahía Lodge is **Hotel Las Ceibas** (Playa Aguacate, cell tel. 313/695-6392 or Medellín tel. 4/331-7440, www.hotellasceibas.com). It has three rooms in two houses set amid gardens; the rooms have pleasant balconies with hammocks for late-afternoon relaxation.

La Bohemia (south of town, no phone, www.labohemiahostal.com, COP$20,000 dorm, COP$50,000 private room) is a hostel in a cheerful wooden house with two dorm rooms and two private rooms, with a shared bath. It's a good choice thanks to the friendly, artsy atmosphere. The hostel is run by the owners of the Sol del Darién tour agency.

SAPZURRO

In Sapzurro, there are quite a few inexpensive lodging options, but fewer restaurants than in Capurganá. Most hotels offer meals, though, and are usually the best bet, as they tend to be open more frequently. **Cabañas Uvali** (in town, cell tel. 314/624-1325, COP$40,000 pp) is a friendly, clean, and straightforward little place in town. It's about a five-minute walk from the beach. **La Posada**

Hostal & Camping (cell tel. 312/662-7599 or 310/410-2245, www.sapzurrolaposada. com, COP$65,000 pp d), close to the path to Capurganá, has one luxury apartment with a view, a dorm-style room, and a large space for camping under a big mango tree. They have a little tiki bar over the water, which can be set up for a romantic dinner under the stars.

The ★ **Resort Paraíso Sapzurro** (cell tel. 313/685-9862, COP$10,000 dorm, COP$50,000 pp d) has basic beachfront cabins. This hostel is more commonly known as "Donde El Chileno" (The Chilean's Place), after the Chilean owner. The hostel can organize oversea transportation directly to Cartagena. Free avocadoes and mangoes are a nice perk. It's located near the path to Capurganá and the entrance to Sapzurro.

The ★ **Sapzurro Reserva Natural Tacarcuna** (on the path to La Miel, cell tel. 314/622-3149 or 320/300-1668, COP$40,000 pp) is a special place for anyone interested in the region's flora and fauna. The two cabins are cute. The owners, Martha and Fabio, offer a botanical garden of native species with nature trails and a butterfly farm. Their other passion is birds: Go behind the house and up the mountain with a pair of binoculars to spot cuckoos, parakeets, owls, antipittas, tanagers, four different types of toucans, and many other species, along with the throngs of migratory birds that arrive between August and November each year. The owners can organize a number of hikes in the area. Don't confuse this natural reserve with the all-inclusive Tacurcuna Hotel near the Capurganá airport.

The ★ **Gata Negra** (cell tel. 314/725-0325, www.lagatanegra.net, COP$50,000) is a cozy guesthouse that also serves Italian food. It's surrounded by fruit trees and jungle. There are two rooms with a shared bath and one with a private bath.

Information and Services

Bring extra cash to Capurganá: There are no ATMs, and credit cards are not accepted in most establishments. To avoid bringing wads of pesos, many hotels will allow (or require) you to make a *consignación* (deposit) to their bank account in advance. That can usually be done from any city in Colombia. The nearest bank, **Banco Agrario** (Cl. Las Flores with Cl. Consistorial, tel. 4/682-8229, 8am-11:30am and 2pm-4:30pm Mon.-Fri.), is in Acandí, a half-hour boat ride south from Capurganá.

Transportation

Capurganá and Sapzurro are accessible only by plane or boat. To get here, you have to either take a flight from Medellín to either the Capurganá airport (near the town center) or Acandí airport (10 minutes outside of Acandí) or take a *lancha* (boat) from Turbo or Acandí. Acandí is the municipality about 17 kilometers (10.5 miles) south of Capurganá. Should the seas be too rough or if a general strike shuts down all transportation options, you may be stuck in the jungle for a couple of days more.

Aerolíneas de Antioquia (www.ada-aero.com.co) serves both Capurganá and Acandí from Aeropuerto Olaya Herera in Medellín. ADA has one flight per day (Mon.-Sat., less than an hour, COP$150,000 and up each way) to Acandí from Medellín. Flights are prone to sell out on long weekends and during high season in December and January and during Semana Santa. The Capurganá airport has been closed for improvements, with an expected reopening in 2017.

To get from Acandí to Capurganá, you'll have to take a horse-drawn cart from the airport to Acandí's docks (a 15-minute trip, COP$6,000), from where you'll take a 30-minute *lancha* (boat) ride to Capurganá (COP$17,000). There is a *lancha* departure at 1pm daily. The seas can be rough at times, so try to get a seat in back to avoid too much jostling from the boat's movements. Keep your camera or other electronics in their cases so they won't be exposed to seawater. Demand a life vest. The return trip from Capurganá to Acandí generally leaves at 7:30am daily.

All boats arrive at the *muelle* (docks) in Capurganá, in the middle of town. Most hotels are within walking distance, although those on Playa Roca are a 15-minute walk away. If you have heavy luggage, ask for a horse (about COP$10,000) when you disembark.

Hotels in Playa Aguacate and Sapzurro are reachable only by taking another *lancha* from the docks in Capurganá, about a 20-minute ride. Those hotels will arrange your transportation from Capurganá in advance.

There are **buses** from Medellín (eight hours), Montería (four hours), and from cities across the Caribbean coast to the rough port city of Turbo on the Golfo de Urabá. It's then possible to take a 2.5- to 3-hour boat ride from Turbo to Capurganá or Acandí. These usually depart daily 7am-8am, costing about COP$60,000. The early-morning departure means that you will probably have to spend the previous night in Turbo. That's not ideal, but most tourists agree that **Residencias La Florida** (Cra. 13 No. 99A-56, Turbo, tel. 4/827-3531, COP$30,000 d) is an acceptable lodging option. It's close to the port, and the hotel staff is quite helpful in arranging your onward transportation.

Do not plan to take a boat from Turbo to Capurganá from December to March. The 2.5-hour journey can be awful due to high winds and unrelenting waves. This is likewise true for the trip from Acandí to Capurganá, although it is a much shorter ride.

There is also a direct **fast boat** service from the town of Necoclí (tel. 4/821-4164 or cell tel. 315/687-4284), which is a convenient option for those coming from Cartagena. It takes 1.5 hours and costs COP$120,000 round-trip. In Necoclí, **Hotel Panorama Suite** (cell tel. 312/702-0813, hotelpanoramanecocli@ gmail.com, COP$40,000 pp d) has 28 rooms and is run by the same people who operate boat transportation to Capurganá.

To return to the mainland from Capurganá, it's best to reserve a day in advance for *lanchas* bound for Acandí or Turbo, especially during peak tourist times. Your hotel should be able to do this for you by calling ahead to the *muelle,* where the contact is Ariel Palacios (cell tel. 312/264-5924).

To travel onward to Panama, you must go to the Colombian **Ministerio de Relaciones Exteriores** (Cl. del Comercio, Capurganá cell tel. 311/746-6234, 8am-5pm Mon.-Fri., 9am-4pm Sat.) to get an exit stamp before leaving Capurganá.

Capurganá is on the edge of the jungle.

San Andrés and Providencia

The beaches of San Andrés and Providencia are pristine and secluded. The waters are an inviting turquoise. Seafood, particularly fresh crab, is always on the menu, accompanied by cold beer.

The San Andrés Archipelago is made up of seven atolls and three major islands: San Andrés, Providencia, and Santa Catalina. San Andrés is 775 kilometers (492 miles) northeast of the Colombian mainland and only 191 kilometers (119 miles) east of Nicaragua. The islands are small: San Andrés, the largest island, has an area of 26 square kilometers (10 square miles), Providencia just 17 square kilometers (6.5 square miles), and Santa Catalina, attached to Providencia by a photogenic pedestrian bridge, is 1 square kilometer (247 acres) in size.

San Andrés is popular with rowdy Colombian vacationers escaping the chilly climes of the Andes. Here, sunbathing, snorkeling, diving, and relaxing are always the order of the day.

Once serving as a base for notorious English pirate Henry Morgan, less developed Providencia—or Old Providence, as English-speaking locals call it—and its tiny tagalong neighbor of Santa Catalina are places to experience how the Caribbean used to be. Here you'll enjoy small bungalow-style hotels, home-cooked creole food, and picturesque palm-lined beaches.

On both islands English and a creole patois are spoken, although Spanish is rapidly taking over in San Andrés and the tourism sector.

HISTORY

Little is known of the early history of San Andrés, Providencia, and Santa Catalina. In pre-Columbian times, the Miskito people of Central America visited the islands but never settled there.

In 1631, 100 Puritans from England founded a colony on Providence Island (the English name for Providencia). Rather than establishing a self-sustaining agricultural community, the colonists imported slaves and established a plantation-based economy. Spaniards attacked the islands in 1641 put an

Previous: view of Providencia from Santa Catalina; sailboat race at Bahía Manzanillo. **Above:** the *coco loco*, the official cocktail of San Andrés.

Look for ★ to find recommended
sights, activities, dining, and lodging.

Highlights

★ **Jardín Botánico:** This well-tended botanical garden sits on a bluff overlooking the turquoise sea. A walk among the native trees, plants, and flowers provides a pleasant break from the beach (page 124).

★ **Snorkeling and Diving off of San Andrés:** Dozens of dive sites among thriving coral formations and steep ocean walls keep divers blissfully busy for days (page 126).

★ **Parque Nacional Natural Old Providence McBean Lagoon:** Paddle through the mangrove lagoons and snorkel offshore among tropical fish at this small national park (page 134).

★ **Beaches on Providencia:** Undertake the tough fieldwork of determining your favorite palm-lined Providencia beach. Your investigations could take several days (page 136).

★ **The Peak:** From the highest point on Providencia, hikers enjoy 360-degree vistas from the jungle toward the deep-blue sea (page 137).

San Andrés and Providencia

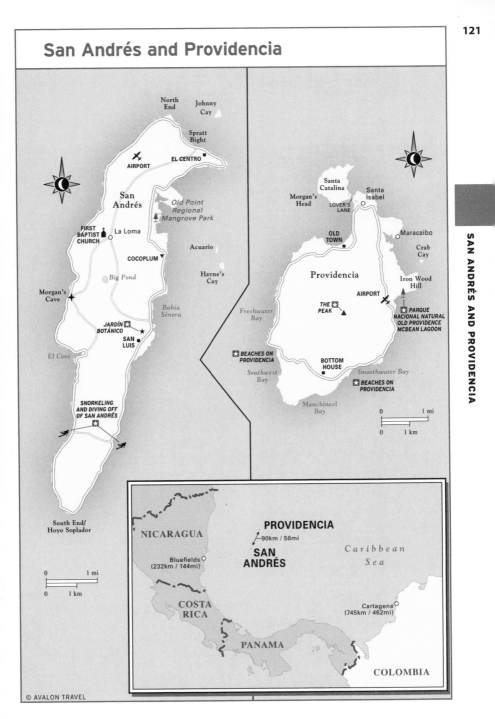

SAN ANDRÉS AND PROVIDENCIA

end to the Puritan experiment. Over the next 50 years, the island was fought over by Spain and England.

In 1821, the archipelago became part of the newly independent Republic of Gran Colombia. During the 19th century, an influx of immigrants from the British Caribbean included many former slaves, who formed the beginnings of the islander community. (These native islanders are sometimes referred to as Raizales, though they themselves don't use this name, which was given to them by mainland Colombians.)

Colombia exerted greater power over the islands in the early 20th century, even forbidding the use of English in official business. In 1953, dictator Gustavo Rojas Pinilla declared San Andrés a free port. This led to a massive influx of outsiders, and the English-speaking native islanders became a minority, losing control of much of their land. Providence, which was not declared a free-trade zone, was spared this onslaught.

The 1991 Colombian constitution gave the islands some autonomy and put an end to immigration from the mainland. Providencia enacted strict zoning and land-ownership regulations that have preserved the islander identity and community.

In recent decades, Nicaragua has contested Colombian jurisdiction over the islands. In 2001, the International Court of Justice reaffirmed Colombian sovereignty over the islands but left the maritime border unresolved. In 2012, the court decided that 70,000 square kilometers (43,500 square miles) of sea surrounding San Andrés that had previously been Colombian were in fact Nicaraguan. For islanders this meant losing traditional fishing areas. The court decision cannot be appealed, but Colombian president Juan Manuel Santos has declared that his country will not abide by the decision until Nicaragua ensures that native islanders have access to their traditional fishing areas.

THE LANDSCAPE

The archipelago covers 280,000 square kilometers (174,000 square miles) of marine area. It includes three major islands, seven atolls, and some well-preserved coral reefs, particularly the barrier reef surrounding Providencia and Santa Catalina, home to more than 80 species of coral and 200 species of fish.

The islands were once covered by forest. Though much has been cleared, especially in San Andrés, significant tracts of forest remain, with cedars, cotton trees, stinkingtoes, birch gums, and other indigenous species. The abundance of fruit-bearing trees and plants includes breadfruit, tamarind, mango, and guava. There are several large, well-preserved mangrove lagoons, notably the McBean Lagoon in Providencia.

The islands support a wide range of reptiles, including snakes, iguanas, geckos, and lizards. Other land animals include crabs, especially the black and shankey crabs, which migrate to and from the sea to spawn, protected by army personnel who block traffic on Providencia's roads during the migration. Four species of protected sea turtles nest here. Approximately 100 bird species have been identified on the islands, but only 18 are resident. The island's only nonhuman land mammals are bats. Dolphins and whales are sighted occasionally.

Despite environmental degradation, especially in San Andrés, the archipelago remains one of the best-preserved corners of the Caribbean. In 2000, the 300,000 square kilometers (186,400 square miles) of the Seaflower Biosphere Reserve became part of UNESCO's "Man and the Biosphere" program, which aims to preserve both biological and ethnic diversity, combining conservation with sustainable use by local communities.

PLANNING YOUR TIME

San Andrés is a possible long-weekend getaway from mainland Colombia; visiting both islands can be accomplished in five nights, breadfruit, Jardín Botánico

expense if you are interested in getting away from it all. Getting to Providencia involves an extra flight, and hotels and restaurants are generally more expensive than in San Andrés (which itself is more expensive than the mainland).

High tourist seasons on both islands are during Christmas and New Year's. It may be hard to find a hotel from mid-December until mid-January. During this time, throngs of Colombian families and a growing number of Brazilians and Argentinians take over San Andrés. Also popular are Semana Santa (Holy Week) and school vacations, which fall between mid-June and August. May and September are quiet. Because it's more difficult to reach, Providencia rarely feels crowded.

The average daily temperature is 27°C (81°F). During the dry season (January-April), water rationing can be necessary, especially in Providencia, where it rains as little as five days per month. The rainy season extends from June until November, when it can rain 20-24 days per month. October is the rainiest month and is also when hurricanes occasionally churn up the warm Caribbean waters. March and April are the best months for snorkeling and diving because the waters are calm. December and January are windy, making snorkeling and diving challenging. Strong winds can prompt airlines to cancel flights into and out of Providencia.

which allows for a relaxed pace. If you want to do some serious diving, plan for at least a week—say three days in San Andrés and four days in Providencia. Wait 24 hours after diving to get in an airplane, due to pressurization concerns.

A visit to Providencia from San Andrés can be a budget buster, but it is well worth the

San Andrés

Surrounded by a large barrier reef, San Andrés is Colombia's Caribbean playground. Here the waters are seven shades of blue, the sandy beaches are white, and *coco locos*, the official island cocktail, are always served. Days here are spent lazing on the beach, island-hopping, snorkeling and diving, and enjoying fresh seafood. For many Colombians, the deals at the many duty-free stores are too good to pass up—and one reason why they visit the island in the first place.

San Andrés has a population of about 75,000, about two-thirds of whom are of mainland Colombian origin. The rest are English- and creole-speaking native islanders, many of whom are descended from Jamaican slaves. There is also a community of "Turcos" or "Arabes," whose roots can be traced to mostly Lebanon and Syria. Their presence on the island is not an insignificant one, as demonstrated by a brilliantly white modern mosque that stands prominently in the commercial center.

Orientation

The island of San Andrés resembles a sea-horse floating gently eastward in the western Caribbean Sea. It is only about 13 kilometers (8 miles) long from top to bottom and 3 kilometers (2 miles) wide, and has a total area of 26 square kilometers (10 square miles). The Circunvalar ring road more or less circles the entire island.

The "town" of San Andrés is usually called the **Centro** or the **North End.** It is in the snout of the seahorse, in the northeast. This is the center of activity and where the majority of the island's restaurants, hotels, and shops (nearly all of which are owned and operated by mainland Colombians) are found. About 1.6 kilometers (1 mile) of the main drag here, Avenida Colombia, is the *paseo peatonal* or *malecón.* Officially known as the Spratt Bight Pathway, it's a delightful pedestrian promenade along the Spratt Bight beach. About two kilometers (1.25 miles) northwest of the Centro is the airport. The west side is quieter, with a handful of points of interest, hotels, and restaurants. The coastline on the west side is all coral; there are no beaches. At the southernmost point of the island is the Hoyo Soplador blowhole. Continuing counterclockwise, the town of **San Luis** extends along the southeastern edge of the island. This area has some good beaches, hotels, and restaurants, and is much more laid-back than the Centro.

The middle part of the island, called **La Loma** (The Hill), is the highest point on the island. The main point of reference here is the stately white First Baptist Church. This area is home to the largest community of native islanders.

SIGHTS

Other than the botanical gardens, the majority of sights in San Andrés are tourist traps. The attractions here are the island's innate pleasures—sun, sand, water, seafood, and tropical drinks.

Spratt Bight Pathway

For many, the first stop in San Andrés is the **Spratt Bight Pathway** (Centro). This pedestrian walkway is the liveliest stretch on the island. It's lined with restaurants, hotels, and souvenir shops on one side and the island's most popular beach, **Spratt Bight,** on the other. In the distance you can spot the palm trees on Johnny Cay.

★ Jardín Botánico

Extending over eight hectares (20 acres) of wilderness, the **Jardín Botánico** (Vía Harmony Hill in front of Hotel Sol Caribe Campo, tel. 8/513-3390, 8:30am-5pm Mon.-Fri., 10am-4pm Sat.-Sun., COP$5,000) is easily the most peaceful place on San Andrés. In this lovely botanical garden run by the Universidad Nacional, you can stroll along several paths and view trees and plants that grow in San Andrés. Of particular interest are the many fruit trees, which include breadfruit, and a section on medicinal plants. From the five-story lookout tower, you can take in an impressive view of the island and its barrier reefs. Guided tours, included in the price of admission, are available (but not required), and take about an hour.

Casa Museo Isleña

Casa Museo Isleña (Km. 5 Av. Circunvalar, tel. 8/512-3419, 8:30am-5pm daily, COP$8,000) is a reconstruction of a typical island wooden house that provides a glimpse into island life in the 19th century. After a required guided tour (15 minutes), your cheerful young guide will tell you "now let's dance!" Reggae dancing is a rather strange component of the museum experience, but then again, it's hard to say no. Those smiling guides are a persuasive lot.

Cueva de Morgan (Morgan's Cave)

It would seem that all caves hidden along the coasts of San Andrés and Providencia are reputed to hold hidden treasures stashed away by notorious pirates. On the western side of San Andrés is **Cueva de Morgan** (Morgan's Cave, tel. 8/513-2946, 9am-6pm daily, COP$10,000), a sort of theme park where Welsh privateer/pirate Captain Henry Morgan allegedly stored some of his loot (but there's no evidence to prove this). There isn't much to see at the cave itself. That's why the park owners added on some reconstructions of traditional wooden island cabins that serve as mini-museums on island culture and ways of life. You visit these on a guided tour that is included in the cost. One is an art gallery where local dancers often perform to calypso beats. Also on the premises is the Coconut Museum, which is a house made out of coconuts. All in all, it's a tourist trap.

Hoyo Soplador

At **Hoyo Soplador** on the island's southern tip, the attraction is a blowhole in the coral where, when the tide and winds are right, water sprays up, reaching heights of more than 10 meters. It can't compare to Old Faithful, but then again, can you order a *coco loco* in Yellowstone? There is no fee to see the hole, but vendors will strongly encourage visitors to purchase something.

First Baptist Church

The white, clapboard **First Baptist Church** (La Loma, no phone, services 7:30pm Thurs. and 10:30am Sun., COP$3,000 donation requested) was built in 1844 and rebuilt before the turn of the 20th century using wood imported from Alabama. It was the first Baptist church established on the island. A guide will tell you the history of the church and allow you to climb up to the bell tower for a commanding view of the island. The Sunday worship service can last several hours. Church members dress up for services, and you'll often see a smattering of tourists in the balcony on Sundays. The church is an excellent place to hear gospel music.

Paradise Farm

Job Saas, a native islander, operates **Paradise Farm** (Cove Seaside, Km. 11 Polly Higgs Rd., tel. 8/513-0798 or cell tel. 315/770-3904, donations accepted). Saas decided to transform the former standard family farm into one with a focus on conservation and the environment. Here you can see animals, such as iguanas and turtles, and plants that are threatened due to overdevelopment on San Andrés. Saas uses the same farming techniques that his family has applied for decades. It is a great initiative on an island where environmental awareness is lacking. Saas welcomes visitors

view from the steeple of the First Baptist Church

to the farm, and, if you are lucky, you can hear his band play.

Big Pond

Managed by a Rastafarian community, the **Big Pond** (La Loma, no phone, no set visiting hours, donations requested) is a pond on the top of La Loma, home to a few domesticated alligators. When called, they will swim close to the shore, where they are fed a diet of white bread. The alligators live in harmony with turtles, and herons watch the action from a tree nearby. You can order a beer at the bar where reggae music blares from speakers. There is no set entry fee, but young men hanging out at the entrance (who are not associated with Big Pond) will insist on a payment. It's expected that you'll pay, but you can negotiate—don't pay more than COP$10,000 per person.

ENTERTAINMENT AND EVENTS
Nightlife

The nightlife scene on San Andrés is big and brash. The most popular nightspots, near Spratt Bight, cater to visiting Colombians. Clubs generally are open from Thursday to Saturday during off-season but every night during high season. Things get cranking around 10pm. The perennial top discos are **Coco Loco** (Av. Colombia, tel. 8/513-1047), **Extasis** (Hotel Sol Caribe, Ave. Colón No. 2-77, tel. 8/512-3043), and **Blue Deep** (Sunrise Hotel).

A relaxing alternative to the club scene is stargazing with beer in hand at **Bar de Kela** (San Luis, no phone, 3pm-midnight daily), a rustic but charming bar that plays reggae, in front of the San Luis Village hotel.

SHOPPING

Ask any Colombian about San Andrés and they will tell you that one of the top things to do here is to go shopping for cheap and duty-free goods. (In fact, Bogotá's shopping district known for its affordable wares, San Andresito, is named in honor of the island.) There are numerous duty-free shops in the Centro, where deals can be had on booze, perfume, watches, and the like. **La Riviera** is the best known of these. It has multiple locations close to the Spratt Bight walkway.

Casa BazArte (San Luis, cell tel. 317/375-4779, 9am-6pm daily) has local handicrafts like papier-mâché (a typical island handicraft), paintings, and wallets made of coconut fiber, among more common Colombian wares. Luly, the owner, can hook you up with local artisans if you're interested. The shop is located in a protected heritage house that's over 90 years old; its cheerful paint job makes it hard to miss.

RECREATION
★ Snorkeling and Diving

San Andrés is surrounded by a well-preserved coral reef teeming with marine life that makes it a diver's and snorkeler's paradise. On the eastern edge is the windward barrier, 15 kilometers (9.3 miles) long and 60-80 meters (200-260 feet) wide, with significant live coral communities. Beyond the reef, the shelf ends abruptly with a vertical wall that drops hundreds of meters. To the west, the windward barrier protects a large marine lagoon that has sea grass cover. The reef on the western, leeward side is a bit less well preserved due to tourism and boat traffic, but it also has beautiful patches of coral and significant marine life. In all, the waters surrounding San Andrés include more than 40 species of corals and 131 species of fish. It is common to see large schools of brightly colored jacks, tangs, grunts, and snapper, as well as barracudas, groupers, and parrot fish. Other marine creatures include turtles, stingrays, moray eels, octopus, squid, and lobster.

A unique feature of San Andrés is that the dives are very close to shore, which means a 10- to 30-minute boat ride maximum. The water is warm and has excellent visibility year-round. The best conditions for diving occur January to May, with stronger winds in June and July. Popular dive sites are The Pyramids, a shallow 4-meter (13-foot) dive with striking anemones and fish; Nirvana, a reef at about 15

divers near San Andrés

318/863-9352, www.karibikdiver.com, two dives COP$170,000), which prides itself on its dive safety. **Sharky Surf Shop** (Sunset Hotel, Km. 13 Carretera Circunvalar, tel. 8/512-0651, www.sharkydiveshop.com) is another reputable agency, whose offerings include a four- to five-day open-water course (COP$800,000) and a mini-course for beginners (COP$140,000). Night diving trips can be arranged by most dive shops for experienced divers.

Other Water Sports

Samuel Raigosa, better known as Chamey, is the kitesurfing guru of San Andrés, and the staff at **Chamey's Náutica** (Km. 4 Vía San Luis, tel. 8/513-2077, cell tel. 317/752-4965) are experts on kitesurfing. A one-hour class costs COP$70,000.

Supported by environmental agencies, **Ecofiwi Turismo Ecológico** (Vía San Luis, Mango Tree sector, cell tel. 316/567-4988 or 316/624-3396, www.sanandresecotourism. com, ecofiwi@gmail.com, 9am-4pm daily, COP$70,000 pp) offers two-hour **kayak tours** of the mangroves in the Old Point Regional Mangrove Park led by local guides. The kayaks are completely transparent, providing kayakers with up-close views of sealife such as upside-down jellyfish, sea cucumbers, sea grass beds, and also birds such as frigate birds, pelicans, herons, and migratory birds. Snorkeling is also part of the tour (equipment included).

Beaches

Some of the best beaches on the island include **Spratt Bight,** near the Centro in front of the pedestrian walkway; **San Luis,** near Chammey Marina; **Cocoplum; Bahía Sonora** (near Rocky Cay) beaches; and the **Parque Regional Johnny Cay.** Out of all of these, the beaches on Johnny Cay, the island off Spratt Bight, are some of the most popular. During peak tourist seasons, on weekends, and on holidays, they get very crowded.

To get to Johnny Cay, you must take a *lancha* (boat) from Spratt Bight on a quick

meters (50 feet) that is teeming with marine life; Trampa Tortuga, a reef at about 15 meters (50 feet) with great visibility; and Blue Wall, on the eastern edge of the windward barrier, which starts at 6 meters (20 feet) and drops to 60 meters (200 feet). It contains magnificent corals and large tube sponges.

Most dive operators also offer short (three hours) introductory courses for beginners, costing around COP$155,000 per person, which allow you to do an easy dive without being certified. There are also many opportunities to do full introductory and advanced courses with certification. A three-day open-water certification course typically costs around COP$800,000.

Highly recommended diving operators on San Andrés include **Banda** (Hotel Lord Pierre, tel. 8/513-1080, www.bandadiveshop. com, two dives COP$185,000, open-water course COP$900,000), where the friendly owner Gloria will help with everything, and German-run **Karibik** (Av. Newball 1-248, Edificio Galeón, tel. 8/512-0101 or cell tel.

15-minute ride. There are always boats (owned by individuals, not organized tour companies) at the ready at Spratt Bight. To arrange a trip, your negotiating skills will be put to the test. Hiring an individual boat can cost up to COP$200,000. The inexpensive option is to take a day tour (COP$20,000). These leave from Spratt Bight by 9:30am every day of the year, returning at around 4pm. In the late afternoon, Johnny Cay clears out, but you can stay until almost 6pm when the last boats leave. It's nice to be one of the last visitors on the island as the sun begins its descent. There are no accommodations options on the island, but there are *coco loco* stands aplenty and some restaurants serving the usual fried fish fare. While there, take a walk around the entire island, where flocks of birds are likely the only company you'll have. It takes about 15 minutes.

On the eastern side of San Andrés, the beaches at **San Luis** and **Rocky Cay** have easy access and great food options. It's possible to wade through the shallow waters to Rocky Cay.

Tours

A popular activity in San Andrés is to take a day tour of some swimming spots just off of the mainland. A standard day tour costs COP$20,000 and leaves at around 9am daily (with return trips departing at 1:30pm and 3:30pm). Tours include a 1.5-hour stop at **El Acuario/La Piscina/Haynes Cay,** where you can wade and swim in waters described as "seven shades of blue." Here, a common attraction is swimming with manta rays, though it's best to avoid participating. On busy days, the rays are handled constantly, being lifted out of the water for snapshots with smiling tourists. They are fed a steady diet of white sandwich bread. The rest of the day is spent on **Johnny Cay,** where you can buy lunch and drinks, and rent snorkeling equipment. There is no need for a guide here, so resist offers to pay for one. **Coonative Brothers** (Spratt Bight Beach, tel. 8/512-3522) offers these tours, as do many of the larger hotels.

Local boaters affiliated with Coonative Brothers also offer day tours with more stops, including a visit to the **San Andrés mangroves** for COP$60,000 per person. There is a minimum of 10 passengers for these tours. Private tours can cost up to COP$200,000, depending on your negotiating skills. Inquire at the Coonative Brothers' beach kiosk.

Parque Regional Johnny Cay

Sustainable Seafood

To protect their sustainability, some seafood should be avoided during certain times of the year, and some should be avoided completely.

Langosta (lobster), *pargo* (snapper), and *caracol pala* (conch) are the three most fished species around San Andrés and Providencia, and are very often found on restaurant menus. It is recommended to avoid ordering conch from June to October (but due to overfishing it's wise to avoid conch entirely), lobster from April until June, and *cangrejo negro* (black crab) from April to July.

Other threatened species include Atlantic bluefin tuna, tarpon, Lebranche mullet, *robalo blanco* (white sea bass), *mero guasa* (goliath grouper), *cherna* (Nassau grouper), and the masked hamlet, which is only found in the waters off Providencia.

To swim with sharks and manta rays in unbelievable crystalline waters, you can take a day tour to the exotic **Cayo Bolívar** (COP$170,000) that's about an hour by boat from San Andrés. The tours leaves at 8am and returns at 5pm. Lunch and drinks are provided. Coonative Brothers also organizes this trip, which, due to the relatively steep cost, attracts fewer customers.

Another option to get out on the water is to take a glass-bottom boat tour with **San Andrés Unlimited** (Tom Hooker Rd. No. 8-75, South End, tel. 8/513-0035 or 8/513-0129, cell tel. 316/889-8701 or 310/625-2938, www.sanandresultd.com). During this tour, the boat makes several stops at coral reefs, sunken ships, and exotic islands. You'll be able to get in the water and snorkel several times to observe sealife. The nearly two-hour tour costs around COP$45,000 per person.

FOOD

Seafood is on every menu in every restaurant in San Andrés. Fish, lobster, crab, and conch are likely to come from the waters off of San Andrés and Providencia. However, *langostinos* (prawns) and *camarones* (shrimp) often come from either the Pacific or from the Cartagena area on the mainland. A Caribbean specialty you'll likely find only on San Andrés, Providencia, and Jamaica is *rondón* (rundown). It is a filling stew that has fish or conch, pig's tail, dumplings, yucca, and other ingredients slow-cooked in coconut milk. All restaurants are beach casual, and most of the larger ones accept credit cards. Service is often laid-back. On Sundays, local women sell food, like fried fish cakes, on the beach in San Luis.

Seafood

North of downtown, the blue-collar **Fisherman's Place** (Cra. 9 No. 1-10 Spratt Bight, tel. 8/512-2774, noon-4pm daily, COP$20,000) is a restaurant run by a cooperative of local fishers. Overlooking the water, it's also close to the airport runway. Try the *rondón* or the lobster.

Ask anyone in town to recommend the best seafood place on the island and a solid majority will mention ★ **La Regatta** (tel. 8/512-0437, www.restaurantelaregatta.com, noon-11pm daily, COP$40,000), next to the Club Náutico. It is open-air and juts out onto the water. For a sampling of the finest of San Andrés seafood, try their Fiesta Náutica, which includes lobster tails, prawns, and crab, or go for the *tesoros del mar*, a filling seafood stew. The restaurant is festively decorated. Reservations are a good idea.

Just far enough from the Centro for a little peace and quiet, **Niko's Seafood Restaurant** (Av. Colombia No. 1-93, tel. 8/512-7535, 11am-11pm daily, COP$30,000) is what a family-run seafood place should be: over the water, not fancy-schmancy, and no lounge music. The house specialties are lobster and coconut lemonade.

The Grog (Rocky Cay, Cocoplum Hotel, tel. 8/513-3244 or cell tel. 311/232-3247, 10am-6pm Wed.-Sun., COP$25,000) is everything you'd expect in a Caribbean seafood restaurant. In an idyllic location on the beach and steps from the water, this is a great spot for a grilled fish lunch on a lazy afternoon.

Although the namesake for **Miss Celia** (Av. Newball and Av. Raizal, tel. 8/513-1062 or 8/512-6495, restaurantemisscelia@gmail.com, noon-10pm daily, COP$30,000) passed away not too long ago, the restaurant continues on in this colorful spot. Located in front of the Club Náutico, Miss Celia is surrounded by flower gardens, and the sounds of local music add to the atmosphere. The restaurant recommends only ordering *rondón* (seafood, pig tail, and yam stew) at lunchtime, as it's a heavy dish. There are also various rice dishes, some with shrimp, some vegetarian; for dessert there's homemade ice cream.

From its simple beachside *cabañas*, it might surprise you that ★ **Donde Francesca** (El Pirata Beach, San Luis, tel. 8/513-0163, cell tel. 318/616-8547, restaurantedondefrancesca@gmail.com, 10am-6pm daily, COP$35,000) serves gourmet food. The varied menu includes *langosta tempura* (tempura lobster, COP$50,000) and *pulpo reducción al balsámico* (balsamic octopus, COP$34,000). The drinks are good, too, like gin cocktails and margaritas, all made from non-bottled ingredients. This may explain why folks arrive for lunch at 11am and don't leave until sundown.

In-the-know locals make a weekly visit to ★ **Restaurante Lidia** (Ground Rd. No. 64-65, San Luis, tel. 8/513-2192) a ritual. It's only open on Sundays and on holiday Mondays. This place gets great reviews from local foodies. Lidia's crab empanadas are recommended.

The **Restaurante Punta Sur** (Km. 15.8, South End, tel. 8/513-0003, cell tel. 312/449-0301, 10am-6pm daily, COP$30,000) is close to the Hoyo Soplador. Sitting on the terrace when the waves come crashing in, it feels like you might be taken out to sea. Bring a bathing suit and chill out in their small pool overlooking the sea. *Arroz con camarones* (rice with shrimp) and grilled lobster are the most popular menu items at this well-liked spot on the southern tip of the island.

International

Mr. Panino (Edificio Bread Fruit Local 106-7, tel. 8/512-3481 or 8/512-0549, 10:30am-10pm Mon.-Sat., 11am-4pm Sun., COP$30,000) is a reliable, somewhat upscale Italian restaurant, popular at both lunch and dinner, but more pleasant in the evening. There is typically a set lunch menu of Colombian fare. It's nice to sit on the high wooden tables in the back. Try their *risotto con langostinos,* a prawn risotto that's a generous plate to share. Service can be chilly.

★ **Gourmet Shop** (Av. Newball in front of Parque de la Barracuda, tel. 8/512-9843, cell tel. 315/770-0140, noon-11pm Mon.-Sat., 6pm-11pm Sun., COP$30,000) is an excellent choice for a break from seafood. The salads, pasta, and other dishes are good, and on every table there is a big bottle of imported spicy chili sauce. With gourmet food items and wine for sale along the walls, and thousands of empty wine bottles decorating the ceiling, it's a cozy place. For something quick, like a slice of pizza, you can try the hole-in-the-wall **Gourmet Shop To Go** (Av. Newball in front of Parque de la Barracuda, tel. 8/512-9843, 11am-3pm daily, COP$15,000) around the corner in the same building.

Margherita e Carbonara (Av. Colombia No. 1-93, tel. 8/512-1050, 11am-11pm daily, COP$30,000) gets packed at night during high season due to its prized location near the big hotels and nightclubs. Stick with the pasta and pizza at this boisterous family-style place.

It's a rarity to find vegetarian options in San Andrés, but **New Dawn Paradise** (Vía Tom Hooker No. 1-107, tel. 8/513-0015, cell tel. 314/444-9418, 11am-3pm Sun.-Fri., COP$15,000) delivers. This simple restaurant is in the modest home of super-friendly Enaida Veloza, who serves vegetarian hamburgers, salads, and the like, as well as baked goods. Many of the vegetables come from her prosperous organic garden.

Cafés, Bakeries, and Quick Bites

Part of the Casablanca Hotel, the groovy

turquoise **Sea Watch Caffé** (Av. Colombia, 7am-11pm daily, COP$18,000) is as close as it comes in Colombia to a New York-style coffee shop. Here you can have a leisurely breakfast as you watch the tourists file by on the walkway out front. They also offer pizza, hamburgers, ceviche, pasta, and desserts.

From the outside, ★ **Coffee Break** (Av. Colombia No. 3-59, in front of Parque de la Barracuda, tel. 8/512-1275, www.coffeebreak. com.co, 7am-11pm daily) often appears empty or even closed. But when you go inside, it's almost always packed with visitors and locals alike sipping on Vietnamese coffee, munching on nachos, or smearing cream cheese on their toasted bagels. Customers here take their time (likely because of the air-conditioning).

A bakery/café popular with locals and visitors alike is **Bread Fruit** (Av. Francisco Newball No. 4-169, outside the Sunrise Hotel, tel. 8/512-6044, 7:30am-8:30pm Mon.-Sat.), named after the breadfruit tree, which is typical to the area. This solid breakfast spot offers outdoor seating and table service.

Miss Carmen is a familiar face on the Spratt Bight walkway, where she has been selling her homemade empanadas, ceviche, and cakes for years. Her stand doesn't really have a name, but you can call it **La Mesa Grande de Carmen** (Av. Colombia pathway).

ACCOMMODATIONS

On this island where tourism is king, lodging options are plentiful, except during high season (mid-December to mid-January, Holy Week, and, to a lesser extent, during school vacations from June to July). Top-end hotels and low-end hostels are not as common as mid- to upper-range all-inclusive hotels.

Most visitors stay on or near the beach on the eastern side of the island, including in quiet San Luis. From here, you can hop on public transportation or hail a cab if you want to go to town, or rent a motorbike, golf cart, jeep (*mulita*), or bicycle. The busy downtown (Centro) of San Andrés can feel claustrophobic, but you'll always be within walking distance of restaurants and services, and

you can often find some good deals in this area. Waterfront hotels here have pools, not beaches. Stay in the north beyond the airport if you prefer more seclusion but still want to be close to the action in the city center.

The western side of the island has coral coastline instead of beaches, and the few hotels cater mostly to divers, so this side feels more isolated.

In the interior of the island are numerous *posadas nativas* (native guesthouses), owned and operated by locals, many of whom have deep roots on the island. Staying at a *posada nativa* is the best way to get to know the local culture. Don't expect fancy amenities.

Renting an apartment offers advantages for those looking for more space, privacy, or the use of a kitchen. **Sol & Mar** (tel. 8/512-5834 or cell tel. 317/665-0273, www.solymarislas. com, two-bedroom apartment COP$450,000 per night) has several fully furnished two- and three-bedroom options, including in quiet Sarie Bay, near the airport. Some of the apartments are in large complexes with access to a swimming pool.

Centro

The Colombian all-inclusive chain Decameron has several properties on the island. Decameron offers optional transportation to the island. Guests can dine at other Decameron locations on the island, but may have to make reservations in advance, which can be a hassle. Wi-Fi is available at an additional cost. The newest, largest, and arguably best Decameron property is the **Royal Decameron Isleño** (Av. Colón Cl. 3 No. 6-106, tel. 8/513-4343, www.decameron.co, COP$660,000 d), with a fantastic location on a quiet stretch along Spratt Bight. During high season, it gets crowded here, but during the off-season, you may just have the facilities, with open-air dining and a pool, practically to yourself.

Decameron Los Delfines (Av. Colombia No. 1B-86, tel. 8/512-7816 or Bogotá tel. 1/628-0000, www.decameron.co, COP$600,000 d), located in town and on the water, is a hotel geared toward couples. It has 39 comfortable rooms and a pool. This is the "boutique" Decameron hotel, but that may be a generous description of this property.

Although it may look retro, blindingly white **Hotel Casablanca** (Av. Colombia No. 3-59, tel. 8/512-4115, www.hotelcasablancacasanandres.com, COP$480,000 d) is a large hotel facing the Spratt Bight Parkway. Of the 91 rooms it offers, 10 are *cabañas*. There is a small pool and, more importantly, a pool bar, Coco's. The hotel has three on-site restaurants. Casablanca gets mixed reviews, but is one of the better options along Spratt Bight.

In the North End, boutique hotel ★ **Casa Harb** (Cl. 11 No. 10-83, tel. 8/512-6348, www.casaharb.com, COP$880,000 d) is by far the most luxurious place to stay in San Andrés. The six suites, lobby, dining area, and spa are thoughtfully decorated with fantastic art and furniture from Morocco to Malaysia, personally chosen by owner Jak Harb. The fabulous on-site restaurant is open to the public (but call first).

On an unassuming street in a quiet neighborhood two blocks from the beach, ★ **Hostal Mar y Mar** (Av. Colombia No. 1-32, Sarie Bay, cell tel. 317/783-6420, www.hostalmarymar.com, COP$190,000 d) offers 10 clean and comfortable rooms. Noise from airplanes may be a nuisance in the mornings for some.

The small hotels in the busy downtown are far more reasonably priced than those with a view to the sea and are just a few blocks away. The most popular choice for backpackers is the five-floor **El Viajero** (Av. 20 de Julio No. 3A-122, tel. 8/512-7497, www.elviajerohostels.com, COP$60,000 dorm, COP$250,000 d), which is part of an Uruguayan chain. It has several air-conditioned gender-separated dorms, as well as private rooms. The top-floor bar serves cold beer and assorted rum drinks, and there are several common areas with wireless Internet and computers. A small breakfast is included, and a kitchen

is provided for guest use. Staff aren't overly friendly, but they can arrange excursions.

It's surprising just how peaceful the **Posada Mary May** (Av. 20 de Julio No. 3-74, tel. 8/512-5669, COP$60,000-110,000 d) is. Every morning you can pick up a cup of coffee in the lovely courtyard that is shaded by a huge avocado tree. On the downside, beds (usually three per room) are on the soft side in the spacious rooms, wireless Internet is sporadic, and in general the place could use an update. Around the corner, **Cli's Place** (Av. 20 de Julio No. 3-47, tel. 8/512-0591, luciamhj@hotmail.com, COP$160,000 d), owned by Cleotilde Henry, has four double rooms in the main house as well as a *cabaña* that accommodates seven people. You will feel at home here.

San Luis

Brightly colored **Cocoplum Hotel** (Vía San Luis No. 43-49, tel. 8/513-2121, www.cocoplumhotel.com, COP$350,000 d) in the San Luis area has the most important feature for a beach hotel: It's actually on the beach, with rooms that are steps from the water. The rooms are generally fine, the food is OK, and service can be chilly.

★ **Ground Road Native Place** (Circunvalar No. 54-88, before the health clinic, tel. 8/513-3887 or cell tel. 313/776-6036, edupeterson1@hotmail.com, COP$50,000 pp) is a comfortable *posada nativa* with five spacious rooms and some large apartments, with air-conditioning and wireless Internet. The *posada* is in the home of friendly Edula and George Peterson and is just a three-minute walk to the beach. The neighborhood is not close to many tourist amenities, but there are always public buses on the main road out front.

Tucked away on a quiet lane is ★ **Villa Verde** (Vía Tom Hooker 1A-24, cell tel. 315/770-0785, temporadasanandres@yahoo.es), a charming guesthouse that offers rooms in the owner's home, an inviting pool surrounded by trees, and camping on the lush grass.

About five minutes to the beach, **Posada Buganvilla** (Vía Tom Hooker No. 3-41, cell tel. 315/303-5474 or 317/804-1952, posadabu-ganvilla@gmail.com, COP$170,000 d) is a cheerfully colored house in a quiet location, with four air-conditioned rooms, tile floors, and shared bathrooms. The guesthouse offers bikes for rent.

La Loma

This neighborhood, home to the island's highest point—hence the name La Loma (The Hill)—is situated in the interior of the island and is almost completely inhabited by English-speaking native islanders, some of whom run *posadas nativas*. A fine option is ★ **Coconut Paradise Lodge** (Vía La Loma, Claymount No. 50-05, tel. 8/513-2926 or cell tel. 301/543-2344, oldm26@hotmail.com, COP$55,000 pp with breakfast), a beautiful turn-of-the-20th-century wooden home with just four rooms. It's close to the botanical gardens and the San Luis beaches. Try for the top-floor room, which has great views and a refreshing breeze. Across the street is **Caribbean Refuge** (Vía La Loma, tel. 8/523-2878 or cell tel. 313/823-3587, COP$50,000 pp) run by Clemencia Livingston. It's a spotless, modern house (though lacking in charm), and Clemencia is a very gracious host.

West

For those interested in diving, ★ **Sunset Hotel** (Km. 13 Circunvalar, cell tel. 318/523-2286, www.sunsethotelspa.com, COP$300,000 d), on the quiet west side of the island, is a great option. It has 16 bright and basic rooms that surround a small pool. While there is no beach, the hotel's dive shop, Sharky's, offers diving lessons and organizes diving excursions. You can go snorkeling in the waters across the street. Weeklong diving packages are a good option. Great sunsets are included at no extra cost. You can also rent bikes here.

INFORMATION AND SERVICES

A **tourist office** (Av. Newball, tel. 8/513-0801, 8am-noon and 2pm-6pm daily) is located between downtown and San Luis, across from Club Náutico. Tourism bureau staff are on hand at a **tourist information kiosk** (intersection of Av. Colombia and Av. 20 de Julio, 8am-7pm daily).

There is a small branch of **Universidad Nacional** (National University, San Luis, tel. 8/513-3310 or 8/513-3311, 8am-noon and 2pm-6pm Mon.-Fri.) here, where the library is open to the public. Anyone is welcome to work or read there.

TRANSPORTATION

San Andrés's **Aeropuerto Gustavo Rojas Pinillas** (ADZ) is very close to many hotels. Cabs to the airport cost COP$10,000. San Andrés is served by all the major Colombian airlines, with most options from Bogotá and Medellín. There are nonstop flights from Cartagena on **VivaColombia** (www.vivacolombia.co) and **Copa** (www.copaair.com); Copa also offers a nonstop flight from Barranquilla. **Air Transat** (www.airtransat.com) operates charter flights between Canada and San Andrés on a seasonal basis.

Public buses serve the entire island; rides cost about COP$2,000 each way. To get to San Luis, flag down a bus from the Parque de la Barracuda just south of the Centro.

Renting a car is possible, but parking is scarce, distances are not far, and, more importantly, there are more fun options than driving a car. Most visitors rent heavy-duty, gas-powered golf carts referred to as *mulas* (literally, mules). **Millennium Rent A Car** (Av. Newball, Parque de la Barracuda, tel. 8/512-3114, 10am-6pm daily) rents standard golf carts (COP$70,000 day) and *mulas* (COP$150,000 day). **Rent A Car Esmeralda** (Av. Colombia, in front of Buxo del Caribe, tel. 8/513-1170 or cell tel. 315/303-7037, 10am-6pm daily) offers similar prices. Although you can rent both golf carts and *mulas* for multiple days, their use is prohibited after 6pm.

Rent a bike at **Bicycle Rental Shop** (Cra. 1B, Sector Punta Hansa, in front of Edificio Hansa Reef, cell tel. 318/328-1790 or 321/242-9328, 8am-6pm daily, COP$45,000/day).

Providencia and Santa Catalina

Secluded palm-lined beaches, gorgeous turquoise Caribbean waters, mellow locals, fresh seafood, and rum drinks make it easy to become smitten with Providencia.

Located about 90 kilometers (56 miles) north of San Andrés, these islands are the easygoing cousins of that hyperactive island. Of volcanic origin, Providencia and Santa Catalina are older islands than San Andrés, and are smaller in area and population than it, having a total area of about 18 square kilometers (7 square miles) and a population of only 5,000. Only 300 people live on minuscule Santa Catalina, an island known as the "Island of Treasures" and which was once home to an English fort.

Orientation

The two islands of Providencia and Santa Catalina combined are about seven kilometers long and four kilometers wide (4 miles by 2.5 miles). A ring road encircles the entire island of Providencia. The harbor/downtown area of Providencia is called **Santa Isabel** and is the center of island activity. Adjacent to this is **Santa Catalina.**

Other settlements on the island are usually referred to by the names of their beaches or bays. The main ones are on the western side of the island: **Manchineel Bay (Bahía Manzanillo),** on the southern end, which has some excellent beaches; **Southwest Bay (Bahía Suroeste);** and **Freshwater Bay (Bahía Aguadulce),** home to most of the island's hotels and restaurants. **Smoothwater Bay (Bahía Aguamansa),** on the southeastern edge of the island, is more remote. Smoothwater is adjacent to **Bottom House (Casa Baja),** which is more residential. **Maracaibo** is on the northeast part of the island, between Santa Isabel and the airport. In the middle of the island is its highest point, **The Peak.**

★ PARQUE NACIONAL NATURAL OLD PROVIDENCE MCBEAN LAGOON

The **Parque Nacional Natural Old Providence McBean Lagoon** (office Jones Point, east of airport, tel. 8/514-8885 or 8/514-9003, www.parquesnacionales.gov.co, oldprovidence@parquesnacionales.gov.co, 9am-5pm daily, COP$14,000 non-Colombians, COP$8,500 Colombians, COP$4,000 students) is a small national park on the northeast coast of the island. It occupies about 1,485 hectares/3,670 acres (1,390 hectares/3,435 acres of that is in the sea). Here you can observe five different ecosystems: coral reefs, sea grass beds, mangroves, dry tropical forests, and volcanic keys.

Crab Cay (Cayo Cangrejo) is one of the main attractions of the park, and it's a convenient spot for some splashing about in the incredibly clear, warm waters. This is a great place for some easy snorkeling, and, in addition to tropical fish, you may see manta rays or sea turtles. A short five-minute nature path takes you to the top of the island. A snack bar on Crab Cay sells water and snacks like ceviche. It is open every day until around 1pm.

Boat tours, organized by all hotels and dive shops, motor around the coast of Providencia, stopping at beaches and at Crab Cay for snorkeling or swimming. These tours depart the hotels at around 9am each morning and cost about COP$35,000 per person. Once you disembark at Crab Cay, you'll have to pay the park entry fee of COP$14,000. Following the stop at Crab Cay, the boats go to Southwest Bay for a seafood lunch, not included in the price of the tour.

Otherwise you can hire a boat for yourself at around COP$350,000 total. Upon arrival at the island, you'll be required to pay the park entry fee. All hotels can arrange this more exclusive option.

The park's **Iron Wood Hill Trail** is a three-kilometer (1.8-mile) round-trip nature trail along which you can explore the tropical dry forest landscape, and will see different types of lizards, birds, and flora. There are nice views from here of the coastline. This path is less popular than the hike to The Peak, but many find it more beautiful. Tourists are encouraged to go with a local guide arranged by the **park's office** (Jones Point, east of airport, tel. 8/514-8885, 8/514-9003, www.parquesnacionales.gov.co, 8am-12:30pm and 2pm-6pm daily, COP$25,000 pp plus park entry fee). But the trail is straightforward, and most visitors simply head off on their own. Be sure to pay the park entry fee before leaving.

An additional activity is to hire a **kayak** and paddle to Crab Cay or through the park's McBean Lagoon mangroves. Passing through the mangroves you'll enter the **Oyster's Creek Lagoon,** where you'll see several species of birds, like blue and white herons and pelicans, as well as crabs, fish, and some unusual jellyfish. This is an interesting trip. Try to go early in the morning or late in the afternoon, as the sun can be brutal. Kayaks can be rented at the **Posada Coco Bay** (Maracaibo sector on the northeastern side of the island, tel. 8/514-8226, cell tel. 311/804-0373, www.posadacocobay.com, COP$30,000). A kayak with a guide costs COP$50,000, and for snorkeling equipment tack on another COP$10,000.

LIGHTHOUSE PROVIDENCIA

Lighthouse Providencia (Hoy's Hill, cell tel. 313/380-5866 or 318/758-1804, www.lighthouseprovidencia.com, 5pm-9pm Mon.-Sat.) is a cultural center/café that's worth a stop. They host a range of cultural activities, including art exhibitions and film showings, all with an environmental bent, including a film on the famous black crab migration that brings the island to a virtual standstill.

ENTERTAINMENT AND EVENTS
Nightlife

Bob Marley never seems to fall out of fashion at **Roland Roots Bar** (Manchineel Bay, tel. 8/514-8417, hours vary). This spot beneath the coconut palms is the perfect place to spend a lazy, sunny day in Providencia. Or go at night, when you can order your rum drink to go and walk to the beach and stargaze, or hang out by a bonfire. On Sunday afternoons, it's a popular spot for locals. Roland's competition is

kayaking through Parque Nacional Natural Old Providence McBean Lagoon

Richard's Place on the beach in Southwest Bay. You can broaden your Caribbean music horizons here with reggae roots, rocksteady, ska calypso, ragamuffin, and soca dub—but more often than not, it's Marley on the sound system. Both bars serve fried fish during the day.

Festivals and Events

In early January of each year (usually a Saturday), the Parque Nacional Natural Old Providence McBean Lagoon organizes the colorful **Festival del Chub** (tel. 8/514-8885 or 8/514-9003, Jan.). Chub is a plentiful but not very popular fish (it can have a strong aroma). The purpose of the festival is to encourage fishers and consumers to choose chub instead of other fish like red snapper, the stocks of which have been depleted throughout the Caribbean. The festival is held at Rocky Point (Punta Rocosa), where chub is widely eaten. In addition to serving dishes like chub burgers and chub ceviche, there is also a sailing race from Southwest Bay to Manzanillo. It's fun to hang out at **Roland Roots Bar** (Manchineel Bay, tel. 8/514-8417) in the morning to watch the sailors ready their boats for the race.

Between April and August each year is when the **black crab migration** takes place. This species of crab lives in the mountainous interior of the island for most of the year, but as the rainy season begins (usually April or May), thousands of the female crabs, carrying up to 120,000 eggs each, make an arduous journey to the sea to deposit their eggs. The migration peaks during nighttime hours, so watch your step. More crabs can be seen on the western side of the island. A second migration occurs a few weeks later, when the young crabs make their trip from the sea up to the mountain. During both migrations, the main road on the island may be closed—enforced by military personnel—as a means of protecting the crabs from vehicles.

SHOPPING

Kalaloo Point Café-Boutique (near Halley View lookout, eastern side of the island, tel. 8/514-8592 or cell tel. 317/387-6448, 10am-8pm Mon.-Sat.) is a cute shop and café in a wooden house that sells tropical dresses by a Colombian designer and various knick-knacks. There's also a small library.

RECREATION
★ Beaches

The best beaches on Providencia can be found generally on the western side of the island. From Manchineel Bay (Bahía Manzanillo) on the southern end to Allan or Almond Bay in the northwest, they are each worth exploring, if you have the time. On these beaches, the waters are calm, the sand golden, and there's always a refreshing breeze.

Manchineel Bay (Bahía Manzanillo), home to Roland Roots Bar, is an exotic beach where you can relax under the shade of a palm tree. (Be careful of falling coconuts.) In **Southwest Bay (Bahía Suroeste),** there are a couple of hotels and restaurants nearby, and you can sometimes see horses cooling off in the water or people riding them along the shoreline. The beaches of **Freshwater Bay** are very convenient to several hotels and restaurants.

The beach at **Allan Bay** (or **Almond Bay**) is more remote. It's notable for its large octopus sculpture on the side of the road (can't miss it) and nicely done walkway down to the beach from the ring road. The beach area is a public park, and there is a snack bar and stand where you can purchase handicrafts. You'll have to either drive to this beach or hitch a ride from a taxi.

A couple of coves on Santa Catalina have some secluded beaches on the path to Morgan's Head, and they offer snorkeling opportunities as well.

Snorkeling and Diving

Providencia, which is surrounded by a 32-kilometer-long (20-mile-long) barrier reef, is a fantastic place to dive or to learn to dive. The water temperature is always warm, and water visibility is usually 25-35 meters (82-115 feet). The best time of year to dive is between June and October. In January, the water can be particularly rough.

Popular diving sites are **Felipe's Place,** made up of several ledges with significant coral and marine life; **Turtle Rock,** a large rock at 20 meters (66 feet) covered with black coral; **Tete's Place,** teeming with fish; **Confusion,** with corals and sponges at 20-40 meters (66-131 feet); and **Nick's Place,** a deep crack in the island's shelf that starts at 18 meters (60 feet) and drops to 40 meters (131 feet). Good snorkeling can be done near **Cayo Cangrejo,** at the small islands of **Basalt** and **Palm Cays,** and around **Morgan's Head** in Santa Catalina, among other places.

The **Hotel Sirius** (Southwest Bay, tel. 8/514-8213, www.siriushotel.net) is serious about diving and offers a PADI certification (COP$850,000) that includes four immersions over open water during a period of five days. They also offer a mini-course (COP$185,000), which includes a double-immersion excursion. Hotel Sirius's diving courses have an excellent reputation.

Felipe Diving (Freshwater Bay, cell tel. 316/628-6664 or 317/805-8684, www.felipediving.com) is also highly recommended. They offer an open-water course (COP$800,000) and rent out snorkeling equipment as well.

Kayaking

For kayak rentals and mangrove tours, contact guide **Israel Livingston Archbold** (cell tel. 318/587-7898). A two-hour tour for two people costs COP$130,000. Israel's tours depart from Posada Coco Bay in Maracaibo.

Hiking
★ THE PEAK

The Peak (El Pico) is the highest point (360 meters/1,181 feet) on Providencia, and from this mountaintop the 360-degree views are impressive. This hike takes about 1.5 hours to the top and less than an hour down. The path to The Peak begins in the middle of the island and meanders along relatively well-marked trails through tropical rainforest and tropical dry forest. You'll likely come across lizards, cotton trees, and maybe a friendly dog who will follow you up to the top and back.

From the top you'll be able to see the barrier reef that extends for 32 kilometers (20 miles) off of the east coast of the island. This reef is the second longest in the Caribbean and is part of the Parque Nacional Natural Old Providence McBean Lagoon.

horses cooling off at Southwest Bay

To get to the starting point, go to the Bottom House (Casa Baja) neighborhood in the southeastern corner of the island just to the east of Manchineel Bay. Although you may come across a sign pointing towards The Peak, roads are not well marked. Ask at your hotel for directions to the starting point.

At the beginning of the walk, follow a path straight ahead, veering towards the right, and five minutes later go towards the right before a two-story house. You'll then go left (not to the right of the concrete well). From here on, you will pass a small garden, then follow a rocky creek straight on, fording it back and forth several times. You'll go through a gate and eventually veer to the left as you begin climbing up the hill. After you cross over a wooden bridge the path becomes steep; hold on to the wooden handrails. Occasional signs identify some of the trees or fauna you might see along the way.

During rainy seasons, the path can become muddy and slippery. Make sure to bring a bottle of water with you. Guides are not necessary for this walk, but it's not impossible to get lost. All hotels can contract a guide for you, and this usually costs around COP$50,000.

Be careful of thorny cockspur trees along the route, which also harbor ferocious ants.

SANTA CATALINA

From atop Santa Catalina island, English colonists and privateers once ruled, keeping their eyes peeled for potential enemies—usually the Spanish Armada or competing Dutch pirates. Today you can see some remains from 17th-century English rule at **Fort Warwick.** It is adjacent to a big rock called **Morgan's Head.** If you squint hard enough, it resembles the head of Henry Morgan, the notorious Welsh pirate and admiral of the Royal Navy who marauded the Spanish New World colonies during the mid-17th century; Morgan captured Santa Catalina from the Spaniards in 1670. Morgan's Head is next to **Morgan's Cave,** where the pirate supposedly hid his loot. You can go snorkeling inside the cave, where you may encounter the occasional shark. Start this hike at the colorful pedestrian bridge that connects Providencia with Santa Catalina in the Santa Isabel area. When crossing the bridge, particularly in the evening, you may be able to spot graceful manta rays in the water. Once on Santa Catalina, take a left and follow the path.

Tours

Paradise Tours (Freshwater Bay, tel. 8/514-8283, cell tel. 311/605-0750, paradisetourscontact@gmail.com) is your one-stop shop, offering tours around the island and snorkeling, diving, and fishing excursions. One of their popular options is the Reefs and Snorkeling Tour (3-4 hours, min. 4 people, COP$85,000), during which you boat to coral reefs around the island, exploring the underwater cities that exist just below the surface. Snorkeling equipment on this tour is extra. A full-day trip to idyllic **El Faro Island** and reef, nine kilometers (5.6 miles) off of Providencia, costs COP$110,000. It's an excellent place for snorkeling in warm, crystalline waters.

On land, Paradise Tours offers several hiking options, such as to The Peak, where you can see coral reefs in the distance; to Manchineel Hill, where you might see wild orchids on your way; and to Iron Wood Hill in the Parque Nacional Natural Old Providence McBean Lagoon. These cost COP$85,000.

A popular excursion is to take a **boat tour** around the island. The tours, departing at around 9am and returning at 3pm, make several stops, including Crab Cay and Santa Catalina. Any hotel can assist you in arranging a tour; boats make the rounds to pick up tourists at various hotels. These tours cost around COP$35,000 per person and usually leave from Freshwater Bay. If you prefer, you can rent a boat for just yourself and your crew; that will cost up to COP$350,000.

Discover Old Providence (Bottom House, cell tel. 318/587-7898 or 316/761-5770, enjoyprovidence.pespo@gmail.com) offers fishing, hiking, and kayak tours in and around Providencia.

A recommended guide who can assist with

lunch with a view at Miss Mary Hotel

transportation on the island is **Bernardo "Big Boy" Henry** (cell tel. 313/811-0121 or 311/853-5166, bbernardhenry@gmail.com). It generally costs about COP$25,000 to get from one part of the island to the other.

FOOD

Providencia is synonymous with fresh Caribbean seafood. A particular specialty here is black crab. These fast-moving crabs live on the interior mountains and descend to the sea en masse once a year to lay their eggs in April or May.

Many restaurants in Providencia do not accept credit cards. Hotel restaurants are open every day, while others often close on Sundays.

Southwest Bay (Bahía Suroeste)

★ **Café Studio** (on ring road, tel. 8/514-9076, 11am-10pm Mon.-Sat., COP$25,000), on the side of the road near Southwest Bay, is a favorite among visitors—and not just because

of their trademark cappuccino pie. Everything is good here, it's open for both lunch and dinner, and it's the best spot for afternoon coffee and dessert. Café Studio has a varied menu with pastas, interesting seafood dishes, and salads. An awesome blues soundtrack plays in the background. It's run by a local and his Canadian wife.

The **Miss Mary Hotel** (tel. 8/514-8454, noon-3pm and 6pm-9pm daily, COP$20,000) has an open-air restaurant overlooking the beach. It's one of the most reliable spots for lunch. On the beach nearby is **Restaurante Arturo** (cell tel. 317/620-0814, 11am-5pm daily, COP$22,000) where the specialty is *rondón* (regional seafood stew). It's open-air and has a relaxed atmosphere.

Freshwater Bay (Bahía Aguadulce)

★ **Caribbean Place** (tel. 8/514-8698, noon-3pm and 6pm-10pm Mon.-Sat., COP$25,000) is one of the best seafood spots in Providencia. Try the fish in ginger-butter sauce or the coconut shrimp, and for dessert, the coconut pie. Cheerfully decorated, it's a great choice for both lunch and dinner.

For a pizza night, try **Blue Coral** (tel. 8/514-8718, 11am-3pm and 6pm-9pm Mon.-Sat., COP$20,000). Though not out of this world, the pizzas and pastas here can taste exotic after several days of seafood. Service is lackluster.

Morgan's Market (8am-noon and 3pm-8pm Mon.-Fri., 9am-noon and 4pm-8pm Sat.-Sun.) is one of the main grocery stores on the island. It's hard to miss, as it's a hub of activity. There's a sandwich and juice stand inside as well.

Santa Catalina and Santa Isabel

For an evening out in Santa Catalina, try ★ **Sea Star Gourmet** (Santa Catalina, cell tel. 316/824-0451, noon-4pm and 6:30pm-9pm Mon.-Fri., noon-4pm Sun., COP$25,000) an open-air restaurant with fine service where you can feast on fish fillets, lobster bathed in a coconut-ginger sauce, or *arroz con cangrejo* (crab stir-fry).

A quirky option is **Don Olivo** (Santa Catalina, cell tel. 310/230-5260), which is made up of a few small tables in front of a wooden house. Monsieur Olivier and his Colombian wife, Amparo, serve Caribbean dishes with a French flair. You have to ring the bell for service, and it's best to call first. Expect to be regaled by stories.

Old Providence Taste (Old Town Bay, to the west of Santa Isabel, tel. 8/514-9028, 11:30am-3pm Mon.-Sat., COP$18,000), on the beach to the west of Santa Isabel, is run by a local sustainable seafood and farming co-op. Each day they offer a different menu, depending on what fishers and farmers bring in. It's the best deal on the island. They can also organize visits to farms and excursions with local fishers.

Maracaibo

The ★ **Deep Blue Hotel Restaurant** (Maracaibo Bay, tel. 8/514-8423, noon-3pm and 6pm-10pm daily, COP$35,000) is the most elegant and pricey restaurant on the island. Menu items are innovative and beautifully presented, and the service is excellent. An impossibly beautiful setting under the stars makes this the perfect place for a special dinner.

ACCOMMODATIONS

Providencia and Santa Catalina offer an array of interesting and comfortable accommodations. Most options are in Freshwater Bay, but each area on this enchanting island has its charms. Note that Internet service is unreliable, and it's best to communicate with hotels via phone call or text message (rather than email) for reservations and inquiries.

Freshwater Bay (Bahía Aguadulce)

There are three affiliated locations of the all-inclusive Decameron chain in Freshwater Bay, but they are locally operated. The least expensive option is **Relax** (Freshwater Bay,

tel. 8/514-8087, COP$100,000 pp). It has a small pool, hot water, and eight rooms, and is near a couple of restaurants and stores. It is across the road from the beach. **Miss Elma** (Freshwater Bay, tel. 8/514-8229 or 8/514-8854, cell tel. 310/566-3773, COP$170,000 d) has just six rooms, all of which overlook the sea, and a restaurant on the beach. **Hotel Posada del Mar** (Freshwater Bay, tel. 8/514-8052, www. posadadelmarprovidencia.com, COP$220,000 pp d) is a 24-room hotel with air-conditioning and a pool. Instead of a beach, a grassy lawn overlooks the water.

Sol Caribe Solar (tel. 8/514-8230, www. solarhoteles.com, COP$175,000 pp) is a chain hotel with around 35 rooms and a pool, with breakfast and dinner buffets included in the cost. There are four rooms with high ceilings and balconies overlooking the water.

Somewhat far from everything is the ★ **Posada Refugio de la Luna** (Bluff, tel. 8/514-8460, providenciarefugiodelaluna@ gmail.com, COP$170,000 d), a guesthouse with just one comfortable and spacious room. Carmeni, the owner, is a papier-mâché artist; her studio is upstairs.

Southwest Bay (Bahía Suroeste)

★ **Hotel Sirius** (tel. 8/514-8213 or cell tel. 318/743-5367, www.siriushotel.net, COP$290,000 d) is a beachside hotel that specializes in diving and snorkeling excursions— but you don't have to be a diver to enjoy your stay here. It offers some huge rooms, and the friendly manager will make every effort to ensure you have a pleasant stay in Providencia.

Cabañas Miss Mary (tel. 8/514-8454, hotelmissmary@yahoo.com, COP$180,000 d) is just steps away from the beach in the southwest part of the island. It has eight rooms, five of which have beach views.

Smoothwater Bay (Bahía Aguamansa)

English writer Sam Cuming (author of *A Short History of Providence and San Andrés*) owns ★ **Windy View Guesthouse** (Bottom

House, tel. 8/514-8750 or cell tel. 310/589-4888, www.windyviewprovidence.blogspot.com or www.providencewindyview.com, COP$120,000 d). This gorgeous spot with two rooms and a nautical feel is brimming with books.

Casa Posada Angels (Smoothwater Bay, cell tel. 321/414-5241, COP$50,000 pp) is a guesthouse managed by Anni, an expat journalist from New Zealand who has lived in the islands for many years. There is one small cabin and a room in the main house. Across the street is a rickety pier and water access that nobody else seems to know about.

For cute accommodations in an A-frame house next to a big mango tree, hang your hat at **Miss Rossi** (Almond Bay, tel. 8/514-8327 or cell tel. 316/315-2350, COP$85,000 pp). There is one room with a double bed and a room with two twins, perfect for a small group.

Maracaibo

By far the most luxurious option on Providencia is ★ **Deep Blue** (Maracaibo Bay, tel. 8/514-8423, www.hoteldeepblue.com, COP$600,000 d). It has 13 rooms of various types, each with a view, and some with Jacuzzis. A deck with a small pool provides spectacular views of the water. There is no beach, and unless you plan on dining exclusively at their elegant restaurant, you will need to find transportation to get to other restaurants and beaches on the island. The friendly and professional staff can organize interesting day trips to nearby islands.

Located directly over the lapping waters on the eastern side of Providencia, **Posada Coco Bay** (Maracaibo, tel. 8/514-8903 or 8/514-8226, posadacocobay@gmail.com, www.posadacocobay.com, COP$180,000 d) is a small guesthouse with five comfortable rooms, three of which are on the water side. The other two (more spacious) options are across the street. You can go snorkeling just outside the hotel, and you can rent kayaks here, but there is no beach. You will have to rent a golf cart or *mula* to get to island restaurants and beaches.

Santa Isabel and Santa Catalina

Providencia is a mostly quiet and relaxed place, but Santa Catalina, a tiny island without any motorized vehicles and just a handful of residents, is exponentially more so.

Posada Santa Catalina (tel. 8/514-8392 or cell tel. 310/842-3278, www.posadasantacatalina.blogspot.com, COP$50,000 pp) uses solar panels for electricity, a rarity in the islands. This guesthouse offers five large rooms, with good beds, set amid fruit trees. The friendly owners grow the medicinal noni fruit here, as well as unusual herbs for teas; you might be able to try some.

Posada Villa Santa Catalina (tel. 8/514-8398 or cell tel. 311/257-3054, www.villasantacatalina.com, COP$50,000 pp d) is a comfortable and clean option with air-conditioning, but it doesn't exude much charm. This guesthouse is next to the Sea Star restaurant.

★ **Posada Sunshine Paradise** (tel. 8/514-8208 or cell tel. 311/227-0333, COP$180,000 d) is a charming guesthouse surrounded by flower gardens, and has four clean rooms. A major selling point is the warm hospitality of the owner, Francisca.

The **Hotel Old Providence** (Santa Isabel, tel. 8/514-8691 or 8/514-8094, COP$100,000 d) is the only option in the "town" area of Santa Isabel. It's close to Santa Catalina and offers basic, comfortable rooms with air-conditioning. Breakfast is not provided.

INFORMATION AND SERVICES

There is a **tourist office** (Santa Isabel, tel. 8/514-8054, ext. 12, www.providencia.gov.co, 8am-noon and 2pm-6pm Mon.-Fri.) in the town area near the port. They may be able to assist with accommodations, including *posadas nativas* (guesthouses owned and operated by locals), and give you some maps. The town has a bank, an ATM, and an Internet café.

In case of an emergency the police can be reached at 112 or 8/514-8000. For medical emergencies, call 125.

Many hotels on the island sell *A Short History of Providence and San Andrés* (COP$30,000), by resident author Sam Cuming. It's a good read for those interested in the mostly forgotten history of these tiny islands.

TRANSPORTATION

There are two ways to travel to Providencia: by plane or by fast catamaran boat service from San Andrés.

Satena (Centro Comercial New Point, Local 206, San Andrés, tel. 8/512-1403 or 8/514-9257, www.satena.com) offers two daily flights—one early-morning flight and one in the late afternoon—to Providencia's **Aeropuerto El Embrujo** (PVA), which is near the Parque Nacional Natural Old Providence McBean Lagoon. Charter flights are usually organized by **Decameron** (Colombian toll-free tel. 01/800-051-0765, www.decameron.co) from San Andrés to Providencia. All flights are on small propeller planes, and there are strict weight limitations. Passengers are only allowed 10 kilograms (22 pounds) in their checked baggage, and each passenger is required to be weighed upon check-in along with their carry-on bag, which makes for an amusing photo op. The average weight per passenger cannot exceed 80 kilograms (176 pounds), including luggage. The flight takes about 35 minutes.

The **Catamaran Sensation** (tel. 8/512-3675 or cell tel. 318/347-2336, www.catamaransanandresyprovidencia.com, COP$140,000 one-way) provides **fast boat service** between San Andrés and Providencia. The trip takes approximately four hours from San Andrés to Providencia (and three hours in the other direction). It provides service Sunday-Monday and Wednesday-Friday during low season. There is greater frequency during high season. Boats leave San Andrés at 8am from the Muelle Toninos and depart Providencia from the docks in Santa Isabel at 2:30pm. The catamaran service, while cheaper than air travel, often gets ghastly reviews due to the rough seas and resulting seasickness among the passengers. When the winds are strong and the waters are choppy between the two islands, especially between June and July and again in December and January, the ride can be extremely rough, requiring boat attendants to constantly circulate among the passengers to distribute seasickness bags. This is especially true on the San Andrés-to-Providencia leg. Waters are normally calmer traveling the other direction.

Taxis are expensive in Providencia, costing around COP$20,000 no matter where you go. *Mototaxis* (motorcycle taxis) are much cheaper and you can find them almost anywhere. You can also flag down passing vehicles and hitchhike (expect to pay a small fee). You can rent *mulas* (gasoline-powered golf carts) and motorbikes in Providencia. All hotels can arrange this. They cost around COP$120,000 for one day. Reputable rental agencies include **Renta Car y Motos Old Providence** (Santa Isabel, tel. 8/514-8369 or cell tel. 313/450-4833, 9am-6pm Mon.-Sat.) and **B&Q Providence Center Hans Bush Felipe** (cell tel. 311/561-1537, hours vary).

Background

The Landscape

Colombia covers a land area of 1.14 million square kilometers (440,000 square miles), roughly the size of Texas and California combined, making it the fourth-largest South American country in area after Brazil, Argentina, and Peru. It is located in the northwest corner of South America, with seacoast on both the Pacific and the Atlantic, and it borders Venezuela, Brazil, Peru, Ecuador, and Panama. The Amazonian departments of Putumayo, Caquetá, Amazonas, and Vaupés in the south of the country straddle the equator.

For a country of its size, Colombia has an astonishing variety of landscapes, including the dense rainforests of the Amazon and the Pacific coast, the vast grassland plains of the Llanos, the lofty Andes Mountains, and the Caribbean islands of San Andrés and Providencia. Colombia's mountainous regions themselves hold a succession of vertically layered landscapes: tropical rainforests at their base, followed by cloud forests at higher elevations, topped by the unique tropical high mountain *páramo* (highland moor) above 3,500 meters (11,480 feet). The country boasts several peaks higher than 5,000 meters (16,400 feet), including Nevado del Ruiz (5,325 meters/17,470 feet) and Pico Cristóbal Colón (5,776 meters/18,950 feet).

GEOGRAPHY

Colombia's Caribbean coast runs 1,760 kilometers (1,100 miles) from the border of Panama to Venezuela, just longer than the California coast. However, the term "Caribe" or "Región Caribe" refers to much more than the narrow strip of coast; it encompasses basically all of Colombia north of the Andes, including a vast area of plains. This region covers 15 percent of the surface of Colombia and is home to 20 percent of the population.

The terrain is mostly low-lying and undulating. Near the border with Panama, the land is covered by dense tropical forests, similar to those on the Pacific coast. Farther east is the Golfo de Urabá, a large, shallow bay. Between the Golfo de Urabá and Cartagena is the Golfo de Morrosquillo, a broad inlet that is 50 kilometers (31 miles) wide. Off the shore of the Golfo de Morrosquillo are two small archipelagos, the Islas de San Bernardo and the Islas del Rosario, with beautiful coral reefs. Inland to the south is a large area of savannas in the departments of Córdoba and Sucre largely devoted to cattle ranching. This area was once covered by dry tropical forests, which have been largely felled.

Bahía de Cartagena, farther east, is a magnificent deep bay that caught the attention of the early Spanish explorers. To the southeast of Cartagena is the lower valley of the Magdalena and Cauca Rivers, a vast expanse of low-lying lagoons and lands prone to seasonal flooding. The Río Magdalena flows into the Caribbean east of Cartagena at the port city of Barranquilla. Farther to the east along the coast is a major mountain range, the Sierra Nevada de Santa Marta. It was formed by the collision of the South American plate and the Caribbean plate to the north and is entirely independent of the Andes. This range is home to Colombia's two highest peaks, the twin Pico Cristóbal Colón and Pico Bolívar (5,776 meters/18,950 feet), and is considered the highest coastal mountain range in the world. The Sierra Nevada de Santa Marta contains the same range of vertically layered landscapes as the Andes, from low-lying

---

Previous: horse-drawn carts, the airport shuttle in Acandí; view of the Sierra Nevada de Santa Marta.

Colombia's National Parks

From undisturbed coral reefs to the Amazonian jungle to snow-covered mountain ranges, Colombia's national park system is a treasure, and making the effort to visit them is worthwhile for any visitor. The country's system of natural parks and protected areas covers more than 14 million hectares (34.6 million acres), around 13.4 percent of the country. It includes 43 Parques Nacionales Naturales (National Natural Parks), which are areas of major ecological interest that have remained largely untouched by human intervention, and 12 Santuarios de Flora y Fauna (Flora and Fauna Sanctuaries), areas that are devoted to the preservation of specific ecosystems. Of the 43 parks, 24 are open for tourism. The rest are officially off-limits, due to lack of infrastructure, security concerns, or in order to respect the territory of indigenous communities.

In 1960, PNN Cueva de los Guácharos, in the southwest, was the first park to be established. The number of parks steadily increased, especially from 1986 to 1990 when President Virgilio Barco doubled the park holdings from roughly 5 million hectares to 10 million hectares (12 million to 24 million acres). In the past few years, the government has again been increasing the number and extension of parks. In 2013 President Juan Manuel Santos doubled the size of the PNN Serranía de Chiribiquete to its present 2.8 million hectares (7 million acres), or three times the size of Yellowstone National Park.

Charged with the considerable task of administering this huge system are a mere 430 rangers—roughly one person for every 33,000 hectares (82,000 acres). Rangers face a great challenge in protecting the parks against threats related to human encroachment, particularly cattle ranching and the planting of illicit crops. There are other threats as well, such as illegal mining and logging. Paradoxically, what has preserved many of the parks until now has been the lack of security due to Colombia's internal conflict. As security conditions improve, there will be increasing pressure on these natural habitats. The Parks Service is actively engaging with the communities that live near the parks and is transferring the operation of much of the ecotourism infrastructure to community-based organizations as part of an effort to enlist local communities in the preservation of the land.

Entry permits and entry fees are only required in a handful of highly visited parks, such as PNN Tayrona, PNN Gorgona, PNN Cocuy, and PNN Los Nevados. At these, you will automatically be charged if you book lodging in advance, or if not, upon arrival. If you want to be meticulous, you can obtain the entry permit and pay entry fees in advance by contacting the **Parques Nacionales** (tel. 1/353-2400, www.parquesnacionales.gov.co) in Bogotá.

tropical forest through cloud forest, Andean forests, *páramo*, and glaciers. There are eight peaks with elevations greater than 5,000 meters (16,400 feet).

Northeast of the Sierra Nevada de Santa Marta is La Guajira, an arid peninsula jutting into the Caribbean. Punta Gallinas, at the tip of La Guajira, is the northernmost point in South America. There are a few low-lying mountain ranges in La Guajira, such as the Serranía de la Macuira (864 meters/2,835 feet), which is covered with rainforest. The Sierra Nevada de Santa Marta and Serranía de la Macuira are biological islands, and their upper reaches are home to numerous endemic species that evolved in isolation.

CLIMATE

Colombia has a typically tropical climate, with no change of seasons. Climate is related primarily to elevation, and there are defined annual precipitation patterns.

In the mountainous areas, temperature decreases approximately six degrees Celsius per every 1,000 meters (3,280 feet) of elevation (or three degrees Fahrenheit per every 1,000 feet). The common designations for the altitudinal zones are as follows: *tierra caliente* (hot lands) is anywhere below 1,000 meters of elevation; *tierra templada* (temperate lands) is anywhere between 1,000 and 2,000 meters; and *tierra fría* (cold land) is anywhere above 2,000 meters. Roughly 80 percent of the country is *tierra caliente,* 10 percent is *tierra templada,* and 7 percent is *tierra fría.*

Cartagena, which is at sea level, has an average temperature of 27.5°C (81.5°F); Medellín, which is at 1,600 meters (5,250 feet), has an average temperature of 22°C (71.5°F); and the capital city of Bogotá, which is built at 2,625 meters (8,612 feet), has an average temperature of 13.5°C (56°F).

Precipitation patterns vary throughout the country. In the Andean region, there are generally two periods of *verano* (dry season, literally "summer"), from December to March and from June to September, and two periods of *invierno* (rainy season, literally "winter"), in April and May and from October to November. On the Caribbean coast, the dry period is from December to April and the rainy season is from May to November. In the Pacific it rains almost the entire year, but there is a slight dry spell from December to March. In the Llanos, there are two very marked seasons: a very dry *verano* from November to March and a very wet *invierno* from April to October. In the Amazon, it rains almost the entire year, but there is a slight dry spell from August to October.

Extreme weather in Colombia is rare, but the country is susceptible to weather phenomena such as El Niño or La Niña, when temperatures in the Pacific Ocean rise or fall, respectively. In 2015-2016, the country was affected by a strong El Niño, which brought prolonged drought.

San Andrés and Providencia are occasionally, and the Caribbean mainland of Colombia rarely, in the path of Atlantic hurricanes from August through October. The last storm of significance was Hurricane Beta in 2005. It caused considerable damage in Providencia.

Plants and Animals

When it comes to biodiversity, Colombia is a place of superlatives. Though representing only 0.2 percent of the earth's surface, it is home to about 10 percent of all the species in the world. The country has an estimated 55,000 plant species, including 3,500 species of orchids. Only Brazil, with seven times the land surface, has as many plant species. Colombia is the country with the greatest number of bird species in the world—about 1,800. It's also home to about 3,200 fish, 750 amphibian species, 500 reptile species, and 450 mammal species. No wonder Colombia was designated as one of 17 so-called megadiverse countries, a select club of countries that are home to an outsized proportion of the world's biodiversity. Other megadiverse countries include Australia, Brazil, China, Democratic Republic of Congo, Indonesia, Madagascar, Mexico, the United States, and South Africa.

This enormous biodiversity is the result of Colombia's location in the tropics, where year-round sunlight and high precipitation are conducive to plant growth, plus the country's mountainous topography with numerous climatic zones and microclimates that have created biological islands where species have evolved in relative isolation. Furthermore, the recent ice ages were not as severe in this part of the world, and as a result many ancient species were preserved. Finally, Colombia's location at the crossroads of Central and South America has further enriched the country's biodiversity.

RAINFOREST

Rainforests are among the most complex ecosystems on Earth. They have a layered structure with towering trees that soar 30-40 meters high (100-130 feet) to form the forest's canopy. Some of the most common rainforest trees are the ceiba, mahogany, myrtle, laurel, acacia, and rubber trees. Occasionally, particularly high trees known as *emergentes* pierce the canopy, reaching as high up as 60 meters

Colombian Fruits

Colombia is a land bursting with exotic fruit. Sold from the back of pickup trucks by farmers on the roadside, overflowing at stalls in colorful markets in every town and village, lined up in neat rows in the produce section at fancy grocery stores and at juice stands—just about anywhere you go, delicious fruit is in reach.

You know pineapple, papaya, mangoes, and bananas, but be sure to try these tropical delights that you may not have encountered outside of Colombia.

- *Pitahaya* (dragon fruit): Looking like a yellow grenade, *pitahayas* have a sweet white meat inside.

- *Guanábana* (soursop): By far the strangest-looking fruit, soursop resemble prehistoric dinosaur eggs. Inside the large green spiky fruit is a milky and slimy flesh. *Guanábana* is great in juices and desserts.

- *Granadilla:* Crack open this orangey-yellow fruit and slurp down the slimy gray contents, seeds and all. It's delicious.

- *Higo* (prickly pear): This green fruit comes from cactus plants and has sweet, if tough, orange-colored meat.

- *Chirimoya* (cherimoya): This green fruit that resembles a smooth artichoke is covered with a smooth, silky skin and filled with delectable, sweet pulp.

- *Níspero* (sapodilla): A fruit with a deep brown color that tastes like a prepared sweet.

- *Mangostino* (mangosteen): Crack open a deep-purple mangosteen and enjoy the sweet segments inside. They're full of antioxidants.

- *Uchuva* (Cape gooseberry): Known in English as Cape gooseberries, these tart yellow berries are a cousin of the tomato and are tasty on their own or in salads, but are often used in jams and sweets.

- *Mamoncillo:* Tough-skinned grapes (don't eat the skin), *mamoncillos* are usually only sold at street markets.

(200 feet). Below the canopy is the *sotobosque*, a middle layer of smaller trees and palms that vie for the sunlight filtering in through the canopy. In the canopy and *sotobosque* there are many epiphytes (plants such as orchids and bromeliads) that have adapted to live on top of trees so as to be nearer to the sunlight. Near the ground live plants that require little sunlight, including ferns, grasses, and many types of fungi. The two main rainforests in Colombia, the Amazon and the Chocó, have the same layered structure, though they have some differences in their flora and fauna.

The Amazon rainforest is home to an impressive array of vertebrates. Over millennia, a large number of canopy-dwelling species evolved. Monkeys, such as the large and extremely agile spider monkey, the woolly monkey, and the howler monkey, evolved prehensile tails that allowed them to move easily from branch to branch. Anteaters, such as the tamandua and the *oso mielero* (giant anteater) and the incredibly cute *kinkajú* (kinkajou), also developed prehensile tails. Other inhabitants of the canopy include sloths, such as the adorable three-toed sloth, whose strategy is not agility but passivity: It eats tree vegetation and is covered with algae that gradually turns the animal green to allow for good camouflage. The canopy is also home to myriad bats and many birds, including exotic eagles, curassows, toucans, woodpeckers, cotingas, and macaws.

Notable is the majestic harpy eagle, with powerful claws and the ability to fly unencumbered through the canopy. It preys on monkeys and sloths, which it kills with the force of its claws. The *tigrillo* (tiger cat) is a small and extremely endangered species. It has a long tail that helps with its balance as it moves from tree to tree.

On the ground, large vertebrates include the extremely endangered tapir, an ancient mammal species that can grow two meters long (over six feet) and weigh 300 kilograms (660 pounds). It is equally at ease on land as in the water. Other land mammals include the giant armadillo, giant anteater, deer, and boars, such as the *saíno* and *pecarí*. Smaller mammals include the *guatín* and *borugo,* both rodents. These animals are often prey to the puma and jaguar, both of which inhabit the Amazon but are difficult to observe in the wild.

The rivers of the Amazon are home to more than 1,500 species of fish, including endangered *pirarucú,* one of the largest freshwater fishes on Earth. There are also dolphins, both pink and gray. The former evolved separately from the oceangoing dolphins when the Amazon was an inland sea. The Amazonian gray dolphins are sea dolphins that adapted to living in freshwater. Other aquatic mammals include the highly endangered manatee and otters.

The Chocó Rainforest is particularly rich in palms, of which 120 species have been identified. In fact, it is sometimes referred to as the "Land of the Palms." The forest also abounds in cycads, ancient plants that have a stout trunk and crowns of hard, stiff leaves. Chocó is also notable for more than 40 species of brightly colored poisonous frogs, known locally as *ranas kokois.* These small frogs

are covered with a deadly poison and have evolved stunning coloration, from bright orange to red, gold, and blue. They are active in the day and therefore relatively easy to spot. Of Colombia's 1,800 species of birds, more than 1,000 have been identified in the Chocó, including a large number of hummingbirds.

Offshore, the Pacific welcomes the annual migration of Antarctic humpback whales. The beaches of the Pacific coast are popular nesting areas for sea turtles, in particular the *tortuga golfina* (olive ridley) and *tortuga carey* (hawksbill) sea turtles. On the island of Gorgona, 35 kilometers (22 miles) from the mainland, an unusual—and quite stunning—species of lizard is the blue anole lizard. Highly threatened, it is found only on Gorgona.

CLOUD FOREST

Rainforests that grow at higher altitudes on the flanks of the Andes are known as montane rainforests or cloud forests because they are often enveloped in mist that results from the condensation of warm air against chillier mountain currents. Unlike the lowland rainforest, cloud forests only have two layers, the canopy and ground layer. Generally, the vegetation is less dense than that in the lowland rainforest. However, it is home to many palms, ferns, and epiphytes, particularly orchids.

The type of cloud forest vegetation is dictated by altitude. *Selva subandina* (sub-Andean forest) vegetation grows between the altitudes of 1,000 and 2,300 meters (3,300-7,500 feet), where temperature varies 16-23°C (61-73°F). Plant species include the distinctive Seussian white *yarumo* with its oversized leaves, as well as cedar, oak, and mahogany trees. Many palms grow here, including the svelte wax palm and *tagua*, which produces a nut that resembles ivory. Ferns include the striking *palma boba* or tree fern. Colombia's premier crop, coffee, is grown at this elevation.

At elevations between 2,300 and 3,600 meters (7,500-12,000 feet), the vegetation is described as *selva Andina* (Andean forest). This vegetation is even less dense and at higher elevations the trees are smaller. *Selva Andina* includes many oak, *encenillo, sietecuero* (glory bush), and pine trees.

Mammals include the spectacled or Andean bear, the only species of bear in South America, the mountain (or woolly) tapir, anteaters, armadillos, sloths, boars, foxes, and *olingos*, small arboreal carnivores of the raccoon family. In 2013, the *olinguito* (small *olingo*), an incredibly cute animal, was declared a new species. Other unusual animals include the slow-moving *guagua loba* and *guatín,* both of which are rodents. In addition, numerous species of monkeys inhabit the cloud forest, including noisy troops of howler monkeys. Birds include many types of *barranqueros* (motmots), including the spectacular blue-crowned motmot. Other common birds include *tángaras* (tanagers), woodpeckers, warblers, parrots, owls, and ducks, including the beautiful white-and-black torrent duck.

PÁRAMOS

Páramos are unique tropical highland ecosystems that thrive above 3,500 meters (11,500 feet), where UV radiation is higher, oxygen is scarcer, and where temperatures vary from minus-2 to 10 degrees Celsius (28-50°F). Due to frequent mist and precipitation, *páramos* are often saturated with water and have many lakes. They are true "water factories" that provide water to many of Colombia's cities, notably Bogotá. Though *páramos* exist throughout the New World tropics, most are located in Colombia. The Parque Nacional Natural Sumapaz, south of Bogotá, is the world's largest *páramo.*

Páramo vegetation includes more than 50 species of *frailejón* (genus *Espeletia*), eerily beautiful plants that have imposing tall trunks and thick yellow-greenish leaves. Other *páramo* vegetation includes shrubs, grasses, and *cojines* (cushion plants). Mammals include the spectacled bear, *páramo* tapir, weasels, squirrels, and bats. The *páramo* is the realm of the majestic black-and-white Andean condor, which has a wingspan of up to three meters (10 feet). The condor, whose numbers had declined almost to the point of extinction, is found in the national parks of the Sierra Nevada de Santa Marta, Sierra Nevada del Cocuy, and Los Nevados. The *páramo* lakes welcome many types of ducks, including the Andean duck, as well as smaller birds.

TROPICAL DRY FORESTS

Tropical dry forests exist in areas where there is a prolonged dry season. The vegetation includes deciduous trees that lose their leaves during the dry season, allowing them to conserve water. Trees on moister sites and those with access to groundwater tend to be evergreen. Before Columbus, this ecosystem covered much of the Colombian Caribbean coast. However, much of it has since been cut down for cattle ranching. Pockets still exist east of the Golfo de Morrosquillo and at the base of the Sierra Nevada de Santa Marta. Tropical dry forests are the most endangered tropical ecosystem in the world.

Though less biologically diverse than rainforests, tropical dry forests are home to a wide variety of wildlife. They were once the stomping ground of the now highly endangered *marimonda*, or white-fronted spider monkey.

TROPICAL GRASSLANDS

Los Llanos (The Plains) of Colombia are covered with lush tropical grasslands. Vegetation includes long-stemmed and carpet grasses in the drier areas and swamp grasses in low-lying humid areas. There are also thick patches of forest throughout the plains and along the rivers (known as gallery forests). These plains are teeming with wildlife, including deer, anteaters, armadillos, tapirs, otters, jaguars, pumas, and *chigüiros* (also known as capybaras), the world's largest rodent. The Llanos are also home to the giant anaconda and to one of the most endangered species on Earth, the Orinoco crocodile, which reaches up to seven meters (23 feet) long.

History

BEFORE COLUMBUS

Located at the juncture of Central and South America, what is now Colombia was a necessary transit point for the migration of people who settled South America. However, because these peoples left few physical traces of their passage, little is known of them. The oldest human objects found in Colombia, utensils discovered near Bogotá, are dated from 14,000 BC. With the expansion of agriculture and sedentary life throughout the territory of present-day Colombia around 1000 BC, various indigenous cultures started producing stunning ceramic and gold work, as well as some monumental remains. These remains provide rich material evidence of their development. Nonetheless, there are significant gaps in the understanding of the history of these early peoples.

From around 700 BC, the area of San Agustín, near the origin of the Río Magdalena in southern Colombia, was settled by people who practiced agriculture and produced pottery. Starting in the 1st century AD, the people of San Agustín created hundreds of monumental stone statues set on large platforms, which comprise the largest pre-Columbian archaeological site extant between Mesoamerica and Peru. By AD 800, this society had disappeared.

In the northwestern plains of Colombia, south of present-day Cartagena, starting in the 1st century AD, the Sinú people constructed a large complex of mounds in the shape of fish bones. These mounds regulated flooding, allowing cultivation in both rainy and dry seasons. During rainy seasons, the water flooded the lower cavities, allowing for cultivation on the mounds; during dry season, cultivation took place in the cavities that had been enriched by the flood waters. These monumental formations are still visible from overhead. By the time of the Spanish conquest, these people no longer inhabited the area.

From AD 500 to 900, the area of Tierradentro, west of San Agustín, was settled by an agricultural society that dug magnificent decorated underground tombs, produced large stone statues, and built oval-shaped buildings on artificial terraces. As in the case of the San Agustín and the Sinú people, it is not known what happened to these people.

At the time of the conquest, present-day Colombia was populated by a large number of distinct agricultural societies that often maintained peaceful trading relations among themselves. The two largest groups were the Muisca people, who lived in the altiplano (highlands) of the Cordillera Oriental, and the Tayrona, who lived on the slopes of the Sierra Nevada de Santa Marta. Other groups included the Quimbaya, who settled the area of the present-day Coffee Region; the Calima, in present-day Valle del Cauca; and the Nariños, in the mountainous areas of southwest Colombia.

These indigenous societies were mostly organized at the village level with loose association with other villages. Only the Muisca and the Tayrona had a more developed political organization. Though these were all agricultural societies, they also engaged in hunting, fishing, and mining and produced sophisticated ceramics and goldwork. Each group specialized in what their environment had to offer and engaged in overland trade. For example, the Muiscas produced textiles and salt, which they traded for gold, cotton, tobacco, and shells from other groups.

The Muiscas, a Chibcha-speaking people, were the largest group, with an estimated 600,000 inhabitants at the time of the Spanish conquest. They settled the Cordillera Oriental in AD 300 and occupied a large territory that comprises most of the highland areas of the present-day departments of Cundinamarca and Boyacá. At the time of the conquest, they were organized into two large confederations:

one in the south headed by the Zipa, whose capital was Bacatá near present-day Bogotá, and another headed by the Zaque, whose capital was at Hunza, the location of present-day Tunja. The Muiscas had a highly homogeneous culture, skilled in weaving, ceramics, and goldwork. Their cosmography placed significant importance on high Andean lakes, several of which were sacred, including Guatavita, Siecha, and Iguaque.

The Tayrona, who settled the slopes of the Sierra Nevada de Santa Marta, were also a Chibcha-speaking people. They had a more urban society, with towns that included temples and ceremonial plazas built on stone terraces, and practiced farming on terraces carved out of the mountains. There are an estimated 200 Tayrona sites, of which Ciudad Perdida (Lost City), built at 1,100 meters (3,600 feet) in the Sierra Nevada de Santa Marta, is the largest and best known. Many of these towns, including El Pueblito in the Parque Nacional Natural Tayrona, were occupied at the time of the Spanish conquest. The Kogis, Arhuacos, Kankuamos, and Wiwas, current inhabitants of the sierra, are their descendants and consider many places in the sierra sacred.

THE SPANISH CONQUEST (1499-1550)

As elsewhere in the New World, the arrival of Europeans was an unmitigated disaster for the Native American societies. Though there were pockets of resistance, on the whole the indigenous people were unable to push back the small number of armed Spanish conquistadores. Harsh conditions after the conquest and the spread of European diseases, such as measles and smallpox, to which the indigenous people had no immunity, killed off millions of natives. The Spanish conquest of present-day Colombia took about 50 years and was largely completed by the 1550s.

In 1499, the first European set foot on present-day Colombia in the northern Guajira Peninsula. In 1510, a first, unsuccessful colony was established in the Golfo de Urabá near the current border with Panama. In 1526, the Spanish established Santa Marta, their first permanent foothold, from where they tried, unsuccessfully, to subdue the Tayronas. In 1533, they established Cartagena, which was to become a major colonial port.

In 1536, Gonzalo Jiménez de Quesada set off south from Santa Marta to conquer the fabled lands of El Dorado in the Andean heartland. After a year of grueling travel up the swampy Río Magdalena valley, 200 surviving members of Jiménez de Quesada's 800 original troops arrived in the Muisca lands near present-day Bogotá. After a short interlude of courteous relations, the Spaniards' greed led them to obliterate the Muisca towns and temples. They found significant amounts of gold, especially in the town of Hunza, but they were, by and large, disappointed. In 1538, Jiménez de Quesada founded Santa Fe de Bogotá as the capital of this new territory, which he called Nueva Granada—New Granada—after his birthplace.

Sebastián de Belalcázar, a lieutenant of Francisco Pizarro, led a second major expedition that arrived in the Muisca lands from the south. Having conquered the Inca city of Quito, Belalcázar and his army traveled north, conquering a vast swath of land from present-day Ecuador to the *sábana* (high plateau) of Bogotá. Along the way, he founded several cities, including Popayán and Cali in 1536. He arrived shortly after Quesada had founded Bogotá. Incredibly, a third conquistador, the German Nikolaus Federmann, arrived in Bogotá at the same time, having traveled from Venezuela via the Llanos. Rather than fight for supremacy, the three conquistadores decided to take their rival claims to arbitration at the Spanish court. In an unexpected turn of events, none of the three obtained title to the Muisca lands: When Bogotá became the administrative capital of New Granada, they came under the sway of the Spanish crown. Other expeditions swept across the Caribbean coast, through current-day Antioquia and the Santanderes.

COLONIAL NUEVA GRANADA (1550-1810)

For most of its colonial history, Nueva Granada, as colonial Colombia was called, was an appendage of the Viceroyalty of Peru. In 1717, Spain decided to establish a viceroyalty in Nueva Granada but changed its mind six years later because the benefits did not justify the cost. In 1739, the viceroyalty was reestablished, with Santa Fe de Bogotá as its capital. It was an unwieldy territory, encompassing present-day Colombia, Venezuela, Ecuador, and Panama. To make it more manageable, Venezuela and Panama were ruled by captain-generals and Ecuador by a president. At the local level, the viceroyalty was divided into *provincias* (provinces), each with a local assembly called a *cabildo*.

Settlement in Nueva Granada occurred primarily in three areas: where there were significant indigenous populations to exploit, as in the case of Tunja in the former Muisca territory; where there were gold deposits, as in Cauca, Antioquia, and Santander; and along trade routes, for example at Honda and Mompox on the Río Magdalena. Cartagena was the main port of call for the biennial convoys of gold and silver sent to Spain. Bogotá lived off of the official bureaucracy and sustained a fair number of artisans. Present-day Antioquia and Santander supported small-scale farming to provide provisions to the gold mining camps. Nueva Granada was one of the least economically dynamic of Spain's New World possessions. The mountainous topography and high transportation costs meant that agricultural production was primarily for local consumption and gold was the only significant export.

Colonial society was composed of a small Spanish and Creole (descendants of Spanish settlers) elite governing a large mestizo (mixed indigenous-white) population. The Spanish had initially preserved indigenous communal lands known as *resguardos*, but the demographic collapse of the native population and intermarriage meant that, unlike in Peru or Mexico, there were relatively few people who were fully indigenous. There were also black slaves who were forced mostly to work in the mines and haciendas (plantations). Society was overwhelmingly Catholic and Spanish-speaking.

Culturally, Nueva Granada was also somewhat of a backwater. Though there was a modest flourishing of the arts, Bogotá could not compete with the magnificent architectural and artistic production of Quito, Lima, or Mexico City. The only truly notable event of learning that took place was the late 18th-century Expedición Botánica (Botanical Expedition), headed by Spanish naturalist José Celestino Mutis, the personal doctor to one of the viceroys. The aim of the expedition was to survey all the species of Nueva Granada—a rather tall order given that Colombia is home to 10 percent of the world's species. However, the expedition did some remarkable research and produced beautiful prints of the fauna and flora.

The late colonial period saw unrest in Nueva Granada. Starting in 1781, a revolt known as the Rebelión de los Comuneros took place in the province of Socorro (north of Bogotá) in present-day Santander as a result of an attempt by colonial authorities to levy higher taxes. It was not an antiroyalist movement, however, as its slogan indicates: ¡Viva el Rey, Muera el Mal Gobierno! ("Long live the king, down with bad government!"). Rather it was a protest against unfair taxes, not much different from the Boston Tea Party. However, it gave the Spanish government a fright. A rebel army, led by José Antonio Galán, marched on Bogotá. Negotiations put an end to the assault, and later the authorities ruthlessly persecuted the leaders of the revolt.

STRUGGLE FOR INDEPENDENCE (1810-1821)

Though there was some ill feeling against the colonial government, as the Rebelión de los Comuneros attests, as well as rivalry between the Spanish- and American-born elites, it was an external event, the Napoleonic invasion of

Spain, that set off the chain of events that led to independence of Nueva Granada and the rest of the Spanish dominion in the New World.

In 1808, Napoleon invaded Spain, took King Ferdinand VII prisoner, and tried to impose his own brother, Joseph, as king of Spain. The Spaniards revolted, establishing a Central Junta in Seville to govern during the king's temporary absence from power. Faced with the issue of whether to recognize the new Central Junta in Spain, the colonial elites decided to take matters in their own hands and establish juntas of their own. The first such junta in Nueva Granada was established in Caracas in April 1810. Cartagena followed suit in May and Bogotá on July 20, 1810. According to popular myth, the revolt in Bogotá was the result of the failure of a prominent Spaniard merchant to lend a flower vase to a pair of Creoles.

Though they pledged alliance to Ferdinand VII, once the local elites had tasted power, there was no going back. Spanish authorities were expelled, and in 1811, a government of sorts, under the loose mantle of the Provincias Unidas de Nueva Granada (United Provinces of New Granada), was established with its capital at Tunja. Bogotá and the adjoining province of Cundinamarca stayed aloof from the confederation, arguing that it was too weak to resist the Spanish. Subsequently, various provinces of Nueva Granada declared outright independence, starting with Venezuela and Cartagena in 1811 and Cundinamarca in 1813.

Several cities remained loyal to the crown, namely Santa Marta and deeply conservative Pasto in the south. From 1812 to 1814 there was a senseless civil war between the Provincias Unidas and Cundinamarca—that is why this period is called the Patria Boba, or Foolish Fatherland. Ultimately, the Provincias Unidas prevailed with the help of a young Venezuelan captain by the name of Simón Bolívar.

After the restoration of Ferdinand VII, Spain attempted to retake its wayward colonies, with a military expedition and reign of terror known as the Reconquista—the Reconquest. The Spanish forces took Cartagena by siege in 1815 and took control of Bogotá in May 1816. However, in 1819, a revolutionary army composed of Venezuelans, Nueva Granadans, and European mercenaries headed by Bolívar arrived across the Llanos from Venezuela and decisively defeated the Spanish army in the Batalla del Puente de Boyacá—the Battle of the Boyacá Bridge—on August 7, near Tunja. The rest of the country fell quickly to the revolutionary army. With support from Nueva Granada, Bolívar defeated the Spanish in Venezuela in 1821. Panama, which had remained under Spanish control, declared independence in 1821. Finally, Bolívar dispatched Antonio José de Sucre to take Quito in 1822, bringing an end to the Spanish rule of Nueva Granada.

GRAN COLOMBIA: A FLAWED UNION (1821-1830)

Shortly after the Battle of Boyacá, the Congress of Angostura, a city on the Río Orinoco in Venezuela, proclaimed the union of Nueva Granada, Venezuela, and Ecuador under the name of the República de Colombia. Historians refer to this entity as Gran Colombia. In 1821, while the fight for independence was still raging in parts of Venezuela and Ecuador, a constitutional congress met in Cúcuta. An ongoing debate about whether a centralist or federalist scheme was preferable resulted in a curious compromise: the República de Colombia assumed a highly centralist form, considered necessary to finish the battle for independence, but left the issue of federalism open to review after 10 years. The document was generally liberal, enshrining individual liberties and providing for the manumission of slaves, meaning that the children of slaves were born free.

Bolívar, who was born in Venezuela, was named president. Francisco de Paula Santander, who was born near Cúcuta in Nueva Granada, was named vice president. Santander had fought alongside Bolívar in the battles for independence of Nueva Granada and was seen as an able administrator. While Bolívar continued south to liberate Ecuador and Peru, Santander assumed the reins of power in Bogotá. He charted a generally liberal course, instituting public education and a curriculum that included avant-garde thinkers such as Jeremy Bentham. However, the highly centralist structure was unsavory to elites in Venezuela and Ecuador, who disliked rule from Bogotá. Shortly after the Congress of Cúcuta, revolt broke out in Venezuela and Ecuador. In 1826, Bolívar returned from Bolivia and Peru, hoping for the adoption in Gran Colombia of the Bolivian Constitution, an unusual document he drafted that called for a presidency for life.

There had been a growing distance between Bolívar and Santander: Bolívar saw Santander as an overzealous liberal reformer while Santander disliked Bolívar's authoritarian tendencies. In 1828, after a failed constitutional congress that met in Ocaña in eastern Colombia, Bolívar assumed dictatorial powers. He rolled back many of Santander's liberal reforms. In September 1828 there was an attempt on Bolívar's life in Bogotá. This was famously foiled by his companion, Manuela Sáenz. The last years of Gran Colombia were marked by revolts in various parts of the country and a war with Peru. In 1830, a further constitutional assembly was convened in Bogotá, but by that point Gran Colombia had ceased to exist: Venezuela and Ecuador had seceded. In March 1830, a physically ill Bolívar decided to leave for voluntary exile in Europe and died on his way in Santa Marta.

CIVIL WARS AND CONSTITUTIONS (1830-1902)

After the separation of Venezuela and Ecuador, what is now Colombia adopted the name República de Nueva Granada. In 1832, it adopted a new constitution that corrected many of the errors of the excessively centralist constitution of Gran Colombia. There was a semblance of stability with the orderly

succession of elected presidents. The elimination of some monasteries in Pasto sparked a short civil conflict known as the Guerra de los Supremos, which lasted 1839-1842. During this war, Conservative and Liberal factions coalesced for the first time, establishing the foundation of Colombia's two-party system. Generally, the Conservative Party supported the Catholic Church, favored centralization, and followed the ideas of Bolívar. The Liberal Party supported federalism and free trade and identified with the ideas of Santander.

The country's rugged topography meant that Nueva Granada was not very integrated into the world economy. Gold, extracted mostly in Antioquia, was the main export. Most of the country eked out its subsistence from agriculture, with trade restricted within regions. This period saw some economic development, such as steam navigation on the Magdalena and Cauca Rivers, and a contract for the construction of the trans-isthmian railroad in Panama, which had yet to secede.

Midcentury saw the rise of a new class of leaders who had grown up wholly under Republican governments. They ushered in a period of liberal reform. In 1851, Congress abolished slavery. In 1853, a new constitution established universal male suffrage, religious tolerance, and direct election of provincial governors. The government reduced tariffs and Nueva Granada experienced a short export-oriented tobacco boom.

Conflicts between radical reformers within the Liberal Party, moderates, and Conservatives led to unrest in various provinces. In 1859, discontented Liberals under Tomás Cipriano de Mosquera revolted, leading to generalized civil war in which the Liberals were ultimately victorious. Once in power, they pushed radical reform. Mosquera expropriated all nonreligious church property, partly in vengeance for church support of the Conservatives in the previous civil war.

The 1863 constitution was one of the world's most audacious federalist experiments. The country was renamed the Estados Unidos de Colombia (United States of Colombia), comprising nine states. The president had a two-year term and was not immediately reelectable. All powers that were not explicitly assigned to the central government were the responsibility of the states. Many of the states engaged in true progressive policies, such as establishing public education and promoting the construction of railroads. This period coincided with agricultural booms in quinine, cotton, and indigo that, for the first time, brought limited prosperity. This period saw the establishment of the Universidad Nacional (National University) and the country's first bank.

In 1880 and then in 1884, a coalition of Conservatives and moderate Liberals, who were dissatisfied with radical policies, elected Rafael Núñez as president. Núñez tried to strengthen the power of the central government, sparking a Liberal revolt. The Conservatives were ultimately victorious and, in 1886, enacted a new centralist constitution that lasted through most of the 20th century. The country was rechristened República de Colombia, the name it has conserved since then. During the period from 1886 through 1904, known as the Regeneración, the Conservative Party held sway, rolling back many of the previous reforms, especially anticlerical measures and unrestricted male suffrage. The Liberal Party, excluded from power, revolted in 1899. The ensuing Guerra de los Mil Días (Thousand Days' War), which raged through 1902, was a terribly bloody conflict. It is not clear how many died in the war, but some historians put the figure as high as 100,000, or an incredible 2.5 percent of the country's population of four million at the time.

One year after the end of the war, Panama seceded. During the late 19th century, there had been resentment in Panama about the distribution of revenues from the transit trade that mostly were sent to Bogotá. However, in 1902 the local Panamanian elites had become alarmed at the lackadaisical attitude of the government in Bogotá regarding the construction of an interoceanic canal. After the failure of the French to build a canal, Colombia had entered into negotiations with the United States. In the closing days of the Guerra de los Mil Días, Colombia and the United States signed the Hay-Terran Treaty, which called for the construction of the canal, surrendering control over a strip of land on either side of the canal to the United States. The Americans threatened that if the treaty were not ratified, they would dig the canal in Nicaragua. Arguing that the treaty undermined Colombian sovereignty, the congress in Bogotá unanimously rejected it in August 1903. That was a big mistake: A few months later, Panama seceded with the support of the United States.

PEACE AND REFORM (1902-1946)

Under the leadership of moderate Conservative Rafael Reyes, who was president 1904-1909, Colombia entered a period of peace and stability. Reyes focused on creating a professional, nonpartisan army. He gave representation to Liberals in government, enacted a protective tariff to spur domestic industry, and pushed public works. During his administration, Bogotá was finally connected by railway to the Río Magdalena. He reestablished relations with the United States, signing a treaty that provided Colombia with an indemnity for the loss of Panama. During the 1920s and 1930s, Colombia was governed by a succession of Conservative Party presidents. Though there was often electoral fraud, constitutional reform that guaranteed minority representation ensured peace.

Expanding world demand for coffee spurred production across Colombia, especially in southern Antioquia and what is now known as the Coffee Region, creating a new class of independent farmers. Improved transportation, especially the completion of the railways from Cali to Buenaventura on the Pacific coast and from Medellín to the Río Magdalena, was key to the growth of coffee exports. In the Magdalena Medio region and in Norte de Santander, U.S.

companies explored and started producing petroleum. Medellín became a center of textile manufacturing. With the country's broken geography, air transportation developed rapidly. The Sociedad Colombo Alemana de Transportes Aéreos (Colombian German Air Transportation Society) or SCADTA, the predecessor of Avianca, was founded in Barranquilla in 1919, and is reputedly the second-oldest commercial aviation company in the world (the oldest is KLM).

In 1930, a split Conservative ticket allowed the Liberals to win the elections. After being out of power for 50 years, the Liberal Party was happy to regain control of the state apparatus. This led to strife with Conservatives long accustomed to power—presaging the intense interparty violence that was to erupt 14 years later.

From 1932 to 1933, Colombia and Peru fought a brief war in the Amazon over the control of the port city of Leticia. The League of Nations brokered a truce, the first time that this body, which was a precursor to the United Nations, actively intervened in a dispute between two countries.

Starting in 1934, Liberal president Alfonso López Pumarejo undertook major social and labor reforms, with some similarities to Roosevelt's New Deal. His policies included agrarian reform, encouragement and protection of labor unions, and increased spending on education. He reduced the Catholic Church's sway over education and eliminated the literacy requirement for male voters. Many of these reforms simply returned the country to policies that had been enacted by Liberals in the 1850s, 80 years prior. In opposition to these policies, a new radical right, with a confrontational style and strains of fascism and anti-Semitism, arose under the leadership of Laureano Gómez.

During World War II, Colombia closely allied itself with the United States and eventually declared war on the Axis powers in retaliation for German attacks on Colombian merchant ships in the Caribbean Sea. The government concentrated those of German descent in a hotel in Fusagasugá near Bogotá and removed all German influence from SCADTA.

LA VIOLENCIA (1946-1953)

In the 1946 elections, the Liberal Party split its ticket between establishment-backed Gabriel Turbay and newcomer Jorge Eliécer Gaitán. Gaitán was a self-made man who had scaled the ladders of power within the Liberal Party despite the opposition of the traditional Liberal elite. He had a vaguely populist platform and much charisma. The moderate Conservative Mariano Ospina won a plurality of votes and was elected to the presidency. As in 1930, the transfer of power from Liberals to Conservatives and bureaucratic reaccommodation led to outbursts of violence.

On April 9, 1948, a deranged youth killed former presidential candidate Gaitán as he left his office in downtown Bogotá. His assassination sparked riots and bloodshed throughout the country, with severe destruction in the capital. The disturbance in Bogotá, known as El Bogotazo, occurred during the 9th Inter-American Conference, which had brought together leaders from all over the hemisphere. Young Fidel Castro happened to be in Bogotá that day, though he had no part in the upheaval.

The assassination of Gaitán further incited the violence that had started in 1946. Over the course of 10 years, an estimated 100,000-200,000 people died in what was laconically labeled La Violencia (The Violence). This conflict was comparable in destruction of human life with the Guerra de los Mil Días, the last civil war of the 19th century. The killing took place throughout the country, often in small towns and rural areas. Mostly it involved loyalists of the predominant party settling scores or intimidating members of the opposite party in order to extract land or secure economic gain. In some cases, the violence was sheer banditry. Numerous, horrific mass murders took place. The police often took sides with the Conservatives or simply turned a blind eye. In response, some Liberals resorted to armed resistance, giving birth to Colombia's first guerrilla armies. The Liberal Party boycotted the 1950 elections, and radical Conservative Laureano Gómez was elected president. His government pursued authoritarian and highly partisan policies, further exacerbating the violence.

DICTATORSHIP (1953-1957)

In 1953, with the purported aim of bringing an end to fighting between Liberals and Conservatives, the Colombian army, under the command of General Gustavo Rojas Pinilla, staged a coup. Rojas was able to reduce, but not halt, the violence, by curtailing police support of the Conservatives and by negotiating an amnesty with Liberal guerrillas. In 1954, Rojas was elected for a four-term period by a handpicked assembly. Incidentally, it was this, nondemocratically elected assembly that finally got around to extending suffrage to women, making Colombia one of the last countries in Latin America to do so. Rojas tried to build a populist regime with the support of organized labor, modeled after Perón in Argentina. His daughter, María Eugenia Rojas, though no Evita, was put in charge of social welfare programs. Though a majority of Colombians supported Rojas at first, his repressive policies and press censorship ended up alienating the political elites.

THE NATIONAL FRONT (1957-1974)

In May 1957, under the leadership of a coalition of Liberals and Conservatives, the country went on an extended general strike to oppose the dictatorship. Remarkably, Rojas voluntarily surrendered power and went into exile in Spain. As a way to put an end to La Violencia, Liberal and Conservative Party leaders proposed alternating presidential power for four consecutive terms while divvying up the bureaucracy on a 50-50 basis. The proposal, labeled the National Front, was ratified by a nationwide referendum and was in effect 1958-1974.

The National Front dramatically reduced the level of violence. After years of fighting, both factions were ready to give up their arms. During this period, thanks to competent economic management, the economy prospered and incomes rose. The government adopted import substitution policies that gave rise to a number of new industries, including automobiles.

By institutionalizing the power of the two traditional parties, the National Front had the unintended consequence of squeezing out other political movements, especially from the left. As a result, during the 1960s a number of leftist guerrilla groups appeared. Some were simply the continuation, under a new name, of the guerrilla groups formed during La Violencia. The Fuerzas Armadas Revolucionarias de Colombia (FARC) was a rural, peasant-based group espousing Soviet Marxism. The Ejército de Liberación Nacional (ELN) was a smaller group inspired by the Cuban revolution. The even smaller Ejército Popular de Liberación (EPL) was a Maoist-inspired group. The Movimiento 19 de Abril (M-19) was a more urban group formed by middle-class intellectuals after alleged electoral fraud deprived the populist ANAPO Party (Alianza Nacional Popular; created by ex-dictator Rojas) of power. During the 1970s and 1980s, the M-19 staged flashy coups, such as stealing Bolívar's sword (and promising to return it once the revolution had been achieved) in 1974 and seizing control of the embassy of the Dominican Republic in Bogotá in 1980.

UNDER SIEGE (1974-1991)
The Drug Trade and the Rise of Illegal Armed Groups

Due to its relative proximity to the United States, treacherous geography, and weak government institutions, Colombia has been an ideal place for cultivation, production, and shipment of illegal drugs, primarily to the

United States. During the 1970s, Colombia experienced a short-lived marijuana boom centered on the Sierra Nevada de Santa Marta. Eradication efforts by Colombian authorities and competition from homegrown marijuana produced in the United States quickly brought this boom to an end.

During the late 1970s, cocaine replaced marijuana as the main illegal drug. Though most of the coca cultivation at the time was in Peru and Bolivia, Colombian drug dealers based in Medellín started the business of picking up coca paste in Peru and Bolivia, processing it into cocaine in Colombia, and exporting the drug to the United States, where they even controlled some distribution at the local level. At its heyday in the mid-1980s, Pablo Escobar's Medellín Cartel controlled 80 percent of the world's cocaine trade. The rival Cali Cartel, controlled by the Rodríguez brothers, emerged in the 1980s and started to contest the supremacy of the Medellín Cartel, leading to a bloody feud.

During the 1980s and 1990s, coca cultivation shifted from Peru and Bolivia to Colombia, mainly to the Amazon regions of Putumayo, Caquetá, Meta, and Guaviare. Initially, leftist guerrillas such as the FARC protected the fields from the authorities in return for payment from the cartels. Eventually, they started processing and trafficking the drugs themselves. Though the guerrillas had other sources of income, such as kidnapping and extortion, especially of oil companies operating in the Llanos, the drug trade was a key factor in their growth. With these sources of income, they no longer needed popular support and morphed into criminal organizations. By the mid-1980s, the FARC had grown into a 4,000-person-strong army that controlled large portions of territory, especially in the south of the country.

During the 1980s and 1990s, the price of land was depressed as a result of the threat posed by the guerrillas. Using their vast wealth and power of intimidation, drug traffickers purchased vast swaths of land, mostly along the Caribbean coast of Colombia, at bargain prices. To defend their properties from extortion, they allied themselves with traditional landowners to create paramilitary groups. These groups often operated with the direct or tacit support of the army.

Colombian campesinos (small farmers), caught in the middle of the conflict between guerrillas and paramilitaries, suffered disproportionately. They were accused by both guerrillas and paramilitaries of sympathizing with the enemy, and the government was not there to protect them. The paramilitaries were particularly ruthless, often ordering entire villages to abandon their lands or massacring the population. The conflict between guerrillas and paramilitaries is at the source of the mass displacement of people in Colombia. According to the Office of the United Nations High Commissioner for Refugees, the number of displaced people in Colombia ranges 3.9-5.3 million, making it the country with the most internal refugees in the world.

Peace Negotiations with the FARC and M-19

In 1982, President Belisario Betancur was elected with the promise of negotiating peace with the guerrillas. The negotiations with the guerrillas got nowhere, but the FARC did establish a political party, the Unión Patriótica (UP), which successfully participated in the 1986 presidential elections and 1988 local elections, managing to win some mayoralties. The paramilitaries and local elites did not want the political arm of the FARC to wield local power. As a result, the UP was subjected to a brutal persecution by the paramilitaries, who killed more than 1,000 party members. In the midst of this violence, Colombia suffered one of its worst natural disasters: the eruption of the Nevado del Ruiz in November 1985, which produced a massive mudslide that engulfed the town of Armero, killing more than 20,000 people.

In 1985, the M-19 brazenly seized the Palacio de Justicia in Bogotá. The Colombian army responded with a heavy hand, and in the ensuing battle, half of Colombia's Supreme

Court justices were killed. Many people, including many cafeteria employees, disappeared in the army takeover, and there is speculation that they were executed and buried in a mass grave in the south of Bogotá. Weakened by this fiasco, leaders of the M-19 took up President Virgilio Barco's offer to negotiate peace. The government set down clear rules, including a cease-fire on the part of the M-19, before talks could proceed. Unlike the FARC, the M-19 was still an ideological movement. The leaders of the M-19 saw that by participating in civil life they could probably gain more than by fighting. And they were right: In 2011 the people of Bogotá elected Gustavo Petro, a former M-19 guerrilla, as their mayor. On March 19, 1990, Barco and the M-19's young leader, Carlos Pizarro, signed a peace agreement, the only major successful peace agreement to date between the authorities and a major guerrilla group.

The Rise and Fall of the Medellín Cartel

Initially, the Colombian establishment turned a blind eye to the rise of the drug cartels and even took a favorable view of the paramilitaries, who were seen as an antidote to the scourge of the guerrillas. For a time, Escobar was active in politics and cultivated a Robin Hood image, funding public works such as parks and housing projects. Rather than stick to his business, as the Cali Cartel did, Escobar started to threaten any official who tried to check his power. In 1984, he had Rodrigo Lara Bonilla, the minister of justice, assassinated. When the government subsequently cracked down, Escobar declared outright war. He assassinated judges and political leaders, set off car bombs to intimidate public opinion, and paid a reward for every policeman that was murdered in Medellín—a total of 657. To take out an enemy, he planted a bomb in an Avianca flight from Bogotá to Cali, killing all passengers on board. The Medellín Cartel planted dozens of massive bombs in Bogotá and throughout the country, terrorizing the country's population. The cartel is allegedly responsible for the assassination of three presidential candidates in 1990: Luis Carlos Galán, the staunchly anti-mafia candidate of the Liberal Party; Carlos Pizarro, the candidate of the newly demobilized M-19; and Bernardo Jaramillo, candidate of the Unión Patriótica.

There was really only one thing that Escobar feared—extradition to the United States. Through bribery and intimidation, he managed to get extradition outlawed, and he negotiated a lopsided deal with the government of César Gaviria: In return for his surrender, he was allowed to control the jail where he was locked up. From the luxurious confines of La Catedral, as the prison was named, he continued to run his empire. In 1992 there was an outcry when it became known that he had interrogated and executed enemies within the jail. When he got wind that the government planned to transfer him to another prison, he fled. In December 1993, government intelligence intercepted a phone call he made to his family, located him in Medellín, and killed him on a rooftop as he attempted to flee. It is widely believed that the Cali Cartel actively aided the authorities in the manhunt.

A New Constitution

The 1990s started on a positive footing with the enactment of a new constitution in 1991. The Constitutional Assembly that drafted the charter was drawn from all segments of the political spectrum, including the recently demobilized M-19. The new constitution was very progressive, devolving considerable power to local communities and recognizing the rights of indigenous and Afro-Colombian communities to govern their communities and ancestral lands. The charter created a powerful new Constitutional Court, which has become a stalwart defender of basic rights, as well as an independent accusatory justice system, headed by a powerful attorney general, which was created to reduce impunity.

COLOMBIA ON THE BRINK (1992-2002)
New Cartels, Paramilitaries, and Guerrillas

Drug cultivation and production increased significantly during the 1990s. The overall land dedicated to coca cultivation rose from 60,000 hectares (148,300 acres) in 1992 to 165,000 hectares (407,700 acres) in 2002. As a result of the government's successful crackdown first on the Medellín Cartel and then on the Cali Cartel, drug production split into smaller, more nimble criminal organizations. During the 1990s, the paramilitaries became stand-alone organizations that engaged in drug trafficking, expanding to more than 30,000 men in 2002. They created a national structure called the Autodefensas Unidas de Colombia, or AUC, under the leadership of Carlos Castaño. The AUC coordinated activities with local military commanders and committed atrocious crimes, often massacring scores of so-called sympathizers of guerrillas.

At the same time, the guerrillas expanded significantly during the 1990s. Strengthened by hefty revenues from kidnapping, extortion, and drug trafficking, they grew to more than 50,000 mostly peasant fighters in 2002. Their strategy was dictated primarily by military and economic considerations and they had little to no public support. At their heyday, the FARC covered the entire country, attacking military garrisons and even threatening major urban centers such as Cali. They performed increasingly large operations, such as attacking Mitú, the capital of the department of Vaupés, in 1998 or kidnapping 12 members of the Assembly of Valle del Cauca in Cali in 2002. The FARC commanders moved around the countryside unchecked. In the territories they controlled, they ruled over civilians, often committing heinous crimes. In 2002, they attacked a church in the town of Bojayá in Chocó, killing more than 100 unarmed civilians, including many children, who had sought refuge there.

Plan Colombia

The increasing growth of drug exports from Colombia to the United States in the 1990s became a source of concern for the U.S. government. From 1994 to 1998, the United States was reluctant to provide support to Colombia because the president at the time, Ernesto Samper, was tainted by accusations of having received campaign money from drug traffickers and because of evidence about human rights abuses by the Colombian army. When Andrés Pastrana was elected president in 1998, the Colombian and U.S. administrations designed a strategy to curb drug production and counteract the insurgency called Plan Colombia. This strategy had both military and social components, and was to be financed jointly by the United States and Colombia. Ultimately, the United States provided Colombia, which was becoming one of its strongest and most loyal allies in Latin America, with more than US$7 billion, heavily weighted towards military aid, especially for training and for providing aerial mobility to Colombian troops. While the impact of Plan Colombia was not immediately visible, over time it changed the balance of power in favor of the government, allowing the Colombian army to regain the upper hand in the following years.

Flawed Peace Negotiations with the FARC

President Pastrana embarked on what is now widely believed to have been an ill-conceived, hurried peace process with the FARC. He had met Manuel Marulanda, the head of the FARC, before his inauguration in 1998 and was convinced that he could bring about a quick peace. Without a clear framework, in November 1998 he acceded to the FARC's request to grant them a demilitarized zone the size of Switzerland in the eastern departments of Meta and Caquetá. In hindsight, it seems clear that the FARC had no interest or need to negotiate as they were at the peak of their military power. Rather, the FARC commanders saw the grant of the demilitarized zone as an opportunity to strengthen their organization.

From the beginning, it became clear that the FARC did not take the peace process seriously. Marulanda failed to show up at the inaugural ceremony of the peace process, leaving a forlorn Pastrana sitting alone on the stage next to a now famous *silla vacilla* (empty seat). They ran the demilitarized zone as a mini-state, nicknamed Farclandia, using it to smuggle arms, hold kidnapped prisoners, and process cocaine. During the peace negotiations, the FARC continued their attacks on the military and civilians. In February 2002, after the FARC kidnapped Eduardo Gechem, senator and president of the Senate Peace Commission, Pastrana declared the end of this ill-advised demilitarized zone and sent in the Colombian army.

A Failed State?

In 2002, the Colombian army was battling more than 50,000 guerrillas and 30,000 paramilitaries, with an estimated 6,000 child soldiers among those groups. The insurgents controlled approximately 75 percent of the country's territory. An estimated 100,000 antipersonnel mines covered 30 of 32 departments. More than 2.5 million people had been internally displaced between 1985 and 2003, with 300,000 people displaced in 2002 alone. Not surprisingly, prestigious publications such as *Foreign Policy* described Colombia at the time as failed state.

REGAINING ITS FOOTING (2002-PRESENT)
Álvaro Uribe's Assault on the Guerrillas

In the 2002 elections, fed-up Colombians overwhelmingly elected Álvaro Uribe, a former governor of Antioquia who promised to take the fight to the guerrillas. Uribe had a real grudge against the FARC, who had assassinated his father. The FARC were not fans of his, either. In a brazen show of defiance, during Uribe's inauguration ceremony in Bogotá on August 7, 2002, the guerrilla group fired various rockets aimed at the presidential palace during a post-swearing-in reception. Several rockets struck the exterior of the palace, causing minor damage (attendees were unaware of the attack), but many more fell on the humble dwellings in barrios nearby, killing 21.

During his first term, Uribe embarked on a policy of Seguridad Democrática, or Democratic Security, based on strengthening the army, eradicating illicit crops to deprive the guerrillas of revenues, and creating a controversial network of civilian collaborators who were paid for providing tips that led to successful operations against the insurgents. The government increased military expenditure and decreed taxes on the rich totaling US$4 billion to finance the cost of the war. Colombian military personnel grew from 300,000 in 2002 to 400,000 in 2007.

From 2002 to 2003, the army evicted the FARC from the central part of the country around Bogotá and Medellín, although that did not prevent them from causing terror in the cities. In February 2003, a car bomb attributed to the FARC exploded in the parking lot of the exclusive social club El Nogal, killing more than 30 people—mostly employees. From 2004 to 2006, the army pressed the FARC in its stronghold in the southern part of the country. Aerial spraying of coca crops brought down cultivated areas from 165,000 hectares (407,700 acres) in 2002 to 76,000 hectares (187,800 acres) in 2006.

In 2006, Uribe was reelected by a landslide, after Congress amended the constitution to allow for immediate presidential reelection. There is clear evidence that the government effectively bribed two congressmen whose votes were necessary for passage of the measure. Uribe interpreted the election results as a mandate to continue single-mindedly pursuing the guerrillas. The FARC came under severe stress, with thousands of guerrillas deserting and, for the first time, the FARC was subjected to effective strikes against top commanders. No longer safe in their traditional jungle strongholds in Colombia, many

FARC operatives crossed the border into Venezuela and Ecuador, causing tension between Colombia and the governments of those countries.

In early 2008, the Colombian military bombed and killed leading FARC commander Raúl Reyes in a camp in Ecuador, causing a diplomatic crisis with that country. Later that year, the military executed Operación Jaque (Operation Checkmate), a dramatic rescue operation in which they duped the FARC into handing over their most important hostages. The hostages released included three U.S. defense contractors and Ingrid Betancur, a French-Colombian independent presidential candidate who was kidnapped by the FARC during the 2002 presidential election as she proceeded by land, against the advice of the military, towards the capital of the former FARC demilitarized zone. In 2008, Manuel Marulanda, founder of the FARC, died a natural death. At that time, it was estimated that the FARC forces had plummeted to about 9,000 fighters, half of what they had been eight years before.

The Colombian army has been implicated in serious human rights abuses. Pressure from top brass to show results in the war against the guerrillas and the possibility of obtaining extended vacation time led several garrisons to execute civilians and present them as guerrillas killed in combat. In 2008, it was discovered that numerous young poor men from the city of Soacha, duped by false promises of work, had been taken to rural areas, assassinated by the army, and presented as guerrillas killed in anti-insurgency operations. This macabre episode—referred to as the scandal of *falsos positives* (false positives)—was done under the watch of Minister of Defense Juan Manuel Santos, who was later elected president of Colombia.

Peace Process with the AUC

From 2003 to 2008, the Uribe government pursued a controversial peace process with the right-wing paramilitaries, the Autodefensas Unidas de Colombia. As part of that process,

an estimated 28,000 paramilitary fighters demobilized, including most of the high-level commanders. In 2005, the Colombian Congress passed the Justice and Peace Law to provide a legal framework for the process. Unlike previous peace laws that simply granted an amnesty to the insurgents, this law provided for reduced sentences for paramilitaries who had committed serious crimes in exchange for full confessions and reparation of victims. Domestic and international observers were extremely skeptical about the process, worrying that the paramilitaries would use their power to pressure for lenient terms. These misgivings were justified by evidence that they used their power of coercion to influence the results of the 2006 parliamentary elections, a scandal referred to as *parapolítica*. Many congresspersons, including a first cousin of Uribe, ended up in prison.

It soon became clear that the paramilitary commanders were not sincere in their commitment to peace. Many refused to confess crimes and transferred their assets to front men. Covertly, they continued their drug-trafficking operations. The government placed scant importance on the truth and reparation elements of the Justice and Peace Law, severely underfunding the effort to redress crimes committed against more than 150,000 victims who had signed up as part of the process. Through 2008, the paramilitaries had confessed to a mere 2,700 crimes, a fraction of the estimated total, and refused to hand over assets. Fed up with their lack of cooperation, in 2008 Uribe extradited 14 top-ranking paramilitary commanders to the United States, where they were likely to face long sentences. However, the extradition severely hampered the effort to obtain truth and reparation for the victims of their crimes.

The difficulty in redressing the crimes against victims has been further troubled by the growth of the dozens of small *bacrim* (*bandas criminals*, or illegal armed groups) who have taken territorial control of former paramilitary areas, intimidating victims who have returned to their rightful lands under the peace process. Many of these *bacrim* inherited the structures of the former AUC groups and employed former paramilitaries.

Social and Economic Transformation

During the past decade, Colombia has made some remarkable strides in improving social and economic conditions. Due to improved security conditions, investment, both domestic and international, has boomed, totaling almost US$80 billion from 2003 to 2012. Economic growth averaged 4.8 percent 2010-2014, a significant increase over the prior decades. The number of people below poverty, as measured by the ability to buy a wide basket of basic goods and services, has declined from 59.7 percent in 2002 to 27.8 percent in 2015. In Colombia's 13 largest cities, which represent 45 percent of the population, poverty has fallen to 18.9 percent. In terms of basic needs, most urban areas are well served in terms of education, health, electricity, water, and sewage. However, there is a wide gap between the cities and rural areas, where 30 percent of the country's population lives. As of 2013, rural poverty stood at 43 percent. Though income inequality has been slowly falling, Colombia still has one of the most unequal distributions of income in the world.

Peace with the FARC

In the 2010 elections, Uribe's former minister of defense, Juan Manuel Santos, was elected president by a large majority. Santos continued to pursue an aggressive strategy against the FARC. Army operations killed Alfonso Cano, the new leader of the FARC, as well as Víctor Julio Suárez Rojas, the guerrillas' military strategist. As evidenced in the diary of Dutch FARC member Tanya Nijmeijer, found by the Colombian army after an attack on a rebel camp, morale within the FARC had sunk to an all-time low.

At the same time, Santos recognized the need to address nonmilitary facets of the violence. In 2011, Congress passed the comprehensive Victims and Land Restitutions Law, meant to rectify Uribe's Justice and Peace Law. This law provides a framework to redress the crimes committed against all victims of violence since 1985.

After a year of secret negotiations, Santos announced the start of peace dialogues with the FARC in October 2012, first in Oslo, Norway, and then in Havana, Cuba. These have proceeded at a slow pace and have covered a large number of topics, including agrarian development and drug trafficking. Former president Uribe and his allies are against this initiative, claiming that a military defeat of the FARC is the best path forward.

At the time of writing, negotiations were entering their final stage, with a focus on grouping the guerrillas in specific areas, disarmament, and demobilization. The government will convene a referendum in 2016 to ratify the agreement. If finalized, this agreement will be an important step toward de-escalating the internal conflict. In March 2016, the ELN, Colombia's second-largest guerrilla group, and the Colombian government announced that they will also begin peace talks.

Government and Economy

Under the 1991 constitution, Colombia is organized as a republic, with three branches of power—the executive, the legislative, and the judicial. The country is divided into 32 *departamentos* (departments or provinces) and the Distrito Capital (Capital District), where Bogotá is located. The departments are in turn divided into *municipios* (municipalities). These *municipios* include towns and rural areas.

The president of the republic, who is both head of state and head of government, is elected for a four-year term. With the exception of the military dictatorship of Gen. Gustavo Rojas Pinilla from 1953 to 1957, presidents have been elected by the people since 1914. In 2005, then-president Álvaro Uribe succeeded in changing the constitution to allow for one immediate presidential reelection. In 2009, he attempted to get the constitution changed once more to allow for a second reelection but was thwarted by the powerful Constitutional Court, which decreed that this change would break the necessary checks and balances of the constitutional framework.

Presidential elections are held every four years in May. If no candidate receives more than 50 percent of the votes, there will be a runoff election. Inauguration of the president takes place on August 7, the anniversary of the Batalla del Puente de Boyacá, which sealed Colombia's independence from Spain.

The legislative branch is made up of a bicameral legislature: the Senado (102 members) and the Cámara de Representantes (162 members). These representatives are elected every four years. Senators are voted for on a nationwide basis, while representatives are chosen for each department and the Distrito Capital. In addition, two seats in the Senate are reserved for indigenous representation. In the Cámara de Representantes, there are seats reserved for indigenous and Afro-Colombian communities as well as for Colombians who live abroad.

All Colombians over the age of 18—with the exception of active-duty military and police as well as those who are incarcerated—have the right to vote in all elections. Women only gained the right to vote in 1954.

POLITICAL PARTIES

Historically Colombia has had a two-party system: the Conservative Party and the Liberal Party. The Conservative Party has traditionally been aligned with the Catholic Church and has favored a more centralized government, and followed the ideas of Simón Bolívar. The Liberal Party favored a federal system of governing, has opposed church intervention in government affairs, and was aligned with the ideas of Gen. Francisco Paula Santander.

The hegemony of the two largest political parties came to a halt in the 2002 presidential election of rightist candidate Álvaro Uribe, who registered his own independent movement and then established a new party called El Partido de la Unidad. Since then, traditional parties have lost some influence. A third party, the Polo Democrático, became a relatively strong force in the early 2000s, capturing the mayorship of Bogotá, but has since faded, leaving no clear representative of the left.

Political parties today have become personality-oriented, and many candidates have been known to shop around for a party—or create their own—rather than adhere to the traditional parties. In 2014, President Juan Manuel Santos won a second term representing the Partido de la Unidad (known as La U), defeating a candidate allied with the founder of La U, former president Álvaro Uribe.

ECONOMY

Colombia has a thriving market economy based primarily on oil, mining, agriculture, and manufacturing. The country's GDP in 2015 was US$274 billion and per capita GDP was US$5,800, placing it as a middle-income country. Growth over the past decade has been a robust 4.7 percent. Inflation has averaged 3.8 percent in the past five years and unemployment has hovered around 10 percent.

During the colonial period and up until the early 20th century, small-scale gold mining and subsistence agriculture were the mainstays of Colombia's economy. Starting in the 1920s, coffee production spread throughout the country and rapidly became Colombia's major export good. Coffee production is of the mild arabica variety and is produced at elevations of 1,000 to 1,900 meters (roughly 3,000-6,000 feet), mostly by small farmers. During most of the 20th century, Colombia emphasized increasing the volume of production, using the Café de Colombia name and mythical coffee farmer Juan Valdez and his donkey Paquita to brand it. A severe global slump in coffee prices during the past decade has led to a reassessment of this strategy and an increasing focus on specialty coffees. Today, coffee represents only 3 percent of all Colombian exports.

Colombia's wide range of climates, from hot on the coast to temperate in the mountains, means that the country produces a wide range of products. Until recently, sugarcane production, fresh flowers, and bananas were the only major export-driven agribusiness. However, improvements in security in recent years have resulted in a boom in large-scale agricultural projects in palm oil, rubber, and soy. Cattle ranching occupies an estimated 25 percent of the country's land. Commercial forestry is relatively underdeveloped, though there is considerable illegal logging, especially on the Pacific coast.

In recent decades, oil production and mining have become major economic activities. The main center of oil production is the Llanos, the eastern plains of Colombia, with oil pipelines extending from there over the Cordillera Oriental to Caribbean ports. Oil currently represents roughly half of all Colombian exports. There are also significant natural gas deposits, mostly dedicated to residential use. Large-scale mining has been focused on coal and nickel, with large deposits in the Caribbean coastal region. With the improvement of security conditions in the past decade, many international firms, such as Anglogold Ashanti, have requested concessions for large-scale gold mining, often with opposition from the community. Illegal gold mining, often conducted with large machinery, is a severe threat to fragile ecosystems, especially in the Pacific coast rainforest.

During the postwar period, Colombia pursued an import substitution policy, fostering the growth of domestic industries such as automobiles, appliances and petrochemical goods. Since the early 1990s, the government has been gradually opening the economy to foreign competition and tearing down tariffs. In recent years, the country has signed free-trade agreements with the United States and the European Union. Today, the country has a fairly diversified industrial sector. The country is self-sufficient in energy, with hydropower supplying the bulk of electricity needs.

Until recently, tourism was minimal because of widespread insecurity and a negative image. Things started to change in the mid-2000s, and the annual number of international visitors has increased from 600,000 in 2000 to over 2 million in 2014. While Bogotá and Cartagena still receive the bulk of visitors, almost the entire country has opened up for tourism, though there are still pockets of no-go zones. This boom in tourism has fostered a growth of community and ecotourism options, often with the support from government. The network of *posadas nativas* (guesthouses owned and operated by locals) is one initiative to foment tourism at the community level, particularly among Afro-Colombians. In recent years, Parques Nacionales has transferred local operation of ecotourism facilities in the parks to community-based associations.

People and Culture

DEMOGRAPHY

Colombia was estimated to have had a population of a little over 46.7 million in 2015 and has the third-highest population in Latin America, behind Brazil and Mexico and slightly higher than Argentina. Around four million Colombians live outside of Colombia, mostly in the United States, Venezuela, Spain, and Ecuador. The population growth rate has fallen significantly in the past two decades and was estimated at 1.04 percent in 2015. The population of the country is relatively young, with a median age of 29.3 years. Average life expectancy is 75.5 years.

Sixty percent of the Colombian population lives in the highland Andean interior of the country, where the largest metropolitan areas are located: Bogotá (9.8 million), Medellín (3.9 million), and Cali (2.6 million). On the Caribbean coast, Barranquilla is the largest metropolitan area (2 million), followed by Cartagena (1.1 million).

It is increasingly an urban country, with around 76 percent of the population living in urban areas. This trend began during La Violencia and accelerated in the 1970s and 1980s. At least 3.9 million persons have been internally displaced due to the armed conflict in Colombia, leaving their homes in rural areas and seeking safety and economic opportunity in large cities.

Most of the population (over 84 percent) is either mestizo (having both Amerindian and white ancestry) or white. People of African (10.4 percent) and indigenous or Amerindian (over 3.4 percent) origin make up the rest of the Colombian population. There is a tiny Romani or Roma population of well under 1 percent of the population, but nonetheless they are a protected group according to the constitution.

There are more than 80 indigenous groups, with some of the largest being the Wayúu, who make up the majority in La Guajira department; the Nasa, from Cauca; the Emberá, who live in the isolated jungles of the Chocó department, and the Pastos, in Nariño. Departments in the Amazon region have the highest percentages of indigenous residents. In Vaupés, for example, 66 percent of the population is of indigenous background. Many indigenous people live on *resguardos*, areas that are collectively owned and administered by the communities.

Afro-Colombians, descendants of slaves who arrived primarily via Spanish slave trade centers in the Caribbean, mostly live along both Pacific and Caribbean coasts and in the San Andrés Archipelago. Chocó has the highest percentage of Afro-Colombians (83 percent), followed by San Andrés and Providencia (57 percent), Bolívar (28 percent), Valle del Cauca (22 percent), and Cauca (22 percent). Cali, Cartagena, and Buenaventura have particularly large Afro-Colombian populations. In the Americas, Colombia has the third-highest number of citizens of African origin, behind Brazil and the United States.

While Colombia has not attracted large numbers of immigrants, there have been periods in which the country opened its doors to newcomers. In the early 20th century, immigrants from the Middle East, specifically from Lebanon, Syria, and Palestine arrived, settling mostly along the Caribbean coast, especially in the cities of Barranquilla, Santa Marta, Cartagena, and Maicao in La Guajira. From 1920 to 1950, a sizable number of Sephardic and Ashkenazi Jews immigrated. Colombia has not had a large immigration from Asia, although in the early 20th century there was a small immigration of Japanese to the Cali area.

RELIGION

Over 90 percent of Colombians identify as Roman Catholics, and it has been the dominant religion since the arrival of the Spaniards.

Happy Monday!

Colombians enjoy a long list of holidays (over 20). With a few exceptions, such as the independence celebrations on July 20 and August 7, Christmas, and New Year's Day, holidays are celebrated on the following Monday, creating a *puente* (literally bridge, or three-day weekend).

During Semana Santa and between Christmas Day and New Year's, interior cities such as Bogotá and Medellín become ghost towns as locals head to the nearest beach or to the countryside. Conversely, beach resorts, natural reserves and parks, and pueblos fill up. Along with that, room rates and airfare can increase substantially.

The following is a list of Colombian holidays, but be sure to check a Colombian calendar for precise dates. Holidays marked with an asterisk are always celebrated on the Monday following the date of the holiday.

- Año Nuevo (New Year's Day): January 1
- Día de los Reyes Magos (Epiphany)*: January 6
- Día de San José (Saint Joseph's Day)*: March 19
- Jueves Santo (Maundy Thursday): Thursday before Easter Sunday
- Viernes Santo (Good Friday): Friday before Easter Sunday
- Día de Trabajo (International Workers' Day): May 1
- Ascensión (Ascension)*: Six weeks and one day after Easter Sunday
- Corpus Christi*: Nine weeks and one day after Easter Sunday
- Sagrado Corazón (Sacred Heart)*: Ten weeks and one day after Easter Sunday
- San Pedro y San Pablo (Saint Peter and Saint Paul)*: June 29
- Día de la Independencia (Independence Day): July 20
- Batalla de Boyacá (Battle of Boyacá): August 7
- La Asunción (Assumption of Mary)*: August 15
- Día de la Raza (equivalent of Columbus Day)*: October 12
- Todos Los Santos (All Saint's Day)*: November 1
- Día de la Independencia de Cartagena (Cartagena Independence Day)*: November 11
- La Inmaculada Concepción (Immaculate Conception): December 8
- Navidad (Christmas): December 25

The numbers of evangelical Christians, called simply *cristianos*, continue to grow, and there are other Christian congregations, including Mormons and Jehovah's Witnesses, but their numbers are small. In San Andrés and Providencia, the native Raizal population—of African descent—is mostly Baptist.

The Jewish community—estimated at around 5,000 families—is concentrated in the large cities, such as Bogotá, Medellín, Cali, and Barranquilla. There are significant Muslim communities, especially along the Caribbean coast, and there are mosques in Barranquilla, Santa Marta, Valledupar, Maicao (La Guajira), San Andrés, and Bogotá.

Semana Santa—Holy or Easter Week—is the most important religious festival in the country, and Catholics in every village, town, and city commemorate the week with a series of processions and masses. The colonial cities of Popayán, Mompox, Tunja, and Pamplona are known for their elaborate Semana Santa processions. Popayán and Mompox in particular attract pilgrims and tourists from Colombia and beyond. In cities such as Bogotá, Cali, and Cartagena, there are multitudinous processions to mountaintop religious sites, such as Monserrate, the Cerro de la Cruz, and El Monasterio de la Popa, respectively.

LANGUAGE

Spanish is the official language in Colombia. In the San Andrés Archipelago, English is still spoken by native islanders who arrived from former English colonies after the abolition of slavery, but Spanish has gained prominence.

According to the Ministry of Culture, there are at least 68 native languages, which are spoken by around 850,000 people. These include 65 indigenous languages, two Afro-Colombian languages, and Romani, which is spoken by the small Roma population.

Three indigenous languages have over 50,000 speakers: Wayúu, primarily spoken in La Guajira; Páez, primarily spoken in Cauca; and Emberá, primarily spoken in Chocó.

Essentials

Getting There

AIR

Most visitors to Colombia arrive by air at the **Aeropuerto Internacional El Dorado** in Bogotá and then take a shorter domestic flight to other destinations in the country. There are also nonstop international flights to the **Aeropuerto Internacional José María Córdova** (MDE) in Medellín and to the airports in Cali, Cartagena, Barranquilla, and Armenia.

There are reliable taxi services at all major points of arrival in Colombia.

Via Bogotá

For those overnighting in Bogotá, there is an array of hotels, including many familiar international chains, along the Avenida El Dorado (Cl. 26), the main artery connecting most of the city with the airport. The city center is a 20- to 30-minute cab ride from the airport.

From North America

Avianca (www.avianca.com) has nonstop flights between Bogotá and Miami, Fort Lauderdale, Orlando, Washington, Los Angeles, and New York-JFK. From Miami there are also nonstops to Medellín, Cali, Barranquilla, and Cartagena.

American (www.american.com) flies between Miami and Dallas and Bogotá; Miami and Medellín; and Cali and Medellín. **Delta** (www.delta.com) flies from Atlanta and New York-JFK to Bogotá; they also fly between Atlanta and Cartagena. **United** (www.united.com) has flights from Newark and Houston to Bogotá.

JetBlue (www.jetblue.com) has nonstop service to Bogotá from Orlando and Fort Lauderdale; to Cartagena from New York and Fort Lauderdale; and to Medellín from Fort Lauderdale. **Spirit** (www.spirit.com) has flights from Fort Lauderdale to Bogotá, Medellín, Cartagena, and Armenia.

Air Canada (www.aircanada.com) operates nonstop flights from Toronto to Bogotá. **Air Transat** (www.airtransat.com) provides seasonal service to Cartagena and San Andrés from Montreal.

From Europe

Avianca (www.avianca.com) has service to Bogotá and Medellín from Madrid and Barcelona, and between Bogotá and London. **Air France** (www.airfrance.com) flies from Paris to Bogotá. **Iberia** (www.iberia.com) serves Bogotá from Madrid, as does **Air Europa** (www.aireuropa.com). **Lufthansa** (www.lufthansa.com) offers service between Bogotá and Frankfurt. **Turkish Airlines** (www.turkishairlines.com) flies between Bogotá and Istanbul. **KLM** (www.klm.com) serves Amsterdam from Bogotá with a stopover in Cali.

From Latin America

Avianca (www.avianca.com) flies to Bogotá from many capitals in Latin America, including Buenos Aires, São Paulo, Rio de Janeiro, Valencia, Caracas, Lima, Santiago, and La Paz in South America; Cancún, Guatemala City, Mexico City, San José, San Juan, San Salvador, and Panama City in Central America; and Havana, Santo Domingo, Punta Cana, Aruba, and Curaçao in the Caribbean. Aerolíneas Argentinas, AeroGal, Aeromexico, Air Insel, Conviasa, Copa, Cubana, LATAM, Gol, TACA, and Tiara Air Aruba also have connections to Colombia.

CAR OR MOTORCYCLE

A growing number of travelers drive into Colombia in their own car or with a rented vehicle. The most common point of entry is at the city of Ipiales on the Pan-American Highway, the site of the Rumichaca border crossing with Ecuador at Ipiales (Tulcán on the Ecuador side). This entry point is open 5am-10pm daily.

On the Venezuelan side, the border at Cúcuta and San Antonio del Táchira is open 24 hours a day. Although there are other border crossings with Venezuela, this is the recommended overland point of entry.

For those taking the Pan-American Highway southbound, note that you will run out of pavement in Panama. In the Darién Gap, the road is interrupted by the Darién mountain range. The road picks up again in the town of Turbo on the Golfo de Urabá. Many travelers ship their vehicle from Panama City to Cartagena, which is not difficult to arrange, and will set you back about $1,000 USD. It takes about 10 days to be able to retrieve your vehicle in Cartagena.

BUS

Frequent buses depart Quito bound for Cali (20 hours) or Bogotá (30 hours). You can also take a taxi from the town of Tulcán to the border at Ipiales and from there take an onward bus to Pasto, Popayán, Cali, or beyond. In Quito contact **Líneas de los Andes** (www.lineasdelosandes.com.co).

BOAT

It is possible to enter the country from Panama, usually via the San Blas Islands. **Blue Sailing** (U.S. tel. 203/660-8654, www.bluesailing.net) offers sailboat trips between various points in Panama to Cartagena. The trip usually takes about 45 hours and costs around US$500. Sometimes, particularly during the windy season between November and March, boats stop in Sapzurro, Colombia, near the border. **San Blas Adventures** (www.sanblasadventures.com, contact@sanblasadventures.com) offers multiday sailboat tours to the San Blas Islands that usually depart from Cartí and end up in the Panamanian border village of La Miel. From there you can walk over the border to Sapzurro and take a *lancha* (boat) from there to Capurganá. There are regular morning boats from Capurganá to both Acandí and Turbo. During the windy season, especially between December and February, this trip can be quite rough.

Getting Around

AIR

Air travel is an excellent, quick, and, thanks to discount airlines such as VivaColombia, economical way to travel within Colombia. Flying is the best option for those looking to avoid spending double-digit hours in a bus or for those with a short amount of time—and sometimes it's cheaper than taking a bus, as well. Airlines have excellent track records and maintain modern fleets.

Bogotá is the major hub in the country, with the majority of domestic **Avianca** (tel. 1/401-3434, www.avianca.com) flights departing from the Puente Aereo terminal (not the main terminal of the adjacent international airport). Other domestic carriers **LATAM Airlines** (Colombian toll-free tel. 01/800-094-9490, www.latam.com), **VivaColombia** (tel. 1/489-7989, www.vivacolombia.co), **EasyFly** (tel. 1/414-8111, www.easyfly.com.co), **Satena** (Colombian toll-free tel. 01/800-091-2034, www.satena.com), and **Copa** (Colombian toll-free tel. 01/800-011-0808, www.copaair.com) depart from the new domestic wing of the international airport.

For Leticia in the Amazon, the Pacific coast destinations of Bahía Solano and Nuquí, La Macarena (Caño Cristales) in Los Llanos, and

San Andrés and Providencia in the Caribbean, the only viable way to get there is by air.

If you plan to fly to Caribbean destinations such as Cartagena, San Andrés, Providencia, and Santa Marta during high tourist season, be sure to purchase your ticket well in advance, as seats quickly sell out and prices go through the roof. If your destination is Cartagena or Santa Marta, be sure to check fares to Barranquilla. These may be less expensive, and that city is only about an hour away. Similarly, if you plan to go to the Carnaval de Barranquilla in February, check fares to both Cartagena and Santa Marta. If you are flying to the Coffee Region, inquire about flights to Pereira, Armenia, and Manizales, as the distances between these cities are short. The Manizales airport, however, is often closed due to inclement weather.

Medellín has two airports: **Aeropuerto Internacional José María Córdova** (in Rionegro) and **Aeropuerto Olaya Herrera.** All international flights and most large airplane flights depart from Rionegro, a town about an hour away from Medellín. The airport is simply referred to as "Rionegro." **Satena** (Colombian toll-free tel. 01/800-091-2034, www.satena.com) and **Aerolíneas de Antioquia-ADA** (Colombian toll-free tel. 01/800-051-4232, www.ada-aero.com) use the Olaya Herrera airport, which is conveniently located in town. This is a hub for flights to remote communities in the western and Pacific region, including Acandí and Capurganá near the Panamanian border.

There are strict weight restrictions for flights to Providencia from San Andrés, which are generally on small planes such as those used by the military-owned Satena airline. These island flights sell out fast.

LONG-DISTANCE BUS

In order to thoroughly cover the country, you will have to hop on a bus at some point—just like the vast majority of Colombians. This is the money-saving choice and often the only option for getting to smaller communities. There are different types of buses, from large coaches for long-distance travel to *colectivos* for shorter distances. *Colectivos* (minivans) are often much quicker, although you won't have much legroom. There are also shared taxis that run between towns, a cramped but quick option. During major holidays, purchase bus tickets in advance if you can, as buses can quickly fill up.

When you arrive at a bus station with guidebook in hand and backpack on, you will be swarmed by touts barking out city names to you, desperately seeking your business on their bus. You can go with the flow and follow them, or, if you prefer a little more control and calm, you can instead walk past them to the ticket booths. Forge ahead and shake your head while saying *gracias.* You can try to negotiate better fares at the ticket booths, as there are often various options for traveling the same route. Find out what time the bus is leaving, if the vehicle is a big bus, a *buseta,* or minivan, and where your seat is located (try not to get stuck in the last row).

Be alert and aware of your surroundings and of your possessions when you arrive at bus stations, are waiting in the bus terminal, and are on board buses. Try to avoid flashing around expensive gadgets and cameras while on board. If you check luggage, request a receipt. During pit stops along the way, be sure to keep your valuables with you at all times.

During most bus rides of more than a few hours' length, you will be subjected to loud and/or violent films. Earplugs, eye masks, and even sleeping pills available at most pharmacies for those long journeys may come in handy, but make sure your possessions are well guarded. Expect the air-conditioning to be cranked to full blast, so have a layer or two at the ready. Pick up some provisions like apples or nuts before departing, because food options are generally unhealthy.

Bus drivers like to drive as fast as possible, and generally have few qualms about overtaking cars even on hairpin curves. Large buses tend to be safer than smaller ones, if only because they can't go as fast.

Buses may be stopped by police, and you

may be required to show or temporarily hand over your passport (keep it handy). Sometimes passengers may be asked to disembark from the bus so that the police can search it for illegal drugs or other contraband. Young males may be given a pat-down. Even if it annoys you, it is always best to keep cool and remain courteous with police officers who are just doing their job.

PUBLIC TRANSPORTATION

For visitors, public transportation networks are most useful in Bogotá, Medellín, and Cali. Many cities, such as Medellín, Cali, Armenia, Bucaramanga, Pereira, Barranquilla, and Cartagena have adopted the Bogotá rapid bus system (BRT) model of the TransMilenio.

Today, buses, such as the SITP bus network in Bogotá, are clean, safe, and only pick up passengers at designated stops. In large cities, you will need to purchase an electronic refillable bus card. These can be purchased at *papelerías* (stationery shops) often close to bus stops and stations.

The free app **Moovit** provides route information for public transportation options in many Colombian cities.

CAR, MOTORCYCLE, OR BICYCLE

Although conditions are improving, driving in Colombia is generally a poor idea for international tourists. Roads are often in a poor state and are almost always just two lanes, speed limits and basic driving norms are not respected, driving through large towns and cities can be supremely stressful, signage is poor, sudden mudslides can close roads for hours on end during rainy seasons, and roads can be unsafe at night.

One exception is the Coffee Region. Here the roads are excellent and often four lanes, distances are short, and traffic is manageable. If you are planning on spending some time visiting coffee farms and idyllic towns, this might be a good option.

Another region where renting a car may make sense is in Boyacá. Here the countryside is beautiful and traffic is manageable.

There are car rental offices in all the major airports in the country. **Hertz** (tel. 1/756-0600, www.rentacarcolombia.co) and the national **Colombia Car Rental** (U.S. tel. 913/368-0091, www.colombiacarsrental.com) are two with various offices nationwide.

Touring Colombia on motorcycle is an increasingly popular option. One of the best motorcycle travel agencies in the country is **Motolombia** (tel. 2/665-9548, www.motolombia.com), based in Cali. A growing number of travelers are motoring the Pan-American Highway, shipping their bikes from Panama or the United States to Cartagena, or vice versa.

Bicyclists will not get much respect on Colombian roads, and there are rarely any bike lanes of significance. In Santander and in Boyacá the scenery is absolutely spectacular, but, especially in Santander, it is often quite mountainous. In the Valle del Cauca, around Buga and towards Roldanillo, the roads are good and flat. Staff at **Colombian Bike Junkies** (San Gil cell tel. 316/327-6101, Medellín cell tel. 318/808-6769, www.colombianbikejunkies.com), based in San Gil, are experts on biking throughout the country, with an emphasis on mountain biking. Another outfitter is **Colombia en Bicicleta** (www.colombiaenbicicleta.com), catering mostly to bike enthusiasts living in Bogotá.

Every Sunday in cities across Colombia thousands of cyclists (joggers, skaters, and dog walkers, too) head to the city streets for some fresh air and exercise. This is the **Ciclovía,** an initiative that began in Bogotá in which city streets are closed to traffic. Except in Bogotá, it may be difficult to find a bike rental place, but you can still head out for a jog. *Ciclorutas* (bike paths) are being built in the major cities as well, and Bogotá has an extensive *cicloruta* network. Again, cyclists don't get much respect from motorists, so be careful!

BOAT

In some remote locations in Colombia the most common way to get around is by *lancha*, or boat. Many of the isolated villages and beaches and the Parque Nacional Natural Utría along the Pacific coast are accessed only by boat from either Bahía Solano or Nuquí. The same goes for Isla Gorgona. To get to this island park, you normally have to take a boat from Guapí or from Buenaventura. All hotels or travel agencies can organize these trips for you.

Although there are some flights from Medellín to the Darién Gap village of Capurganá, it is often more convenient to either fly to the town of Acandí and take a boat onward to Capurganá or take a boat from Turbo or Necoclí. Waters can be rough, especially from November to March. Don't risk this trip if you have a bad back, as the boat ride can be jarring.

In the Amazon region, the only way to get from Leticia to attractions nearby, including Puerto Nariño and the eco-lodges on the Río Yavarí, is by a boat on the Amazon, which is a memorable experience. All boats leave from the *malecón* (wharf) in Leticia.

The fabulous beaches of Islas del Rosario, off the coast of Cartagena, are accessed only by boat from the Muelle Turístico or from the docks in Manga. The same goes for Barú, although you can technically drive there. If visiting Mompox from Cartagena, you'll need to take a ferry from the town of Magangué along the mighty Río Magdalena.

Visas and Officialdom

PASSPORTS AND VISAS

U.S. and Canadian citizens do not need a visa for visits to Colombia of less than 90 days. You may be asked to show a return ticket.

There is an exit tax (Tasa Aeroportuaría Internacional) of around US$37 (COP$122,000). This is often automatically tacked onto your ticket price, but the airline agents will let you know upon check-in. If you are visiting for under 60 days, you are exempt. Prior to check-in, inquire with the airline if you qualify for an exemption. You may be directed to the Aeronáutica Civil booth across from the airline check-in counter, where you'll show your passport to get an exemption stamp.

To renew a tourist visa, you must go to an office of **Migración Colombia** (www.migracioncolombia.gov.co) to request an extension of another 90 days.

CUSTOMS

Upon arrival in Colombia, bags will be spot-checked by customs authorities. Duty-free items up to a value of US$1,500 can be brought in to Colombia. Firearms are not allowed into the country, and many animal and vegetable products are not allowed. If you are carrying over US$10,000 in cash you must declare it.

Departing Colombia, expect a pat-down by police (looking for illegal drugs?) at the airport. In addition, luggage may be screened for drugs, Columbian art, and exotic animals.

EMBASSIES AND CONSULATES

The **United States Embassy** (Cl. 24 Bis No. 48-50, tel. 1/275-2000, http://bogota.usembassy.gov) is in Bogotá, near the airport. In case of an emergency, during business hours contact the **U.S. Citizen Services Hotline** (business hours tel. 1/275-2000, after-hours and weekends tel. 1/275-4021). Non-emergency calls are answered at the American Citizen Services Section from Monday through Thursday 2pm-4pm. To be informed of security developments or emergencies during your visit, you can enroll in the Smart Traveler Enrollment Program (STEP) on the U.S. Embassy website. In Barranquilla, there is a **Consular Agency**

Office (Cl. 77B No. 57-141, Suite 511, tel. 5/353-2001 or tel. 5/353-2182), but its hours and services are limited.

The **Canadian Embassy** (Cra. 7 No. 114-33, Piso 14, tel. 1/657-9800, www.canadainternational.gc.ca) is in Bogotá. There is a **Canadian Consular Office** (Bocagrande Edificio Centro Ejecutivo Oficina 1103, Cra. 3, No. 8-129, tel. 5/665-5838) in Cartagena. For emergencies, Canadian citizens can call the **emergency hotline** (Can. tel. 613/996-8885) in Canada collect.

Accommodations and Food

HOSTELS

Hostels catering to backpackers are a relatively new phenomenon, and more are offering private rooms for those not interested in sharing a dorm room with strangers. Young people are drawn to hostels, but an increasing number of older travelers opt for hostels, as these, in addition to offering budget accommodations, are also the best places for information on activities. Most hostel staff speak English. **Hostel Trail** (www.hosteltrail.com) is a good resource for information on Colombian hostels. Hostels generally maintain updated information on their Facebook pages.

HOTELS

Midrange hotels are often harder to find and their quality can be unpredictable. Beds can be uncomfortable, rooms may be small, views might be unappealing, and service hit-or-miss. Spanish is the most prevalent language spoken at these types of accommodations.

High-end hotels, including international brands, are in all large cities. In tourist centers such as Cartagena and Santa Marta, boutique hotels are good options for those seeking charm. Expect courteous service and comfort. The only place to expect international television channels and access for travelers with disabilities are at high-end international hotels.

VALUE-ADDED TAX EXEMPTION

Non-Colombian visitors are exempt from IVA, a sales tax, which is around 16 percent. To qualify for the exemption, you must make your hotel reservation by email or phone from abroad, there must be at least two services included (such as the room fee and an included breakfast), and you must show proof of being in Colombia for less than six months.

FOOD AND DRINK

In Bogotá and Cartagena especially, Colombian foodie culture is alive and well, and visitors will have a wealth of excellent dining options—if they don't mind the occasional Manhattan prices.

While seafood, especially *pescado frito* (fried fish), is de rigueur in the Caribbean and along the Pacific, in the interior beef and chicken rule. In the Medellín area, the famed and hearty *bandeja paisa* is a dish made of red beans cooked with pork, white rice, ground meat, *chicharrón* (fried pork rinds), fried egg, plantains (*patacones*), chorizo, *hogao* sauce, *morcilla* (black pudding), avocado, and lemon. In Bogotá, the dish for cool evenings is *ajiaco*, a chicken and potato soup. In rural areas, the typical lunchtime meal will include soup and a main dish (*seco*) such as *arroz con pollo* (chicken with rice). Eat what you can, but foreigners are forgiven if they can't finish a plate.

Vegetarians have decent options available to them, especially in tourist centers. A can of lentils can be a helpful travel companion in rural areas. In coastal areas it will be hard to avoid eating fish.

Be sure to try the many unusual fruits and juices in Colombia. Juice is either served in water or in milk, and sometimes has a lot of sugar. The same goes for freshly squeezed lemonade.

Coffee, usually served as *tinto* (shots of

espresso mixed with water), can be down-right dismal in rural areas, where it is served very sweet. For a good cup of coffee, head to a national brand like Juan Valdez or Oma. Non-coffee drinkers will enjoy *aromatica,* herbal tea that is typically served after dinner.

Colombia is a major chocolate producer and has some award-winning local brands, such as Hunter's Chocolate, which works with small farmers in different regions including the Sierra Nevada and near Tumaco.

Breakfast almost universally consists of eggs, bread or *arepas*, juice, and coffee. Fresh fruit is not that common at breakfast. *Arepas* are important in Colombia: Every region has its own take on these starchy corn cakes. *Arepas* in Medellín are large, thin, and bland, while *arepas* in other parts of the country can be cheese-filled.

Travel Tips

ACCESS FOR TRAVELERS WITH DISABILITIES

Only international and some national hotel chains offer rooms (usually just one or two) that are wheelchair-accessible. Hostels and small hotels in secondary cities or towns will not. Airport and airline staff will usually bend over backwards to help those with disabilities, if you ask.

Getting around cities and towns is complicated, as good sidewalks and ramps are the exception, not the rule. Motorists may not stop—or even slow down—for pedestrians.

WOMEN TRAVELING ALONE

Along the Caribbean and Pacific coasts especially, women traveling alone should expect to be on the receiving end of flirting and various friendly offers by men and curiosity by everyone. Women should be extra cautious in taxis and buses. Always order taxis by phone and avoid taking them alone at night. While incidents are unlikely, it is not a fantastic idea to go out for a jog, a walk on a remote beach, or a hike through the jungle on your own. Walking about small towns at night alone may elicit looks or comments. Don't reveal personal information, where you are staying, or where you are going to inquisitive strangers. There have been incidents in the past with single women travelers in remote areas of La Guajira.

GAY AND LESBIAN TRAVELERS

Colombia has some of the Western Hemisphere's most progressive laws regarding the rights of LGBT people. The Constitutional Court legalized same-sex marriage in 2016 after a torturous, decades-long struggle marked by court victories, legislative defeats, and much debate. Same-sex couples still cannot adopt children in Colombia, although individuals can.

Colombia is a fairly tolerant country, especially in its large cities. Bogotá is one of the most gay-friendly cities on the continent, with a large gay nightlife scene and city-supported LGBT community centers. In many neighborhoods, passersby don't blink an eye when they see a gay couple holding hands on the sidewalk.

The Caribbean region is generally less open to homosexuality, and this is especially true in rural areas. Nevertheless, the main cities of the region—Cartagena, Barranquilla, and Santa Marta—have gay clubs and are home to active LGBT communities. All bars and clubs, while catering to men, are welcoming to gay women and to straight people. In the San Andrés Archipelago, homophobia is the norm among the native islanders, although violence against gay travelers is unheard of. The online guide **Guia GAY Colombia** (www.guiagaycolombia.com) has a listing of meeting places for LGBT people throughout the country.

Discrimination, especially against

transgender people and even more so against trans sex workers, continues to be a problem in many cities and towns, in particular in Cali and the Caribbean. The award-winning nonprofit group **Colombia Diversa** (www.colombiadiversa.org) is the main advocate for LGBT rights in the country, with **Caribe Afirmativo** (www.caribeafirmativo.lgbt) focusing its efforts on the Caribbean region.

Gay men in particular should be cautious using dating apps, keep an eye on drinks at nightclubs, and avoid cabs off the street when departing clubs.

Same-sex couples should not hesitate to insist on *matrimonial* (double) beds at hotels. Most hotels in cities and even in smaller towns and rural areas are becoming more clued in on this. At guesthouses, hostels, and at some midsized hotels, front desk staff may charge if you invite a guest to the room. At large international hotels and at apartments for rent, this is never the case.

CONDUCT AND CUSTOMS

Colombians are generally friendly to visitors and are often inquisitive about where you are from and how you like Colombia so far. This is most often the case in rural areas. Colombians are also quite proud of their country, after emerging from decades of armed conflict.

With acquaintances and strangers alike, it is customary to ask how someone is doing before moving on to other business. You're even expected to issue a blanket *buenos días* ("Good morning") in the elevator. When greeting an acquaintance, it's customary to shake hands (between men) or give an air kiss on the cheek (for women), although this is mostly the case in urban areas, especially with the upper crust.

Colombians are comfortable with noise—expect the TV to always be on and music blasting almost everywhere. Many Colombians you meet will ask about your family. Family ties are very important to Colombians. Sundays often mean lunch in the countryside with nuclear and extended family members.

While tourists get a pass on appearance, it's preferred that men avoid wearing shorts, especially at restaurants, except on the Caribbean coast. Dress up, like the locals do, when going out on the town.

Indigenous cultures are much more conservative, and women are expected to refrain from showing much skin.

Health and Safety

VACCINATIONS

There are no vaccination requirements for travel to Colombia. At present, proof of vaccination is no longer required in the national parks (namely Parque Nacional Natural Tayrona). However, having proof of vaccination may make life easier, especially if you plan on traveling onward to Brazil or other countries.

The Centers for Disease Control (CDC) recommends that travelers to Colombia get up-to-date on the following vaccines: measles-mumps-rubella (MMR), diphtheria-tetanus-pertussis, varicella (chicken pox), polio, and the yearly flu shot.

DISEASES AND ILLNESSES
Malaria, Zika, Chikungunya, and Dengue Fever

In low-lying tropical areas of Colombia, mosquito-borne illnesses such as malaria, dengue fever, chikungunya, and Zika are common. It is best to assume that there is a risk, albeit quite small, in all areas of the country.

Malaria is a concern in the entire Amazon region and in the lowland departments of Antioquia, Chocó, Córdoba, Nariño, and Bolívar. There is low to no malarial risk in Cartagena and in areas above 1,600 meters (5,000 feet). The Colombian Ministry of Health estimates that there are around 63,000 annual cases of malaria in the country, 20 of which result in death. Most at risk are children under the age of 15. Malaria symptoms include fever, headache, chills, vomiting, fatigue, and difficulty breathing. Treatment involves the administration of various antimalarial drugs. If you plan on spending a lot of time outdoors in lowland tropical areas, consider taking an antimalarial chemoprophylaxis.

The number of cases of **dengue fever** in Colombia has grown from 5.2 cases per 100,000 residents in the 1990s to around 18.1 cases per 100,000 in the 2000s. It is another mosquito-borne illness. The most common symptoms of dengue fever are fever; headaches; muscle, bone, and joint pain; and pain behind the eyes. It is fatal in less than 1 percent of the cases. Treatment usually involves rest and hydration and the administration of pain relievers for headache and muscle pain. **Chikungunya virus** has similar symptoms to dengue, and an infection, involving painful aches, can last for several months. It is spread, like dengue, by the *Aedes aegypti* mosquito, often during daytime.

Zika virus is the latest scare to grip South America, and is a concern to pregnant women, as there is a link between the virus and birth defects. Pregnant women should avoid traveling to low-lying areas (under 2,000 meters/6,000 feet), where Zika is present. This includes much of Colombia. Symptoms include fever, rash, joint pains, and conjunctivitis.

The Centers for Disease Control (www.cdc.gov) remains the best resource on health concerns for worldwide travel.

PREVENTION
Use mosquito nets over beds when visiting tropical areas of Colombia. Examine them well before using, and if you notice large holes in the nets request replacements. Mosquitoes tend to be at their worst at dawn, dusk, and in the evenings. Wear lightweight, long-sleeved, and light-colored shirts, long pants, and socks, and keep some insect repellent handy.

DEET is considered effective in preventing mosquito bites, but there are other, less-toxic alternatives, most available from online retailers.

If you go to the Amazon region, especially during rainy seasons, take an antimalarial prophylaxis starting 15 days before arrival, continuing 15 days after departing the region. According to the CDC, the recommended chemoprophylaxis for visitors to malarial regions of Colombia is atovaquone-proguanil, doxycycline, or mefloquine. These drugs are available at most pharmacies in Colombia with no prescription necessary.

Altitude Sickness
The high altitudes of the Andes, including in Bogotá (2,625 meters/8,612 feet), can be a problem for some. If arriving directly in Bogotá, or if you are embarking on treks in the Sierra Nevada del Cocuy or in Los Nevados, where the highest peaks reach 5,300 meters (over 17,000 feet), for the first couple of days take it easy and avoid drinking alcohol. Make mountain ascents gradually if possible. You can also take the drug acetazolamide to help speed up your acclimatization. Drinking coca tea or chewing on coca leaves may help prevent *soroche,* as altitude sickness is called in Colombia.

Traveler's Diarrhea
Stomach flu or traveler's diarrhea is a common malady when traveling through Colombia. These are usually caused by food contamination resulting from the presence of *E. coli* bacteria. Street foods, including undercooked meat, raw vegetables, dairy products, and ice, are some of the main culprits. If you get a case of traveler's diarrhea, be sure to drink lots of clear liquids, avoid caffeine, and take an oral rehydration solution of salt, sugar, and water.

Tap Water
Tap water is fine to drink in Colombia's major cities, but you should drink bottled, purified,

or boiled water in the Amazon, the Pacific coast, the Darién Gap, La Guajira, and San Andrés and Providencia. As an alternative to buying plastic bottles, look for *bolsitas* (bags) of water. They come in a variety of sizes and use less plastic.

MEDICAL SERVICES

Colombia has excellent hospitals in its major cities. Over 20 hospitals in Colombia (in Bogotá, Medellín, Bucaramanga, and Cali) have been listed in the *América Economía* magazine listing of the top 40 hospitals of Latin America. Four hospitals were in the top 10. Those were the **Fundación Santa Fe de Bogotá** (www.fsfb.org.co), the **Fundación Valle del Lili** (www.valledellili. org) in Cali, the **Fundación Cardioinfantil** (www.cardioinfantil.org) in Bogotá, and the **Fundación Cardiovascular de Colombia** (www.fcv.org) in Floridablanca, near Bucaramanga. For sexual and reproductive health issues, **Profamilia** (www.profamilia. org.co) has a large network of clinics that provide walk-in and low-cost services throughout the country.

Aerosanidad SAS (tel. 1/439-7080, 24-hour hotline tel. 1/266-2247 or tel. 1/439-7080, www.aerosanidadsas.com) provides transportation services for ill or injured persons in remote locations of Colombia to medical facilities in the large cities.

Travel insurance is a good idea to purchase before arriving in Colombia, especially if you plan on doing a lot of outdoor adventures. One recommended provider of travel insurance is **Assist Card** (www.assist-card.com). Before taking a paragliding ride or white-water rafting trip inquire to see whether insurance is included in the price of the trip—it should be.

CRIME

Colombia is safe to visit, and the majority of visitors have a wonderful experience in the country. For international travelers, there is little to worry about when it comes to illegal armed groups today. The threat of kidnapping

of civilians and visitors has been almost completely eliminated.

Even in the worst of times, places like Cartagena and Bogotá have always been less affected by violence from the armed conflict plaguing the rest of the country. Now, with implementation of a peace deal between FARC guerrillas and the Colombian government within the realm of possibility, the outlook is brighter than ever. However, uncertainty remains and smaller groups of former paramilitaries (*bacrim*) and guerrillas operate in some cities and towns, while drug lords and dangerous gangs rule marginalized urban areas.

There are still places to avoid, even along the peaceful Caribbean coast. In the northwest, avoid the jungle and rural areas in and around Parque Nacional Natural Los Katios in the Darién region, as well as the Parque Nacional Natural Paramillo in Córdoba. On the eastern side of the country, the Catatumbo region, along the Venezuelan border, remains volatile. In the rest of the country, hot spots include much of the Amazonian rainforest (with the notable exception of Leticia and Puerto Nariño), areas near La Macarena in Meta (but Caño Cristales is safe), rural areas of Cauca (Popayán and Tierradentro are fine), rural areas near Tumaco and Buenaventura on the Pacific coast, and much of the Chocó jungle (except for tourist areas of Bahía Solano, Nuquí, and the capital city of Quibdó).

For updated travel advisories, check the website of the **U.S. Embassy** (http://bogota. usembassy.gov/) in Bogotá. The embassy always errs on the side of caution.

Street Crime

Cell phone theft continues to plague much of the country. Keep wallets in front pockets, be aware of your surroundings, and keep shopping bags and backpacks near you at all times. Muggings in major cities are not unheard of, but are quite rare. Be alert to your surroundings late at night.

Always order cabs instead of hailing them

off the street. Fortunately, taxi crimes have diminished greatly in recent years, in no small part due to the advent of apps like Uber and Easy Taxi.

Police

From just about anywhere in the country, the police can be reached by dialing 123 on any phone. Otherwise, many parks are home to neighborhood police stations, called CAI (Centros de Atención Inmediata). Authorities may not be able to do much about petty theft, however.

Recreational Drugs

In Colombia, the legal status of the use, transport, and possession of recreational drugs can be best described as murky. A 1994 high court decision legalized a "personal dose" of recreational drugs for adults. The sale of drugs is prohibited. An attempt by President Uribe to criminalize recreational drugs failed in 2005. In practice, police may harass those caught with drugs, in addition to confiscating drugs, and may solicit bribes.

Medical use of marijuana was legalized in 2015.

Information and Services

MONEY
Currency

Colombia's official currency is the peso, which is abbreviated as COP. Prices in Colombia are marked with a dollar sign, but remember that you're seeing the price in Colombian pesos. COP$1,000,000 isn't enough to buy a house in Colombia, but it will usually cover a few nights in a nice hotel!

Bills in Colombia are in denominations of $1,000, $2,000, $5,000, $10,000, $20,000, $50,000, and $100,000. Coins in Colombia got a makeover in 2012, so you may see two different versions of the same coin amount. Coins in Colombia are in denominations of $50, $100, $200, $500, and $1,000. The equivalent of cents is *centavos* in Colombian Spanish.

Due to dropping oil prices, the Colombian peso has devalued to record levels, making the country a bargain for international visitors. In 2016, one US dollar was the equivalent of COP$3,000.

Most banks in Colombia do not exchange money. For that, you'll have to go to an exchange bank, located in all major cities. There are money changers on the streets of Cartagena, but the street is not the best place for safe and honest transactions.

Travelers checks are not worth the hassle, as they are hard to cash. Dollars are sometimes accepted in Cartagena and other major tourist destinations. To have cash wired to you from abroad, look for a Western Union office. These are located only in major cities.

Counterfeit bills are a problem in Colombia, and unsuspecting international visitors are often the recipients. Bar staff, taxi drivers, and street vendors are the most common culprits. It's good to always have a stash of small bills to avoid getting large bills back as change. Tattered and torn bills will also be passed off to you, which could pose a problem. Try not to accept those.

Consignaciones

Consignaciones (bank transfers) are a common way to pay for hotel reservations (especially in areas such as Providencia and remote resorts), tour packages or guides, or entry to national parks. It's often a pain to make these deposits in person, as the world of banking can be confusing for non-Colombians. On the plus side, making a deposit directly into the hotel's bank account provides some peace of mind because it will diminish the need to carry large amounts of cash. To make a *consignación* you will need to know the recipient's bank account and whether that is a *corriente* (checking) or *ahorros* (savings) account, and you will need to show some identification and probably have to provide a fingerprint. Be sure to hold onto the receipt to notify the recipient of your deposit.

ATMs

The best way to get cash is to use your bank ATM card. These are almost universally accepted at *cajeros automáticos* (ATMs) in the country. *Cajeros* are almost everywhere except in the smallest of towns or in remote areas. Withdrawal fees are relatively expensive, although they vary. You can usually take out up to around COP$300,000-500,000 (the equivalent of around US$150-250) per transaction. Many banks place limits on how much one can withdraw in a day (COP$1,000,000).

Credit and Debit Cards

Credit and debit card use is becoming more prevalent in Colombia; however, online credit card transactions are still not so common except for the major airlines and some of the event ticket companies, such as www.tuboleta.com or www.colboletos.com. When you use your plastic, you will be asked if it's *credito* (credit) or *debito* (debit). If using a *tarjeta de credito* (credit card) in restaurants and stores, you will be asked something like, *"¿Cuantas cuotas?"* or *"¿Numero de cuotas?"* ("How many installments?"). Most visitors prefer one *cuota* (*"Una, por favor"*). But you can have even your dinner bill paid in up to 24 installments! If using a *tarjeta de debito,* you'll be asked if it is a *corriente* (checking) or *ahorros* (savings) account.

Tipping

In most sit-down restaurants in larger cities, a 10 percent service charge is automatically included in the bill. Waitstaff are required to ask you, *"¿Desea incluir el servicio?"* ("Would you like to include the service in the bill?"). Many times restaurant staff neglect to ask international tourists about the service inclusion. If you find the service to be exceptional, you can leave a little extra in cash. Although tipping is not expected in bars or cafés, tip jars are becoming more common. International visitors are often expected to tip more than Colombians. In small-town restaurants throughout the country, tipping is not the norm.

It is not customary to tip taxi drivers. But if you feel the driver was a good one who drove safely and was honest, or if he or she made an additional stop for you, waited for you, or was just pleasant, you can always round up the bill (instead of COP$6,200 give the driver COP$7,000 and say *"Quédese con las vueltas por favor"* ("Keep the change"). Note that sometimes a "tip" is already included in the fare for non-Colombian visitors!

In hotels, usually a tip of COP$5,000 will suffice for porters who help with luggage, unless you have lots of stuff. Tips are not expected, but are certainly welcome, for housekeeping staff.

Value-Added Tax

Non-Colombian visitors are entitled to a refund of value-added taxes for purchases on clothing, jewelry, and other items if their purchases total more than COP$300,000. Save all credit card receipts and fill out Form 1344 (available online at www.dian.gov.co). Submit this to the **DIAN office** (tel. 1/607-9999) at the airport before departure. You may have several hoops to go through to achieve success. Go to the DIAN office before checking your luggage, as you will have to present the items you purchased.

INTERNET AND TELEPHONES

Being connected makes travel throughout Colombia so much easier. Free Wi-Fi is available at most hotels, restaurants, and cafés in major cities. An important Spanish phrase to learn is *"Como es la contraseña para el wifi?"* ("What's the password for the Wi-Fi?")

Obtaining a SIM card for your cell phone will ensure connectivity in all but the most remote locations. Sometimes low-tech phones work better than smartphones in very rural or remote locations like Providencia. SIM cards (*datos de prepago*) are available at mobile-phone carriers in all major towns and cities. Three main cell phone companies are Claro, Movistar, and Tigo.

Facebook and Whatsapp are often the best bets for contacting hotels, restaurants, and shops.

The telephone country code for Colombia is 57. Cell phone numbers are 10 digits long, beginning with a 3. To call a Colombian cell phone from abroad, you must use the country code followed by that 10-digit number. Landline numbers in Colombia are seven digits long. An area code is necessary when calling from a different region. To call a landline from a cell phone, dial 03 + area code + 7-digit number. To reach a cell phone from a landline, dial 03 + 10-digit number.

Resources

Spanish Phrasebook

Knowing some Spanish is essential to visit Colombia, as relatively few people outside the major cities speak English. Colombian Spanish is said to be among the clearest in Latin America. However, there are many regional differences.

Spanish commonly uses 30 letters—the familiar English 26, plus four straightforward additions: ch, ll, ñ, and rr, which are explained in "Consonants," below.

PRONUNCIATION

Once you learn them, Spanish pronunciation rules—in contrast to English—don't change. Spanish vowels generally sound softer than in English. (*Note:* The capitalized syllables below receive stronger accents.)

Vowels

a like ah, as in "hah": *agua* AH-gooah (water), *pan* PAHN (bread), and *casa* CAH-sah (house)

e like ay, as in "may:" *mesa* MAY-sah (table), *tela* TAY-lah (cloth), and *de* DAY (of, from)

i like ee, as in "need": *diez* dee-AYZ (ten), *comida* ko-MEE-dah (meal), and *fin* FEEN (end)

o like oh, as in "go": *peso* PAY-soh (weight), *ocho* OH-choh (eight), and *poco* POH-koh (a bit)

u like oo, as in "cool": *uno* OO-noh (one), *cuarto* KOOAHR-toh (room), and *usted* oos-TAYD (you); when it follows a "q" the u is silent; when it follows an "h" or has an umlaut, it's pronounced like "w"

Consonants

b, d, f, k, l, m, n, p, q, s, t, v, w, x, y, z, ch pronounced almost as in English; **h** occurs, but is silent—not pronounced at all

c like k as in "keep": *cuarto* KOOAR-toh (room), *casa* KAH-sah (house); when it precedes "e" or "i," pronounce **c** like s, as in "sit": *cerveza* sayr-VAY-sah (beer), *encima* ayn-SEE-mah (atop)

g like g as in "gift" when it precedes "a," "o," "u," or a consonant: *gato* GAH-toh (cat), *hago* AH-goh (I do, make); otherwise, pronounce **g** like h as in "hat": *giro* HEE-roh (money order), *gente* HAYN-tay (people)

j like h, as in "has": *Jueves* HOOAY-vays (Thursday), *mejor* may-HOR (better)

ll like y, as in "yes": *toalla* toh-AH-yah (towel), *ellos* AY-yohs (they, them)

ñ like ny, as in "canyon": *año* AH-nyo (year), *señor* SAY-nyor (Mr., sir)

r is lightly trilled, with tongue at the roof of your mouth like a very light English d, as in "ready": *pero* PAY-roh (but), *tres* TRAYS (three), *cuatro* KOOAH-troh (four)

rr like a Spanish r, but with much more emphasis and trill. Let your tongue flap. Practice with *burro* (donkey), *carretera* (highway), and Carrillo (proper name), then really let go with *ferrocarril* (railroad)

Note: The single small but common exception to all of the above is the pronunciation of Spanish **y** when it's being used as the Spanish word for "and," as in "Ron y Kathy." In such case, pronounce it like the English ee, as in "keep": Ron "ee" Kathy (Ron and Kathy).

Accent

The rule for accents, the relative stress given to syllables within a given word, is straightforward. If a word ends in a vowel, an n, or an s, accent the next-to-last syllable; if not, accent the last syllable.

Pronounce *gracias* GRAH-seeahs (thank you), *orden* OHR-dayn (order), and *carretera* kah-ray-TAY-rah (highway) with stress on the next-to-last syllable.

Otherwise, accent the last syllable: *venir* vay-NEER (to come), *ferrocarril* fay-roh-cah-REEL (railroad), and *edad* ay-DAHD (age).

Exceptions to the accent rule are always marked with an accent sign: (á, é, í, ó, or ú), such as *teléfono* tay-LAY-foh-noh (telephone), *jabón* hah-BON (soap), and *rápido* RAH-pee-doh (rapid).

BASIC AND COURTEOUS EXPRESSIONS

Colombians use many courteous formalities. Whenever approaching anyone for information or some other reason, do not forget the appropriate salutation—good morning, good evening, etc. Standing alone, the greeting *hola* (hello) can sound brusque.

Hello. *Hola.*
Good morning. *Buenos días.*
Good afternoon. *Buenas tardes.*
Good evening. *Buenas noches.*
How are you? Colombians have many ways of saying this: *¿Cómo estás/como está? ¿Qué hubo/Qu'hubo? ¿Cómo va/vas? ¿Que tal?*
Very well, thank you. *Muy bien, gracias.*
Okay; good. *Bien.*
Not okay; bad. *Mal.*
So-so. *Más o menos.*
And you? *¿Y Usted?*
Thank you. *Gracias.*
Thank you very much. *Muchas gracias.*
You're very kind. *Muy amable.*
You're welcome. *De nada.*
Goodbye. *Adiós.*
See you later. *Hasta luego. Chao.*
please *por favor;* (slang) *por fa*
yes *sí*

no *no*
I don't know. *No sé.*
Just a moment, please. *Un momento, por favor.*
Excuse me, please (when you're trying to get attention). *Disculpe.*
Excuse me (when you've made a mistake). *Perdón. Que pena.*
I'm sorry. *Lo siento.*
Pleased to meet you. *Mucho gusto.*
How do you say . . . in Spanish? *¿Cómo se dice . . . en español?*
What is your name? *¿Cómo se llama (Usted)? ¿Cómo te llamas?*
Do you speak English? *¿Habla (Usted) inglés? ¿Hablas inglés?*
Does anyone here speak English? *¿Hay alguien que hable inglés?*
I don't speak Spanish well. *No hablo bien el español.*
Please speak more slowly. *Por favor hable más despacio.*
I don't understand. *No entiendo.*
Please write it down. *Por favor escríbalo.*
My name is . . . *Me llamo . . . /Mi nombre es . . .*
I would like . . . *Quisiera . . . /Quiero . . .*
Let's go to . . . *Vamos a . . .*
That's fine. *Está bien.*
All right. *Listo.*
cool, awesome *chévere, rico, super*
Oh my god! *¡Dios mío!*
That's crazy! *¡Qué locura!*
You're crazy! *¡Estás loca/o!*

TERMS OF ADDRESS

When in doubt, use the formal *Usted* (you) as a form of address.
I *yo*
you (formal) *Usted*
you (familiar) *tú*
he/him *él*
she/her *ella*
we/us *nosotros*
you (plural) *Ustedes*
they/them *ellas* (all females); *ellos* (all males or mixed gender)

Mr., sir *señor*
Mrs., madam *señora*
miss, young lady *señorita*
wife *esposa*
husband *esposo*
friend *amigo/a*
girlfriend/boyfriend *novia* (female); *novio* (male)
partner *pareja*
daughter; son *hija; hijo*
brother; sister *hermano; hermana*
mother; father *madre; padre*
grandfather; grandmother *abuelo; abuela*

TRANSPORTATION

Where is . . . ? *¿Dónde está . . . ?*
How far is it to . . . ? *¿A cuánto queda . . . ?*
from . . . to . . . *de . . . a . . .*
How many blocks? *¿Cuántas cuadras?*
Where (Which) is the way to . . . ? *¿Cuál es el camino a . . . ? ¿Por dónde es...?*
bus station *la terminal de buses/terminal de transportes*
bus stop *la parada*
Where is this bus going? *¿A dónde va este bús?*
boat *el barco, la lancha*
dock *el muelle*
airport *el aeropuerto*
I'd like a ticket to . . . *Quisiera un pasaje a . . .*
round-trip *ida y vuelta*
reservation *reserva*
baggage *equipaje*
next flight *el próximo vuelo*
Stop here, please. *Pare aquí, por favor.*
the entrance *la entrada*
the exit *la salida*
(very) near; far *(muy) cerca; lejos*
to; toward *a*
by; through *por*
from *de*
right *la derecha*
left *la izquierda*
straight ahead *derecho*
in front *en frente*

beside *al lado*
behind *atrás*
corner *la esquina*
stoplight *el semáforo*
turn *una vuelta*
here *aquí*
somewhere around here *por aquí*
there *allí*
somewhere around there *por allá*
road *camino*
street *calle, carrera*
avenue *avenida*
block *cuadra*
highway *carretera*
kilometer *kilómetro*
bridge; toll *puente; peaje*
address *dirección*
north; south *norte; sur*
east; west *oriente (este); occidente (oeste)*

ACCOMMODATIONS

hotel *hotel*
hostel *hostal*
Is there a room available? *¿Hay un cuarto disponible?*
May I (may we) see it? *¿Puedo (podemos) verlo?*
How much is it? *¿Cuánto cuesta?*
Is there something cheaper? *¿Hay algo más económico?*
Is breakfast included? *¿Está incluido el desayuno?*
single room *un cuarto sencillo*
double room *un cuarto doble*
private room *una habitación privada*
double bed *cama matrimonial*
single bed *cama sencilla*
with private bath *con baño propio*
television *televisor*
window *ventana*
view *vista*
hot water *agua caliente*
shower *ducha*
towels *toallas*
soap *jabón*
toilet paper *papel higiénico*
pillow *almohada*

blanket *cobija*
sheets *sábanas*
air-conditioned *aire acondicionado*
fan *ventilador*
swimming pool *piscina*
gym *gimnasio*
bike *bicicleta*
key *llave*
suitcase *maleta*
backpack *mochila*
lock *candado*
safe *caja de seguridad*
manager *gerente*
maid *empleada*
clean *limpio*
dirty *sucio*
broken *roto*
(not) included *(no) incluido*

FOOD

I'm hungry. *Tengo hambre.*
I'm thirsty. *Tengo sed.*
Table for two, please. *Una mesa para dos, por favor.*
menu *carta*
order *orden*
glass *vaso*
glass of water *vaso con agua*
fork *tenedor*
knife *cuchillo*
spoon *cuchara*
napkin *servilleta*
soft drink *gaseosa*
coffee *café, tinto*
tea *té*
drinking water *agua potable*
bottled carbonated water *agua con gas*
bottled uncarbonated water *agua sin gas*
beer *cerveza*
wine *vino*
glass of wine *copa de vino*
red wine *vino tinto*
white wine *vino blanco*
milk *leche*
juice *jugo*
cream *crema*
sugar *azúcar*

cheese *queso*
breakfast *desayuno*
lunch *almuerzo*
daily lunch special *menú del día*
dinner *comida*
the check *la cuenta*
eggs *huevos*
bread *pan*
salad *ensalada*
lettuce *lechuga*
tomato *tomate*
onion *cebolla*
garlic *ajo*
hot sauce *ají*
fruit *fruta*
mango *mango*
watermelon *patilla*
papaya *papaya*
banana *banano*
apple *manzana*
orange *naranja*
lime *limón*
passion fruit *maracuyá*
guava *guayaba*
grape *uva*
fish *pescado*
shellfish *mariscos*
shrimp *camarones*
(without) meat *(sin) carne*
chicken *pollo*
pork *cerdo*
beef *carne de res*
bacon; ham *tocino; jamón*
fried *frito*
roasted *asado*
Do you have vegetarian options? *¿Tienen opciones vegetarianas?*
I'm vegetarian. *Soy vegetarian(o).*
I don't eat ... *No como ...*
to share *para compartir*
Check, please. *La cuenta, por favor.*
Is the service included? *¿Está incluido el servicio?*
tip *propina*
large *grande*
small *pequeño*

SHOPPING

store *tienda*
supermarket *supermercado*
shopping center/mall *centro
commercial* (abbreviated C.C.)
cash *efectivo*
money *dinero*
credit card *tarjeta de crédito*
debit card *tarjeta de débito*
money exchange office *casa de cambio*
What is the exchange rate? *¿Cuál es la
tasa de cambio?*
How much is the commission? *¿Cuánto
es la comisión?*
Do you accept credit cards? *¿Aceptan
tarjetas de crédito?*
credit card installments *cuotas*
money order *giro*
How much does it cost? *¿Cuánto
cuesta?*
expensive *caro*
cheap *barato; económico*
more *más*
less *menos*
a little *un poco*
too much *demasiado*
value-added tax *IVA*
discount *descuento*

HEALTH

Help me please. *Ayúdeme por favor.*
I am ill. *Estoy enferma/o.*
Call a doctor. *Llame un doctor.*
Take me to ... *Lléveme a ...*
hospital *hospital, clínica*
drugstore *farmacia*
pain *dolor*
fever *fiebre*
headache *dolor de cabeza*
stomachache *dolor de estómago*
burn *quemadura*
cramp *calambre*
nausea *náusea*
vomiting *vomitar*
medicine *medicina*
antibiotic *antibiótico*
pill *pastilla, pepa*
aspirin *aspirina*

ointment; cream *ungüento; crema*
bandage (big) *venda*
bandage (small) *cura*
cotton *algodón*
sanitary napkin *toalla sanitaria*
birth control pills *pastillas
anticonceptivas*
condoms *condones*
toothbrush *cepillo de dientes*
dental floss *hilo dental*
toothpaste *crema dental*
dentist *dentista*
toothache *dolor de muelas*
vaccination *vacuna*

COMMUNICATIONS

Wi-Fi *wifi*
cell phone *celular*
username *usuario*
password *contraseña*
laptop computer *portátil*
prepaid cellphone *celular prepago*
post office *los correos/4-72*
phone call *llamada*
letter *carta*
stamp *estampilla*
postcard *postal*
package; box *paquete; caja*

AT THE BORDER

border *frontera*
customs *aduana*
immigration *migración*
inspection *inspección*
ID card *cédula*
passport *pasaporte*
profession *profesión*
vacation *vacaciones*
I'm a tourist. *Soy turista.*
student *estudiante*
marital status *estado civil*
single *soltero*
married; divorced *casado; divorciado*
widowed *viudado*
insurance *seguro*
title *título*
driver's license *pase de conducir*

AT THE GAS STATION

gas station *estación de gasolina*
gasoline *gasolina*
full, please *lleno, por favor*
tire *llanta*
air *aire*
water *agua*
oil (change) *(cambio de) aceite*
My ... doesn't work. *Mi ... no funciona.*
battery *batería*
tow truck *grúa*
repair shop *taller*

VERBS

Verbs are the key to getting along in Spanish. They employ mostly predictable forms and come in three classes, which end in *ar, er,* and *ir,* respectively:

to buy *comprar*
I buy, you (he, she, it) buys *compro, compra*
we buy, you (they) buy *compramos, compran*

to eat *comer*
I eat, you (he, she, it) eats *como, come*
we eat, you (they) eat *comemos, comen*

to climb *subir*
I climb, you (he, she, it) climbs *subo, sube*
we climb, you (they) climb *subimos, suben*

Here are more (with irregularities indicated):
to do or make *hacer* (regular except for *hago,* I do or make)
to go *ir* (very irregular: *voy, va, vamos, van*)
to walk *caminar*
to wait *esperar*
to love *amar*
to work *trabajar*
to want *querer* (irregular: *quiero, quiere, queremos, quieren*)
to need *necesitar*
to read *leer*
to write *escribir*

to send *enviar*
to repair *reparar*
to wash *lavar*
to stop *parar*
to get off (the bus) *bajar*
to arrive *llegar*
to stay (remain) *quedar*
to stay (lodge) *hospedar*
to rent *alquilar*
to leave *salir* (regular except for *salgo,* I leave)
to look at *mirar*
to look for *buscar*
to give *dar* (regular except for *doy,* I give)
to give (as a present or to order something) *regalar*
to carry *llevar*
to have *tener* (irregular: *tengo, tiene, tenemos, tienen*)
to come *venir* (irregular: *vengo, viene, venimos, vienen*)

Spanish has two forms of "to be":
to be *estar* (regular except for *estoy,* I am)
to be *ser* (very irregular: *soy, es, somos, son*)

Use *estar* when speaking of location or a temporary state of being: "I am at home." *"Estoy en casa."* "I'm happy." *"Estoy contenta/o."* Use *ser* for a permanent state of being: "I am a lawyer." *"Soy abogada/o."*

NUMBERS

zero *cero*
one *uno*
two *dos*
three *tres*
four *cuatro*
five *cinco*
six *seis*
seven *siete*
eight *ocho*
nine *nueve*
10 *diez*
11 *once*
12 *doce*
13 *trece*

14 *catorce*
15 *quince*
16 *dieciséis*
17 *diecisiete*
18 *dieciocho*
19 *diecinueve*
20 *veinte*
21 *veinte y uno* or *veintiuno*
30 *treinta*
40 *cuarenta*
50 *cincuenta*
60 *sesenta*
70 *setenta*
80 *ochenta*
90 *noventa*
100 *cien*
101 *ciento y uno*
200 *doscientos*
500 *quinientos*
1,000 *mil*
10,000 *diez mil*
100,000 *cien mil*
1,000,000 *millón*
one-half *medio*
one-third *un tercio*
one-fourth *un cuarto*

TIME
What time is it? *¿Qué hora es?*
It's one o'clock. *Es la una.*
It's three in the afternoon. *Son las tres de la tarde.*
It's 4 a.m. *Son las cuatro de la mañana.*
six-thirty *seis y media*
quarter till eleven *un cuarto para las once*
quarter past five *las cinco y cuarto*
hour *una hora*
late *tarde*

DAYS AND MONTHS
Monday *lunes*
Tuesday *martes*
Wednesday *miércoles*
Thursday *jueves*
Friday *viernes*
Saturday *sábado*
Sunday *domingo*

today *hoy*
tomorrow *mañana*
yesterday *ayer*
day before yesterday *antier*
January *enero*
February *febrero*
March *marzo*
April *abril*
May *mayo*
June *junio*
July *julio*
August *agosto*
September *septiembre*
October *octubre*
November *noviembre*
December *diciembre*
week *una semana*
month *un mes*
after *después*
before *antes*
holiday *festivo*
long weekend *puente*

WEATHER
How's the weather today? *¿Cómo está el tiempo hoy?*
It's beautiful today. *Está muy bonito hoy.*
It's so hot! *¡Qué calor!*
It's sprinkling. *Está lloviznando.*
It's raining. *Está lloviendo.*
temperature *temperatura*
sun *sol*
cloud/cloudy *nube/nublado*
rain *lluvia*
rainstorm *aguacero*
moon *luna*
tide *marea*

LANDMARKS
museum *museo*
church *iglesia*
building *edificio*
tower *torre*
statue *estatua*
park *parque*
square *plaza*

Suggested Reading

HISTORY

Bushnell, David. *The Making of Modern Colombia: A Nation in Spite of Itself.* Berkeley: University of California Press, 1993. Mandatory reading for students of Colombian history. Bushnell, an American, is considered the "Father of the Colombianists."

Hemming, John. *The Search for El Dorado.* London: Joseph, 1978. Written by a former director of the Royal Geographical Society, this book explores the Spanish gold obsession in the New World. It's a great companion to any visit to the Gold Museum in Bogotá.

Lynch, John. *Simón Bolívar: A Life.* New Haven, CT: Yale University Press, 2007. This biography of the Liberator is considered one of the best ever written in English, and is the result of a lifetime of research by renowned English historian John Lynch.

Palacios, Marco. *Between Legitimacy and Violence: A History of Colombia, 1875-2002.* Durham, NC: Duke University Press, 2006. Written by a Bogotano academic who was a former head of the Universidad Nacional, this book covers Colombia's economic, political, cultural, and social history from the late 19th century to the complexities of the late 20th century, and drug-related violence.

THE DRUG WAR AND ARMED CONFLICTS

Bowden, Mark. *Killing Pablo: The Hunt for the World's Greatest Outlaw.* New York: Grove Press, 2001. This account of U.S. and Colombian efforts to halt drug trafficking and terrorism committed by drug lord Pablo Escobar was originally reported in a 31-part series in *The Philadelphia Inquirer.*

Dudley, Steven. *Walking Ghosts: Murder and Guerrilla Politics in Colombia.* New York: Routledge Press, 2004. Essential reading for anyone interested in understanding the modern Colombian conflict, this book is written by an expert on organized crime in the Americas.

Gonsalves, Marc, Tom Howes, Keith Stansell, and Gary Brozek. *Out of Captivity: Surviving 1,967 Days in the Colombian Jungle.* New York: Harper Collins, 2009. Accounts of three American military contractors who were held, along with former presidential candidate Ingrid Betancourt, by FARC guerrillas for over five years in the Colombian jungle.

Leech, Garry. *Beyond Bogotá: Diary of a Drug War Journalist in Colombia.* Boston: Beacon Press, 2009. The basis for this book is the author's 11 hours spent as a hostage of the FARC.

Otis, John. *Law of the Jungle: The Hunt for Colombian Guerrillas, American Hostages, and Buried Treasure.* New York: Harper, 2010. This is a thrilling account of the operation to rescue Ingrid Betancourt and American government contractors held by the FARC. It covers the flip side of *Out of Captivity.*

NATURAL HISTORY

Hilty, Steven L., William L. Brown, and Guy Tudor. *A Guide to the Birds of Colombia.* Princeton, NJ: Princeton University Press, 1986. This massive 996-page field guide to bird-rich Colombia is a must for any serious bird-watcher.

McMullan, Miles, Thomas M. Donegan, and Alonso Quevedo. *Field Guide to the Birds of Colombia.* Bogotá: Fundación ProAves,

2010. This pocket-sized field guide published by ProAves, a respected bird conservation society, is a more manageable alternative to Hilty's guide.

ETHNOGRAPHY

Davis, Wade. *One River: Explorations and Discoveries in the Amazon Rain Forest*. New York: Simon & Schuster, 1997. From the author of *The Serpent and the Rainbow*, this is a rich description of the peoples of the Amazonian rainforest, and the result of Davis's time in the country alongside famed explorer Richard Evan Schultes.

Reichel-Dolmatoff, Gerardo. *Colombia: Ancient Peoples & Places*. London: Thames and Hudson, 1965. A thorough anthropological investigation of the indigenous cultures across Colombia by an Austrian-born anthropologist who emigrated to Colombia during World War II.

———. *The Shaman and the Jaguar: A Study of Narcotic Drugs Among the Indians of Colombia*. Philadelphia: Temple University Press, 1975. An examination of shamanic drug culture in Colombia, particularly among indigenous tribes from the Amazon jungle region.

ARCHITECTURE

Escovar, Alberto, Diego Obregón, and Rodolfo Segovia. *Guías Elarqa de Arquitectura*. Bogotá: Ediciones Gamma, 2005. Useful guides for anyone wishing to learn more about the architecture of Bogotá, Cartagena, and Medellín.

TRAVEL

Lamus, María Cristina. *333 Sitios de Colombia Que Ver Antes de Morir*. Bogotá: Editorial Planeta Colombiana, 2010. Colombian version of *1,000 Places to See Before You Die* (only available in Spanish).

Mann, Mark. *The Gringo Trail*. West Sussex: Summersdale Publishers, 2010. A darkly comic tale of backpacking around South America.

Nicholl, Charles. *The Fruit Palace*. New York: St. Martin's Press, 1994. A wild romp that follows the seedy cocaine trail from Bogotá bars to Medellín to the Sierra Nevada and a fruit stand called the Fruit Palace during the wild 1980s. The English author was jailed in Colombia for drug smuggling as he conducted research for the book.

PHOTOGRAPHY AND ILLUSTRATED BOOKS

Often only available in Colombia, coffee-table books by Colombian publishers Villegas Editores and the Banco de Occidente are gorgeous, well done, and often in English. Save room in your suitcase for one or two.

Cobo Borda, Juan Gustavo, Gustavo Morales Lizcano, and César David Martínez. *Colombia en Flor*. Bogotá: Villegas Editores, 2009. This book features fantastic photographs of flowers you will see in Colombia.

Davis, Wade, and Richard Evans Schultes. *The Lost Amazon: The Photographic Journey of Richard Evans Schultes*. Bogotá: Villegas Editores, 2009. A fantastic journey deep into the Amazonian jungle by famed explorer Richard Evans Schultes.

Díaz, Hernán. *Cartagena Forever*. Bogotá: Villegas Editores, 2002. A tiny little book of stunning black-and-white images of the Cartagena of yesteryear, by one of Colombia's most accomplished photographers.

Díaz, Merlano, Juan Manuel, and Fernando Gast Harders. *El Chocó Biogeográfico de Colombia*. Banco de Occidente Credencial Cali, 2009. A spectacular trip through the unique and biodiverse Chocó region.

Freeman, Benjamin, and Murray Cooper. *Birds in Colombia*. Bogotá: Villegas Editores, 2011. Dazzling photographs of native bird species found in Colombia, a veritable birding paradise.

Hurtado García, Andrés. *Unseen Colombia*. Bogotá: Villegas Editores, 2004. Photos and descriptions of the many off-the-beaten-track destinations in the country.

Montaña, Antonio, and Hans Doering. *The Taste of Colombia*. Bogotá: Villegas Editores, 1994. A thorough survey of Colombian cuisine by region, with recipes included.

Ortiz Valdivieso, Pedro, and César David Martínez. *Orquídeas Especies de Colombia*. Bogotá: Villegas Editores, 2010. Jaw-dropping photos of orchids, from the unusual to the sublime, found in the forests of Colombia.

Rivera Ospina, David. *La Amazonía de Colombia*. Cali: Banco de Occidente Credencial, 2008. An excellent souvenir of your visit to the Amazon region.

———. *La Orinoquía de Colombia*. Cali: Banco de Occidente Credencial, 2005. One of the least visited areas of Colombia is the Río Orinoco basin in the Llanos and Amazon regions.

Various. *Colombia Natural Parks*. Bogotá: Villegas Editores, 2006. Gorgeous photos from all of Colombia's spectacular national parks.

Villegas, Liliana. *Coffees of Colombia*. Bogotá: Villegas Editores, 2012. Everything you'd like to know about Colombian coffee in one charming and compact book.

Villegas, Marcelo. *Guadua Arquitectura y Diseño*. Bogotá: Villegas Editores, 2003. Profiles of minimalistic and modern constructions throughout Colombia, all made from *guadua*.

FICTION

Caballero, Antonio. *Sin Remedio*. Bogotá: Alfaguara, 2006. A novel about a struggling poet in 1970s Bogotá by one of Colombia's best-known columnists.

Espinosa, Germán. *La Tejedora de Coronas*. Bogotá: Alfaguara, 2002. This novel contains the remembrances of Genovevea Alcocer, who, during the 18th century, left her native Cartagena to travel the world. Considered one of the most beautiful works of Latin American literature from the 20th century.

Franco, Jorge. *Rosario Tijeras*. New York: Siete Cuentos, 1999. An acclaimed suspense novel that takes place in violent Medellín in the 1980s.

García Márquez, Gabriel. *Innocent Eréndira and Other Stories*. New York: Harper, 2005. A collection of short stories, including a memorable tale of poor Eréndira and her awful grandmother.

———. *Love in the Time of Cholera*. New York: Alfred A. Knopf, 1988. A Colombian love and lovesickness story set in a fictitious version of Cartagena.

———. *One Hundred Years of Solitude*. New York: Harper, 2006. One of the Nobel Prize-winning author's classic novels, this book tells the story of the Buendía family from the fictitious town of Macondo.

Isaacs, Jorge. *María*. Rockville, MD: Wildside Press, 2007. Considered one of the most important Latin American romantic novels of the 19th century, this love story takes place among the sugarcane fields near Cali.

Sánchez Baute, Alonso. *Líbranos del Bien.* Bogotá: Alfaguara, 2008. The incredible account of how two friends from the Caribbean coastal city of Valledupar became powerful adversaries.

Vallejo, Fernando. *Our Lady of the Assassins.* London: Serpent's Tail, 2001. A novel that takes place in Medellín, about a gay writer who returns to his violent hometown, where he falls in love with a young contract killer.

Internet and Digital Resources

ACCOMMODATIONS
Hostel Trail
www.hosteltrail.com
Run by a Scots couple living in Popayán, this is an excellent resource on hostels throughout South America.

BIRDING
ProAves
www.proaves.org
Excellent website for the largest birding organization in the country.

CARTAGENA
This Is Cartagena
www.ticartagena.com
Experience Cartagena like a local.

ECOTOURISM
Aviatur Ecoturismo
www.aviaturecoturismo.com
Package tours of the Amazon, PNN Tayrona, PNN Isla Gorgona, and more are available from one of Colombia's most respected travel agencies.

Colombia Oculta
www.colombiaoculta.org
This group offers a year-round calendar of weekend excursions to some of Colombia's most exotic locations.

Fundación Malpelo
www.fundacionmalpelo.org
This nonprofit organization works to protect Colombia's vast maritime territory, including the Santuario de Flora y Fauna Malpelo.

Fundación Natura
www.natura.org.co
The Fundación Natura operates several interesting ecotourism reserves in the country.

Parques Nacionales Naturales de Colombia
www.parquesnacionales.gov.co
Colombia's national parks website has information on all of the natural parks and protected areas in the country.

EMBASSIES AND VISAS
Colombian Ministry of Foreign Affairs
www.cancilleria.gov.co
The website for the Ministry of Foreign Affairs offers information on visas and other travel issues.

U.S. Embassy in Colombia
http://bogota.usembassy.gov
The Citizen Services page often has security information for visitors, and is where you can register your visit in case of an emergency.

ENTERTAINMENT, CULTURE, AND EVENTS
Banco de la República
www.banrepcultural.org
The site for this nationwide cultural organization contains information on upcoming activities in 28 different cities.

Tu Boleta
www.tuboleta.com
The top event-ticket distributor in the country, Tu Boleta is a good way to learn about concerts, theater, parties, and sporting events throughout Colombia.

Vive In
www.vive.in
This site provides updated information on restaurants, entertainment, and cultural events in Bogotá.

HISTORY AND HUMAN RIGHTS ISSUES

Centro de Memoria Histórica
www.centrodememoriahistorica.gov.co
This is an excellent website on the human toll of the Colombian conflict.

CIA World Factbook Colombia
www.cia.gov
On this up-to-date site, the CIA offers background information on Colombia.

Colombia Diversa
www.colombiadiversa.org
The website for Colombia Diversa, the country's top human rights organization, offers information and resources.

International Crisis Group
www.crisisgroup.org
The website for this independent nonprofit group provides in-depth analysis of the human rights situation in Colombia.

LANGUAGE COURSES

Spanish in Colombia
www.spanishincolombia.gov.co
This official government website offers information on places to study Spanish in Colombia.

NEWS AND MEDIA

The City Paper Bogotá
www.thecitypaperbogota.com
The City Paper is Colombia's largest English-language newspaper, published monthly.

Colombia Calling
www.richardmccoll.com/colombia-calling
This weekly online radio program covers all things Colombia from an expat's perspective.

Colombia Reports
http://colombiareports.co
This site, unaffiliated with any political or social organization, publishes Colombian news in English.

El Espectador
www.elespectador.com.co
One of Colombia's two national newspapers, *El Espectador* publishes online and print editions.

El Tiempo
www.eltiempo.com
El Tiempo is the country's leading newspaper.

La Silla Vacia
http://lasillavacia.com
On this blog, political insiders dish about current events.

Revista Semana
www.semana.com
Semana is the top newsmagazine in Colombia.

TRANSPORTATION

Moovit
http://moovitapp.com
This app will help you figure out public transportation in Bogotá.

SITP
www.sitp.gov.co
This is the official website of the ever-improving public bus system in Bogotá.

Tappsi
https://tappsi.co
To order a safe taxi in Colombia's large cities, first upload this excellent app.

TRAVEL INFORMATION
Colombia Travel
www.colombia.travel
This is the official travel information website of Proexport, Colombia's tourism and investment promotion agency.

Pueblos Patrimoniales
www.pueblospatrimoniodecolombia.travel
Find a pueblo that suits your needs at this informative website.

Index

List of Maps

Photo Credits

Acknowledgments

Mil gracias to: Eduardo Osorio of Fontour; Gustavo Toro of COTELCO Colombia; Enrique Stellabatti of PROCOLOMBIA and his team; Carlos Mario Tamayo and staff at Parques Nacionales de Colombia; Rainbow Nelson; Cristina Zapata and Miguel Velasquez; Richard McColl; Claudia Mejía; Claudia Buendía; Walter Nocua; Elena Posada; Marco Chiandetti; Alonso Sánchez; Amado Ariza; and Vio Barco.

Also Available

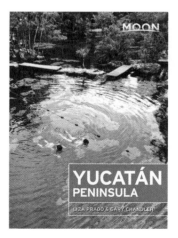

MAP SYMBOLS

▦▦▦	Expressway	○	City/Town	✈	Airport	⚲	Golf Course
▦▦▦	Primary Road	◉	State Capital	✖	Airfield	🅿	Parking Area
▦▦▦	Secondary Road	⊛	National Capital	▲	Mountain	▟	Archaeological Site
-------	Unpaved Road	★	Point of Interest	✛	Unique Natural Feature	⬛	Church
———	Feature Trail	•	Accommodation	⚘	Waterfall	⛽	Gas Station
- - - - -	Other Trail	▾	Restaurant/Bar	⬩	Park	◯	Glacier
··········	Ferry	■	Other Location	⬛	Trailhead	▧	Mangrove
▦▦▦	Pedestrian Walkway					▱	Reef
▮▮▮▮	Stairs	Λ	Campground	⛷	Skiing Area	▭	Swamp

CONVERSION TABLES

°C = (°F - 32) / 1.8
°F = (°C x 1.8) + 32
1 inch = 2.54 centimeters (cm)
1 foot = 0.304 meters (m)
1 yard = 0.914 meters
1 mile = 1.6093 kilometers (km)
1 km = 0.6214 miles
1 fathom = 1.8288 m
1 chain = 20.1168 m
1 furlong = 201.168 m
1 acre = 0.4047 hectares
1 sq km = 100 hectares
1 sq mile = 2.59 square km
1 ounce = 28.35 grams
1 pound = 0.4536 kilograms
1 short ton = 0.90718 metric ton
1 short ton = 2,000 pounds
1 long ton = 1.016 metric tons
1 long ton = 2,240 pounds
1 metric ton = 1,000 kilograms
1 quart = 0.94635 liters
1 US gallon = 3.7854 liters
1 Imperial gallon = 4.5459 liters
1 nautical mile = 1.852 km

MOON CARTAGENA & COLOMBIA'S CARIBBEAN COAST

Avalon Travel
An imprint of Perseus Books
A Hachette Book Group company
1700 Fourth Street
Berkeley, CA 94710, USA
www.moon.com

Editor: Leah Gordon
Series Manager: Kathryn Ettinger
Copy Editor: Brett Keener
Graphics Coordinator: Rue Flaherty
Production Coordinator: Rue Flaherty
Cover Design: Faceout Studios, Charles Brock
Interior Design: Domini Dragoone
Moon Logo: Tim McGrath
Map Editor: Mike Morgenfeld
Cartographer: Brian Shotwell
Proofreader: Ashley Benning
Indexer: Rachel Kuhn

ISBN-13: 978-1-63121-427-1
ISSN: 2473-5833

Printing History
1st Edition — November 2016
5 4 3 2 1

Text © 2016 by Andrew Dier.
Maps © 2016 by Avalon Travel.
All rights reserved.

Some photos and illustrations are used by permission and are the property of the original copyright owners.

Front cover photo: View looking up at historic colonial balconies and a church in Cartagena, Colombia © Jesse Kraft / Alamy Stock Photo
Back cover photo: View of crystal clear Caribbean water on the island of San Andres y Providencia, Colombia © Jesse Kraft /123rf.com

Printed in Canada by Friesens